SURVIVING IN A NEGATIVE WORLD

Things Happen for a Reason

Tanya Creedon

authorHOUSE®

AuthorHouse™
1663 Liberty Drive
Bloomington, IN 47403
www.authorhouse.com
Phone: 1-800-839-8640

First published by AuthorHouse   06/21/2011

ISBN: 978-1-4567-6446-3 (e)
ISBN: 978-1-4567-6447-0 (hc)
ISBN: 978-1-4567-6448-7 (sc)

Library of Congress Control Number: 2011906794

Printed in the United States of America

Editing done by:
Kayla Creedon and
Jamie Trescavage

Thanks to Kayla Creedon and Jamie Trescavage for all their help in editing my book.

I dedicate this book to my mother,

Sara L. Swanson, LPN.

She did the best she could

in raising us,

It just took me many years to

realize it.

Sara L. Swanson

1/07/1947 – 9/20/2000

I do have to admit, the childhood that I had made me a better parent to my children. I feel sorry for those that grew up thinking it is normal to abuse their children because of what they went through. Thank God I knew the difference between right and wrong. One day I hope there will no longer be abuse in this world. The more we talk about it the more people will learn it is wrong.

My Childhood and My Reviews on Life

July 5, 2010 @ 10:05am (a)

We are always thinking of ways to improve ourselves and our lives. For me I started writing. I don't know why it took me so long to realize this. For others, they read, go to church, travel to find meanings, and talk to others for help and comfort.

I tried all those except the traveling. I can't afford that. They just didn't work. It's nice to be able to find help these days but back then before they believed you, you had to answer questions over and over again to make sure you weren't lying.

All my life before my mom passed away, I was called a martyr, miss goody two shoes, and other names that at the moment slipped my mind. The person who did this to me was my mother of all people. I guess she didn't like the fact that I tried so hard to do things right. I didn't want anybody to be mad at me, so I tried to impress them or I tried to keep a low profile.

Writing this book, I hope, will help me to overcome the negativities in my life and to encourage others to step up and take control over their own lives. I can't live in the past anymore. That's all I can remember and it sucks. Life is so hard to understand sometimes, but we must continue on and try to find a way to be happy and productive in our lives.

"Please, whatever you do, don't let others try to control you, step all over you, and put you down. These people have no right to be this way towards you. Just walk away and don't look back."

I've been dealing with my own "demons" ever since I was born, everyone has. Did you know it took me 41 years to figure this out? I thought I was put on this earth to have everyone adore me, help me and to love me. I didn't understand why it was the opposite. I thought I was special and everyone will be there for me. At the beginning it was that way. I felt so much love from my mom and my dad. I was happy, but after a couple of years being on Earth, things changed. That's where my story starts.

Ok, let's get this clear and out of the way. People that are apart of your life and are around you are there to encourage you, support you, and love you through your life, so you won't have to be alone to make your decisions. "Yes", I say strongly, "you will make decisions that will make you feel the world is falling apart around you. It will be hard to deal with and if you don't have the proper support system, it will not help to get you out of this slump you're in. It will probably take years to get out". I should know, I'm going through it right now.

These people; you shouldn't assume are there to take care of you. They are there to support you. I myself don't have this. If I do, it's not that big of a support system. I grew up in a very negative environment. It took me just about all my life to realize I've been doing this all wrong. Now I have to figure out how to fix it or how to make it right so I can enjoy the rest of my life without negativity. If you don't have a spiritual out look in your life you wouldn't understand. The more negativity you surround yourself with, the harder your life experience is. Anything that affects you negative or not, will somehow affect everyone else in one way or another, even if you don't feel it or see it. So, keep that in mind when your in your car cutting in front of somebody, honking your horn, or riding someone's ass; that's negativity and it's not only affecting the person you are doing this to, in one way it's affecting everyone else.

I started writing about 10 years ago. I told my favorite Uncle what I was doing. He said," Writing a book isn't a job, and to be able to sell a lot of copies, you would have to have someone famous to help promote it. You would have to have a company to publish it. You have to have something interesting to write about." I thought highly of my Uncle and still do. So,

I stopped writing. I thought to myself maybe he's right. Anyways, who would read my book?

You know what? I love my Uncle. He's a realist. And sometimes we clash because I'm not a realist I'm more of an idealist. But without him, life would be three times more difficult to deal with. He keeps me focused on the issues that need to be dealt with and he always shows that he cares for me. All he is doing right now is supporting me and helping me make up my own mind of what to do with my life. I hope that when this book is published and he reads it, he won't be mad at me.

I don't like it when the people I love and care about are mad at me. It hurts deep down inside. My Uncle has never laid a hand on me or showed any abuse towards me, which still is kind of confusing because my mom was abusive. They were raised in the same house. All I can come up with is we were a burden to mom, so my Uncle and his parents were the ones I truly loved. I'm so happy to have had them in my life.

All my life I've written little things here and there. Then I would stop for some reason or another. Maybe that's what I'm supposed to do. I'm supposed to write. All my life I've had problems with grammar, spelling and making sense in my writings. I'm afraid I'll fail in this as well. My English teacher in college failed me and told me I wouldn't amount to anything. This was coming out of a Catholic Priest, of all people. Talk about a let down. I never finished college because of him. I'm afraid of people ignoring my book when they find out that someone with learning disabilities wrote it. This is what I had to deal with all my life. People look at you differently when they find out.

So, my first book will be about my life. Well most of it and what I can remember that is, then I'll go from there. I want people to know me and what I went through. That way if something happens in their life that is similar to mine, they'll have an idea how to cope with what is going on with them and know they aren't alone.

I'm not a reader. I love to watch T.V. and movies. I will, however, read a fantasy or Sci-Fi book if it has really caught my fancy. I love country music but not as much as my T.V. My newest fetish is gaiaonline.com. I've been involved in it for a year now; I'm so addicted to it. I have a close net of friends on there. I met some of them the first day I joined. Most of them are younger than I, but they seem not to mind. I can spend all my time there because there's nothing else to do. Oh my, they are getting free advertising from me.

I don't have a degree in psychology, matter of fact I don't have a degree in anything except early mechanics which isn't much at all these days, but I do have the experience in this life to help others if I can. I'm not a well known author who knows how to write and grammar check. I'm just a regular person who wants to let others know what I went through. Maybe God wants me to write and it's my calling, I haven't a clue, but I'm doing it right now.

My Childhood

It's weird, when you're a baby, you can remember bits and pieces of it. I mean the senses – what feelings you have and learn what they mean. I believe when you're born into this world, you already know how to be, how to comprehend everything around you. You just have to be born to someone who will enjoy and love to support you in your life's journey.

I didn't really pay attention to my life until I was about two years of age. I guess it's probably because life was simple and easy and loving. Then things gradually started to change. My dad wasn't around that much. I didn't get the attention I used to get. My mom didn't seem to care anymore. Things weren't the same. I started reacting to it. I didn't talk, (well, didn't want to talk) and couldn't walk.

My mom and someone else, it could have been my dad, decided to put some sevens in my 7-up can, to encourage me to walk. I remember crawling back and forth to my mom and this other person, taking sips of 7-up. Then the taste changed, it reminded me of medicine. I didn't like it. But they made me drink it. All I can remember is drinking a couple of sips out of it. I felt funny and I thought I was crawling to mom so she can hold me; I saw her clapping her hands smiling and saying "you're walking". I fell into her arms and fell asleep. What ever you do, don't give babies alcohol!!! Adults may think its fun and entertaining but to a baby it's not. It's disgusting and it makes them feel sick. I had a picture of it to prove it, but I don't know where it went to.

I didn't feel like talking, there was nothing to talk about. So, why would you worry about a baby who didn't talk yet? I could feel everything and see everything. There wasn't any need for it. I got everything from mom or dad. They knew what I always wanted and needed somehow. (My mom told me I was lazy) Eventually I started to talk.

Mom, Dad, my sister (Gayle) and I went to a friend's house. I liked it there. They had a pond in the back yard with a turtle and fish. Plus they had a pool too.

I remember being in the pool with my family. It was nice and bright outside with the sun reflecting off the light blue water into my eyes, I tried to protect my eyes with my arm. I like the water. For some reason we got out. My dad sat down under the homemade porch, it had palm leaves on the roof. I was left with him; my mom took Gayle inside the house. I started walking towards the pool. My dad said "Don't go in the pool, you don't know how to swim yet." I saw a ball on the side of the pool. I sat down with my legs over the edge of the pool and they were in the water. I went to grab the ball and the ball moved so I leaned over to grab it and I fell in the pool. I sank, I couldn't go up, I tried, I couldn't breath, and then I felt the water going in my lungs. I'll tell you this, drowning is so painful. The burning in your chest, like you have a bad case of bronchitis. Then I blacked out. I woke up screaming because my chest still hurt a lot and I saw my dad over me and my mom right beside me. I was 2 ½ or 3 at the time. Mom told me years later that it was my dad's fault. "He didn't watch you closely enough. He was so tied up with the newspaper that he forgot all about you." She told me that it was her that screamed out to my dad and he realized what happened and dove in to the pool to get me. She said "You could have been in the pool for 5 minutes but I don't know." She was shocked that I remembered this stuff.

I asked my Dad about it. He said "Tanya, I was watching you. I let you have your space. I warned you about the pool. When I saw you jump, I jumped in right after you. It was so quick. I got you breathing within 3 minutes." Dad was even shocked that I remembered.

July 9th 9:30am

I called my Dad the other day to verify my memories about that day. He

6

changed his story. He told me; I was on the side of the pool, sitting there. He got distracted and looked away for a brief moment. Then he turned back around and didn't see me. He looked in the pool and I was there at the bottom just jumping up and down, moving all over the place. Dad grabbed me. He said "You didn't drown. I got you before that." I asked him about the ball, he said he didn't recall a ball. Then I asked him, "Where were you?" he said, "I was in the pool." I asked "How old was I?" he said "3". When he told me that – I was a little bit confused. I thought to myself, how come I remember it differently? There was silence between us; I was trying to think of something to say. So, I said; "You weren't in a chair reading a newspaper?" He started laughing a little and said "No at that time newspaper wasn't important to me." (It just now dawned to me it might have been Sandy in the chair reading a newspaper) I said; "So, my learning disabilities weren't caused by my drowning?" He said; "No, and stop saying you drowned. Your disabilities were caused by your mother's drinking all the time while she was pregnant with you and your sister." In shock I said "Oh, wow, ok, that explains everything."

"I remember going somewhere before kindergarten to learn how to speak and move my hands. I only remember a little bit about that. Do you have any knowledge about the school I went too?" He said "No, but I'm not surprised you had to go. Even, though you were a happy baby, you didn't want to do anything." Then there was silence again. He said, "Look I got to get going." I said, "Well, if I need to call and ask questions, can I? I'm writing a book about my life." I heard him chuckle and he said "Yeah, I guess so." I told him I had nothing better else to do. So we said our good bye's and love ya's and hung up the phone. I'm still looking back at that moment. I can still feel the water going into my chest. Maybe when my dad was pulling me up a little bit of water got in. That's what I can come up with anyways. Or maybe my dad didn't want to tell me the real truth. Hmmm, makes you wonder, huh?

Here's another little thing I did. I will have to call my dad to see if he was there or not, to determine if he was still with us and how old I was. I remember cutting my chin with a razor. I was trying to shave like my dad. I didn't scream, but I was scared that mom would hit me. So, I tried to flush the razor down the toilet and try to stop the bleeding myself. In the process of doing that I flooded the bathroom, made a mess with toilet paper, blood, and water. It was everywhere, in the tub, walls, toilet, floor, sink, and mirror. My mom knocked at the door, I freaked out and started screaming, trying to hold door closed. That didn't work, mom pushed opened the door, saw the mess and saw me. Frantically she asked what happened. I tried to tell her, but I guess she didn't understand. She cleaned me up and took me to the doctors. I had to get five stitches, which wasn't fun at all. I struggled against the doctor and the nurse. They gave me a shot to calm me down. That wasn't fun either, they weren't gentle at all. I guess I survived that because I'm still here.

My dad and mom got divorced when I was 3. After that I didn't see my dad that much. Matter of fact, I hardly remember very much after that; just bits and pieces until the age 8. I remember dad coming to my 4th birthday, he bought me an orange race car. I played with it the whole entire day. I was happy. My dad got me something and I'm going to keep it forever. But, something happened. My mom took me out of it, I heard yelling. I saw my dad take the car away. He came back, I ran to him tugging on him to go get my car back. He picked me up took me to the swing set, kneeled down and said, "Don't worry sweetie, you'll get it back later, I promise." He started swinging me....

One day I came across a picture of me in my car and the memory came back. I think I was about 12 years old. I asked mom what happened to my car. She told me that I ran it into a wall and I ruined it. A little later I asked my dad what happened to my car. He told me that mom made him take it back because I was a little girl and not a boy. He didn't want to but he took it back. So I believe what my dad said. I remember it like it was yesterday.

Since my dad didn't come around much after the divorce, I would cry constantly. My mom would yell at me to stop crying, sometimes she would send me to my room until I stopped crying. She never held me or tried to calm me down. Sometimes she would hit me and say here's something to cry about, now go to bed. Some nights I would go to bed without eating dinner.

We moved to South Dakota, to an apartment complex. It had stairs and to make it interesting to us, mom would get us to sing the fire truck song, I think it was. I remember the feeling and the motion of it but not the lyrics of the song to get us to walk up the stairs.

My next door neighbor was my age, but I can't remember his name. He was my best friend in the whole world. We would go to each other's places to play. You couldn't tear us apart…. I would tell him my deepest secrets. Even the times I'd get into trouble. He told me a couple of tricks to make mom feel guilty, but they never worked. He came to my Birthday party. I was unhappy at one point. I think it was because I didn't get what I wanted. I got a crying doll instead. Mom made me wear a dress and I hated them with a passion, but my best friend was sitting next to me so I cheered up a little.

It seemed like it wasn't my party. I couldn't do what I wanted and mom controlled everything. So, I just spaced out for a while and pretend I wasn't there like I was an empty shell. I found a way to deal with unpleasant situations. I just froze or emptied my mind and just shut down. It was easy. I tried to tell and show my best friend what I do when I get yelled at or punished. But he didn't catch on. He just laughed at me, saying it was silly, but to me it worked very well. I found a way to manage my life in a way, so for most of my party I wasn't really there. It was mom's party anyway.

Mom met this guy named Kent. I remembered him because he drilled his name into us. She married him; well that's what she said. When they would fall asleep, my sister and I would leave our room and go to the kitchen to find something to eat and to drink. Mom would keep her favorite breath mints on top of the fridge. My sister at the time was only 3 and she climbed up there and got the breath mints. We ate a few and hoping mom didn't notice. The next night all hell broke lose. Mom asked Kent if he took some of her breath mints he said no. Then she turned to us, we just shrugged our shoulders. Kent grabbed us and sat us next to him with a belt and threatened to spank us if we didn't tell him. So we told him. He made us sing the Indian song: One little, two little, three little Indians… four little, five little, six little Indians,…seven little, eight little, nine little Indians… ten little Indian boys…. That's all I can remember. If we couldn't sing the song all the way we would get hit. We were crying and crying we tried to sing it all, he was about to hit us and mom told him no, they had enough. We went to bed. My sister and I hardly ever talked to him again.

One day, mom had to leave and she couldn't find a babysitter so Kent said he would baby-sit for her. So my sister and I were playing in our room. He called us in to the living room. He didn't have any clothes on except his underwear. We asked where his clothes were. He said "they are dirty; I took them to the laundry room. They'll be clean soon. Come here, let's play a game." He made us sit on his lap. I didn't like that to well, so I struggled to get away. I did and I ran to my room. I heard my sister screaming, I was yelling and crying to get her to come here. After a little while she came running into our room, we shut the door pushed our bed against the door. He was yelling at us to open it. We climbed on our dresser to look out the window to see if we can see our mom. We stayed there for a long time, I asked her if he hurt her, she said yes. It was almost dark and we heard the front door open. Mom was yelling at Kent, I guess he fell asleep on the couch without his clothes on. She came to our door, knocked softly, and said, "Open the door pumpkins". We replied with a no. Then I heard more yelling and the front door slamming. My sister and I were screaming and crying and then we heard a knock at the door again. Mom said "He's gone now and he won't come back anymore. You can open the door now." Even though we were exhausted my sister and I got enough energy to move the bed a little for mom to come in. She turned on the light and we ran to her and we cried together. She said nothing like this will ever happen again. Mom took us to the doctor's to make sure we were okay. I was okay, but my sister on the other hand had signs of redness.

My friend saw me in the hallway and ran to me. He told me he heard us crying and he wanted to come over to see how I was but his mom wouldn't let him saying it was none of their business. I told him, I wished he did show up, then none of this would have happened. Mom's voice changed when she was talking to his mom. I guess she was pretty upset that her neighbors didn't do anything. But I've found that a lot of people are like that. They don't want to get involved or don't want to be bothered when it came to arguments and violence. In a way it kept my friend safe but in the long run we got hurt. Look, if by any chance you hear arguing, things being broken, someone you know is crying, don't wait for everything to calm down to see if every thing's okay. Go and stop it. If you're scared to do that call the police and have them stop it. Abuse is an invasion of your personal being. Absolutely no one deserves to get hit or get insulted with words. If you are in that situation get out of it now and get help. If you don't know who to turn to ask a friend or call Human Resources and if it's really bad call the police.

Next thing I knew it, we were driving very far away, and we ended up somewhere in the country. We moved to a farm away from everyone. I didn't see mom packing up our things or anything like that. There was no sign of moving again. It's like we just got up and left. Mom was good at doing that.

Nothing but fields upon fields of grass and what ever else was growing there. I remember taking a bus to school vaguely but that's all I remember about that. The house was old, a lot of yard to play in. It had cows, pigs, and a lot of cats. Inside the house there wasn't electricity or running water. The bathroom was outside and it stank. I know the kitchen really well. She would make me clean the dishes at the age of 5. What kind of mother would do that? To warm up the water, mom would put some water in a pan and heat it up on the wood stove. Anyways, the kitchen had a wood stove which was used to heat the house, and cook too. I had to put wood in it once in a while as well. We had to take baths in the kitchen in a big bucket or tub or what ever you want to call it. Once a week mom would take us to town. She would play bingo and we would try to as well. She was really good at it. On one of the nights we were supposed to go out, we couldn't, there were cows all over the driveway and around our car. Mom told us to sit on the fence and don't get off until she told us too, the cows can be dangerous. So we sat there. Mom went inside to call the farmer. She came back outside and stood by us. Talking to us about what cows do and what they are good for. She even told us about a time in her life where she would tip the cows in the middle of the night, while they slept. She warned us not to do that because it's very dangerous and the cows will get mad. She told us that the cows sometimes would have trouble getting back up and if they couldn't get back up, they would die from suffocation. She told us how the cow had two stomachs and that's why they eat all the time. She said "All they do is eat, sleep, and poop that's it." We got to pet one cow because it came to us. It felt weird, very course and soft at the same time. The farmer got there and moved the cows out of the way and we left. Mom stopped at a store on the way to where we were going and I remember picking out a packet of Chiclets and my sister I believed picked out a pack of Wrigley's gum in the yellow pack.

Mom met someone and brought him home. I don't know much about him. I remember seeing them run upstairs and there were a lot of laughs. My sister and I were in the living room playing with these plastic round things with four legs. You can build off them, make them as tall as you want or try to make a building with them. It was getting dark, and mom came down with a candle and said it was time for bed. So we followed her upstairs. The next morning, we saw this guy sitting on the couch smoking a cigarette, asking mom what was for breakfast. Mom said, "Well the kids are having cereal, I have to go get milk from a cow." She went outside and the man followed. I was sitting on the living room floor with my sister playing with those blocks. I heard yelling; I looked up and saw two shadow figures outside the covered window. I saw this guy grab my mom and hit her really hard in the face. I ran outside and started hitting him; he got a hold of me and threw me against the house wall. Mom yelled, "Get out, get out! You son of a Bitch!" He left. The farmer came running up when he heard the noise. On the porch I found a tooth. I picked it up and gave it back to mom. She had lost one of her front teeth. The police showed up and took pictures of mom. She went to the dentist and they fixed her tooth. I guess all they had to do was put it back in. This is all I can remember about this event. Next thing I knew, we were packing up our things and moving once again.

We moved to a house next door to a hospital and a few blocks away from a school. I started school in the fall. So two weeks before school started, she would walk me to school back and forth, so I can get use to the routine. I would be starting Kindergarten.

The first week of school mom would walk me to school and walk me back. Then after that I had to do it by myself. I was constantly late to school. One day the principal came to my class, took me to his office and had a chat with me. He brought out the wooden paddle and showed it to me. He said "Tell your mother, if you're late to school one more time, you'll be spanked with this." I told my mom, and she said, "Well then, don't be late". The next day, I realize I was going to be late to school. I got to this house that was next to the school, I looked and all the kids were going in. I thought to myself if they see me I will get into trouble and I don't want to get into trouble, so I ducked behind the bushes in the houses yard and waited. Trying to figure out how I was going to fix this. The person who lived in the house came outside and I ran away to the school. I didn't know what else to do. I went to my room, but the teacher wouldn't let me in and she sent me to the office. The principal paddled my bottom. He sent me back to my classroom crying. I couldn't sit down, so I laid my chest on top of my desk, my legs and feet holding me up and I cried and cried. The teacher yelled at me to stop crying and to start doing my work or she'll call the principal again. I didn't listen. I couldn't do anything. I was in so much pain, I didn't know what else to do. Another teacher heard the noise and came to check. She saw me at my desk and saw the teacher yelling at me. She came in and grabbed me, then took me to the nurse. On the way there, I was trying to get away screaming, "Don't take me to the principal's please." She stopped, kneeled down and said "We are going to the nurse to call your mother. Now be quiet so the principal doesn't hear you." I was lying in the nurse's bed and my mom came in. I don't know how they kept it quiet from the principal. The nurse told her what happened and I wasn't able to concentrate at school today. My mom looked at me, put her hand on my chin and asked are you all right. It took all the energy in me to try not to cry but it didn't work, I started to cry real hard and said no. My mom told the nurse to take care of me for a few more minutes and that she had to talk to the principal. I said no, no please no. Mom said "Don't worry I won't let that man touch you again." I heard her yelling all the way across the hall way. Then she came in got me and we went home. I took a few days off of school. Then she took me to school a couple of times. The last time she picked me up at school, she told me that I will be able to walk to school now. She got the principal fired and that my teacher will be treating me a lot better. The teacher would yell for me outside every morning to get my attention. She would wait there until I got to the door. I was never late to class again, though technically I was. A few weeks went by. I was happy, enjoying school, playing in the school yard, then one day I was playing on the jungle gym bars. I slipped and hit my head on the bar and fell to the ground. I got a black eye from it. The kids around me laughed at me. They didn't get help. I just laid there crying and holding my face. Then someone yelled at everyone to stop and get away; then picked me up and took me to the nurses. It was really painful. I had a black eye for about a month. The kids stopped playing with me. I had no idea why.

One day on the way home two boys stopped me. They were a couple of grades higher than I. They wanted me to pull up my skirt so they can see under it. I told them no. They threatened to beat me up if I didn't. I still said no. So they started punching me, hitting me, pushing me down. I covered my face with my arms and curled my legs up, to try to lessen the blows. A high school kid comes up, throws the boys off me and told them to leave me alone. They ran off. He picked me up and helped me walk home. He said he knows the boys and he'll talk to their parents for me. I don't remember

his name. Mom was waiting for me on the porch, she saw me walking with this boy and saw some of my clothing ripped. The boy said he had to pull a couple of boys off me. My mom was even more worried for me at this point. She asked him if he could walk me home for awhile. He said sure, not a problem. He walked with me for about three weeks. The last day he walked with me, he said that it was time for him to go. He couldn't walk with me anymore and not to worry, no one will hurt me again. I started to cry, he made me feel safe and I was going to lose that. I didn't want to go to school anymore, I was afraid, but mom made me go anyways.

We had cats and one day mom noticed we had skin rashes all over. Gayle had it real bad on top of her head and ears. I only had blotches of it. Not to bad. Mom took us to the doctors, the doctor didn't know what it was and sent us to a friend of his that was a Veterinarian and that's where we found out we had ringworm, so we had to put cream all over us. One day, I was walking home from school, I saw a white truck outside our house and a person taking a cat to it. I started running to him and screaming, "What are you doing with my cat?" Mom came out and said, "I was hoping this would be done before you came home. Our cats got sick with ringworm and they can't be saved. They had to take the cats." I was so upset, I cried; I prayed to God, please take me home. I don't want to be here anymore. Please!!!! Then I fell asleep. When I woke I was hoping I wasn't here anymore, but I was wrong. I felt disappointed at the fact that God didn't take me back home. I was sad for a very long time. I didn't talk to anyone and I kept to myself.

I was taking my sweet time getting home, I wasn't in a rush. I got to the steps to my house and there was a lady sitting on the porch with dark sun glasses on. Mom opened the screen door and said "Meet our new roommate, her name is Ruth. She'll be staying with us for a little while. Now say hello." I said hello and ran into the house. Another big surprise, in the living room there was this big, huge dog. A Saint Bernard!!! I looked at mom and asked, "Is he ours, can we keep him?" Mom said "We are only taking care of him for a while, until his owner finds a place to stay. So don't get too attached to him." My sister and I had so much fun with him. We tried riding him; he didn't like that at all. He tried to snip at us, but we knew he didn't want us to ride him so we stopped doing that. We would give him hugs and when he was lying on the floor we would put our heads on him and lay down with him. He was so soft, if I could I would lay there all day long.

Ruth came in from outside she had to have mom help her in. In her hand was a cane, a white long cane with red at the bottom. She sat down in a rocking chair and mom put the T.V. on. Ruth took her glasses off. I saw her eyes. I said, "What happened to your eyes?" She said "What, what do you mean?" I said " Your eyes are almost all white." She said "Oh, that. Well, I'm blind, I can't see. I haven't been able to see since childhood." OH, I said. "Do they hurt?" She chuckled and said. "No, they don't bother me." I remember mom taking her to places and helping her out every once in a while. We would eat dinner together at the table and Ruth would ask how our day went. She seemed like a very nice person. I started to like her and looked forward to coming home just to see her and to sit next to her. One day I came home and she wasn't there anymore. I asked mom where she was. Mom told me she was at the hospital and doesn't look like she'll be coming home. I started to cry. I loved her, she was nice to me. To this day I still think of her. I really don't know what happened to her, I can only speculate.

The dog was finally gone and that made me sad as well. Mom said it was about time because the dog ate her out of house and home and she didn't know how much more she could take of him.

At the end of kindergarten, Mom told us we were moving back to Tucson Arizona. I didn't want to move. So I packed up all our things (my sister and I) that I can carry and move out. We went a couple of blocks, my mom's neighbor saw us walking and pushing our things. She asked "What's wrong, why are you running away?" I said "My mom is moving back to Tucson and we don't want to go. So, can we move in with you? She said "Let's have some cookies and milk and we'll talk about it." My sister and I were sitting there, eating and drinking our milk and cookies, and then the lady came in and started asking questions, like she was worried about us and was trying to be our friend type of thing. Then we heard the door bell. We didn't think anything about it because we thought we walked pretty far away and didn't think mom knew her. Boy, were we wrong. She found us, the lady called her and told her where we were at and to wait a little while, while we ate our cookies.

The outcome of my baby years were down right negative. No child should ever go through what I went through. I can't believe I remembered all this. I know there's more but I have no one to tell me about it. However, my Dad did say that one time mom left us at the babysitters for over six weeks and the babysitter finally called him to pick us up. But when he showed up, Mom was there, so he left us with her. Sometimes I do blame my Dad for not being there for us. If he was there maybe things would have been better. I thought that way for years. It's really not good to dwell over the past. Remembering the past is all right as long as it doesn't interfere with your life, but in a positive way instead. Like learning from the mistakes and possibly make things better for yourself or others that may enter into your life later on. How would you handle it in this situation? Well, I grew up hating my mom and being very afraid of her. That's how I handled living with her. My sister, that's another story. She didn't handle it too well. She started making up another world for herself. As I continue to tell my story I'll continue to write about her. Let's just say, I'm the lucky one. It's really too bad that you can't read this book when you are a baby. It would help you handle the negativity in your life. God gave my mom an opportunity to love, cherish, and care for us to the best of her ability, instead she just gave up and did what ever she wanted and didn't think about the consequences her actions would be towards her children. I cannot tell you how many times I have screamed out to God to help me and asking him, "Why me?" Maybe I was put here to open my mom's heart and show her what life is supposed to be. Or maybe I was put here to experience this difficult life, either set forth by me or my mother. I will only know when I finally go home.

Going Back to Arizona

It was a very long drive for two children ages of 5 and 6. Mom didn't stop at any hotels, only at restaurants, gas stations and rest stops. We would sleep in the car. The car was a 1968 Camaro two door and the color was baby blue. Someone made a bed mat for the back seat so it would act like a full bed. It folded up and was able to be placed on the floor against the two front seats.

All I remember is that my sister and I had to find stuff to keep us entertained and busy so we wouldn't bother mom while she was driving. I've got to hand it to mom; she knew how to pack a car with children. I think that's the only time I felt comfortable around her. We had coloring books, road games, and dolls (paper dolls out of a book and regular dolls). She packed snacks for us to have when we got hungry.

One late night mom pulled into a rest stop to get some sleep. I didn't feel like sleeping, I wanted to play. So, I told mom I needed to go to the bathroom. She said fine just take you sister too and hurry back. Well, on the way to the bathroom we played hop scotch and tag. When we got done with the bathroom, we played on the way back to the car. I tried to open the car door but it wouldn't open. I tapped on the window to get mom's attention. She didn't budge. I banged on the window, still nothing. So we just sat next to the car, trying not to cry. A truck came driving in and parked not to far from us. A guy got out of the truck; he saw us sitting next to the car and asked us if we needed help. I just told him, "I couldn't wake mom up so we can get back in." He said, "Let me try." He really banged on the window, it sounded like he was going to break the glass. It startled mom, she jumped up and almost hit her head on the car ceiling. I laughed a little. She got her glasses on and looked outside. The guy pointed to us and mom opened the door and we got in. I had no problem falling a sleep. With stress I get very tired easily and just want to sleep. So that worked out just fine for her. In the old days, everyone trusted everyone. There was hardly any violence to worry about. I trusted everyone, even the ones I shouldn't. I looked for the good in everyone. I even gave them chance after chance to change their ways. So, I wasn't really afraid when that guy came up to us.

Mom had a big coffee can with a lid on it in the car. When she didn't feel like stopping at the rest stops, she'd tell us to go in the can. At first I had no idea how to do that. I just looked at mom like she was crazy. How would you even come up with something like that? She told us to sit on the can and go. That image has been stuck in my head for the whole entire time of my existence. That was so embarrassing to me. I felt it was wrong. I didn't want anybody to watch me go to the bathroom, especially while riding in a car. Mom said in the old days they would do that in the wagons so they didn't have to stop for anything. Why? It's not like they were going very fast. They can just jump off, go to the nearest bush and go, then run to catch up to the wagon. At six years old, you come up with some strange ideas, but it makes sense. I asked my sister to hold up the blanket for me and I would do it for her. Can you imagine a six year old and a five year old going in a can, while the car is moving? I didn't like it back then, but today I have to chuckle about it. What my mom came up with sometimes was shocking and unheard of, but it worked.

The trip only took a couple of days, since it seems like she was driving almost all the time. We only ate twice a day and had snacks constantly during the driving parts. Mom didn't believe in sodas for us, so we had water or juice. Mom use to tell us soda is bad for you and I want the very best for my kids. We just thought she was mean.

My sister and I had our fights in the car and mom would yell at us to stop, can't you see I'm driving or she'll yell, If I have to stop this car you two are going to get it. One time when she was yelling at us we were watching the way she was driving and she hit a huge bird. I started to cry, well, scream. Mom killed a living thing. I couldn't believe it. Mom pulled over got out of the car, walked around to the front of the car to check things out. She put her right hand on the hood of the car leaned over and looked. She straightened up started going back to driver side and stopped and looked down the road. She got back in the car, looked at us and said, "Stop crying now, everything is all right. The bird didn't suffer." I asked mom if I can see the front of the car when we stop, and she said no.

That was my first experience of witnessing something dying right before my eyes. I'll never forget that. This day, I look back and thought to myself: if that ever happened to my kids and they acted like that, I would have taken them out of the car and held them until they calmed down and explain to them that things happen for a reason. I believe in that saying with all my heart. Maybe God put the bird there, to warn mom to slow down and pay attention to your children and she didn't see it. I look at things all around me. I look for signs if there is any to try to figure what to do next if I need help with something.

We made it to Tucson and ended up staying at my mom's friend's house, Cathy. She has two girls, Kimberly and Cassey, of her own. Cathy's house was huge. It was two stories high and had a lot of rooms. She told mom she was welcome to stay as long as she wants. The first night, to celebrate our return to Tucson, we had Kentucky Fried Chicken with all the works.

After we ate, we went to the living room to watch some T.V. I started feeling weird and so did my sister. We didn't feel to good. So, Cathy told mom to take us up to bed. Kimberly and Cassey came up with us. I guess they were curious about what was going on. Mom took our temperatures, it was fine. So she asked the girls to watch us while she went down stairs to get something. I started to feel like I was going to puke. Kimberly told me to lye down and the feeling will pass that way. Nope, it didn't. I puked all over her. Hey, she was standing right in front of me, where else was I going to do it? She went screaming and crying down the hall. I went to the bathroom and continued to throw up. While I was in there, I heard all kinds of commotion. I heard a knock on the door. It was mom asking if I was okay and I yelled no. She opened the door, came in and said, "You know, that wasn't nice of you to do that to Kimberly. We are their guest in their home. Why did you do that?" All I could say was that she was in my way. She knew I felt like I was going to puke, it's not my fault. Why did she assume it was my fault? Why couldn't she just be a mom for once and take care of us like she'd cared for us?

At this point I was losing my fluids in both ends. I was sitting on the toilet and puking in a garbage can. I was thirsty and I asked mom for some water, and she told me no and to wait a while. "We have to see if you throw up anymore." She helped me back to bed.

I fell asleep.... Mom came in to take my temperature and she said I had a fever. I was in bed for a couple of days, mostly sleeping and going to the bathroom. The first day I had to have help going to the bathroom. I was so weak; Mom seemed to act like it was a big chore to take care of me, like she didn't want to have anything to do with me. I was a burden to her. So I cried a lot, I didn't understand why she treated me this way.

I knew down deep inside myself that mothers and fathers are suppose to be affectionate; loving, caring people. They are suppose to be there for you unconditionally when you're sick and they are suppose to comfort you and encourage you to get well. I just wanted mom to love us. I was always after her for attention, most of the time I didn't get it. All I wanted was to be held and to be told that everything was going to be all right.

I finally got better and mom found a place to live in, so we moved there. It had a big back yard with a huge tree and some cacti, no grass just a lot of dirt. The yard was closed off with a wooden fence. There was an open garage with an entrance to the inside of the house. When you first walk in there's the laundry room, then you go through the door way and you end up in the dining room. Look to your right you see the Kitchen. There's a window over the sinks and it was a very bright kitchen. On the other side of the Kitchen, there's a front door. As you walk through the dinning room you come into the living room. Nice and big, the carpet was a mustard color and walls were yellow and there's a sliding door going to the back yard. On the other side of the living room, next to the dinning room there's a counter on the wall. Right when you come into the living room, glance to the right there's a hallway leading to a bathroom and further down three bedrooms. They didn't have carpet but tile instead. I thought I was going to have my own room. I was excited about that. It turned out that I had to share my room with my sister and the other room was for a roommate. One of mom's rules was never to go into her room without her permission.

So, living in that house I never knew what her room looked like. I had glances when she would open the door while I was around her, but never really had any idea what it looked like.

We were settling down in our new home. I liked it there and it was very comfortable. One day mom told us we were going to New York to visit Nana and Granddad and we were going to fly on a plane. I got excited and scared at the same time. "A plane! Wow!" Well, we were invited to go to my Uncles wedding in the summer of 1974, our first plane ride that I could remember. It was so exciting to be able to do something with mom without worrying about anything. Back then, everyone was nice and willing to help each other. On the plane the stewardess always had something for us to do. We got to meet the captain of the plane. We got our own wings. I was so proud of them. Back then they allowed smoking in the planes so that's what mom did, smoke and drank Tab. Mom didn't say or do anything to us on the plane. I guess she was satisfied at the fact that someone else was watching us. She took advantage of that.

My sister Gayle was 5 and I was 6. Gayle was going into kindergarten and I first grade. I totally forgot about this until I asked my Uncle what year he was married. I know we were there because I remember watching the wedding ceremony. I hate to say this but I didn't like it to well. My favorite Uncle getting married to someone I didn't know. But I had to stand there for my Grandparents and my mom. But I have to admit to this day when I look back, my Uncle was very much happy and in love. The wedding was in Reading, Connecticut at Nana and Granddad's home by the Little Forest. At the end of the ceremony, Will and Yee hammered a plaque on a tree with their name and the date of when they got married. I believe to this day it's still there. The Little Forest had little statuses all over the place and one was standing and holding a stick as a flute. This one showed the entrance to the forest and it was one of my favorites. The others were weird, but I guess it had to do with Asian relics, but it was nice to explore the forest and wonder what it all meant. I was told to not touch them or move them because they had their own special meaning and they might break so I didn't, but I did just stand there a lot and day dreamt about what they meant. I never did find out. This part of my life started the future events of our lives. I look at it this way, if my Uncle never married at Nana's and Granddad's place, we would have never been asked to visit every summer.

After all the excitement ended, everything seemed quiet and calm. We woke up happy, ate with others at every meal, did things with each other. Then one day mom said it was time to get ready to go home. I started to cry, I just didn't want to leave. I wanted to stay. Mom said school was starting soon and we had to get ready for it. I asked her why we couldn't go to school there and stay with Nana and Granddad. Mom got mad and stormed out of the room. A few minutes later, Nana comes in and explains that she was too old to take care of us all the time and it was best we went with mom. She promised us that we would be able to visit her and Granddad when ever it was possible. She gave us a hug and said now stop your crying and cheer up and that little girls aren't suppose to cry. Gayle and I went to the bathroom to rinse our faces, like mom had taught us, so no one would know we were crying. We came out and it was dinner time and Nana looked at us like she was stunned and then looked at mom. I guess she didn't think we would recover that quickly.

The next morning we were off to the airport to go back home. Nana and Granddad walked us to the terminal and sat with us until the plane came. I gave them big hugs and didn't want to let go and I started to cry. Mom took us and we were pulled into the hallway to the plane. I could see Nana looking and watching so I waved to her. We were still crying when we got to the seats. A stewardess notices and came over to ask if everything was alright. Mom told her, "Yes, they are going to miss they're grandparents that's all."

We got home and everything went back to normal in my eyes. We had to be quiet in the mornings, and when mom woke up we had to be quiet. When the phone rang we had to be quiet, when it was dinner time we had to be quiet. Mom didn't want to hear from us at all. I actually looked forward to bed time. Dreaming was one of my escapes from what we went through.

I didn't like the way mom was treating us. I just wanted her to pay attention to us and play with us.

Our new school was about to start. Mom took us there to register. Then we went to the doctor's to get shots. I didn't like that at all. Mom told us to get over it, that it's part of life.

Mom took us to school by walking us to it. She did this for a couple weeks. Then one day she told me it was up to me to take my sister to school and not to stop and talk to strangers. So I had another school to go to. GREAT, I was not looking forward to that….

Roommate

Mom's roommate was a guy named Grant, I think. Well, he would prefer to be called Gwen. He didn't like being a guy, so he tried very hard to cover that up by dressing like a girl. He would help mom take care of us while she was gone. I didn't know where she went, but he took better care of us than she did.

Gwen would wake Gayle and I up in the morning. When she/he did, she would say, "Shhhh, be very quiet we don't want to wake up your mother." So we tipped toed our way to the living room. Gwen had our school clothes ready, and we took turns going to the bathroom to change and brush our teeth and hair. Well, Gwen helped Gayle because she was still too young to do it herself. Gwen had our breakfast ready, too. While we ate our breakfast she would make our lunch. She would do this for us everyday that I could remember.

I hated walking back and forth to school. In the mornings it wasn't bad, but on the way home it was hard. The heat got to me many times. I never packed water in my back pack, never thought of it. I would try to find faster ways home everyday because of the heat. I finally found one, alley ways. The alley where my house was had a German Shepard that would bark every time someone would go in the alley and pass his house. Every time I would walk by I would say, "It's just your neighbor. Don't worry and calm down." I couldn't see the dog. The fence was all wood and very tall. I only knew it was a German Shepard because one day I saw the owner walking the dog in the alley through a hole in my fence.

Mom or Gwen would pick Gayle up at school because she only had half days. I have no idea what happens when I'm not around her, so the first year of school there I walked home alone. Hey, I was used to it. I still didn't like the heat. I couldn't wait to get home so I can get something to drink, sit down, and relax from the heat.

Gwen would have something waiting for me to drink and snack on when I got home. She asked me if I had homework and would sit down and try to help me. I hated homework, sometimes it was hard for me to understand it and I would get frustrated a lot. Sometimes I would get so mad that I start to cry. But with Gwen, she was patient and helped even if it took hours for me to understand. We would take breaks so I could calm down and try to focus.

One night around 7pm, I was still having problems figuring out my homework. Mom came home unexpectedly and saw me doing my home work. She asked "Why didn't you finish you homework before dinner?" I said, "I took a break, it's too hard for me to figure out. So, Gwen said to take a break and eat maybe it'll be easier after." Mom didn't like that too well. She started screaming at me. "What? You know the rules. Homework first, chores second, dinner third, and free time last. Why can't you do what I ask you to do?" She grabbed my homework and looked at it. "You can't figure this out? What's wrong with you?" She throws the work on the table and was about to back hand me then Gwen grabbed her hand.

"Sally, you don't need to that. She's trying the best she can. Let me just help her a little." Mom went to her room for the rest of the night.

Gwen put her hand on my forehead and brushed back my hair. "Don't worry Tanya, everything with will be fine. Let's try to get this homework done and then you can go to bed."

After I went to bed, I heard mom yelling at Gwen. "You have no right to tell me what I'm supposed to do with my kids. This is my family and not yours. Please don't interfere again." Gwen just said, "I'm here to help you and I thought an extra bonus I would help your children too. I'm just trying to make it easier for everyone." Things went back to "normal" if you care to look at it that way.

Halloween was coming; mom bought a couple of huge pumpkins. She asked us to draw faces on them so she can cut them out. She said we had to clean them out though. Mom cut the top of the pumpkin off for us. We had to scoop out the pulp and the seeds. I kind of liked doing stuff with mom because this was the time she didn't yell or hit us. Mom told us to separate the seeds from the pulp so we did that. She started to wash the seeds just with water to get the slime off and I threw away the pulp. She had us watch her set the oven for 350, and spread the seeds on the cookie sheet, then put salt on them. Then she put them in the oven. Mom turned around and said, "Now in ten minutes we'll check on them. If they are golden brown on top then we will take them out and flip them, salt them and put them back in the oven." While we were waiting, we started finishing the pumpkins. What a mess, but we were having fun. Ten minutes later, we went to the kitchen and she made us stand far back from the stove. She opened it, pulled out the tray and said, "Look at the seeds. See how golden brown they are?" She then proceeded to flip the pumpkin seeds and put them back in the oven. We cleaned up the mess we did with the pumpkins, mom put candles inside the pumpkins and lit them, then put the top on them and placed them outside in the front. They were cool looking. Then mom blew out the candles and said, "We have to save the candles for Halloween." I understood that. Gayle and I smiled, went back in and sat at the dinning room table and waited for the pumpkin seeds to get done. That was torture, I couldn't wait for them. I never had pumpkin seeds before. I was so excited. Then the time came and Mom took the seeds out, put them in a bowl and said, "We have to wait for a few minutes for them to cool." I'm thinking to myself, "What? I don't know if I can handle this any longer." She put the seeds in the middle of the table gave us a napkin and put a spoonful of seeds on it. Oh My God, were they good. I wanted more but she said no, let's save some for tomorrow. My sister and I went to bed happy. I believe that's the way it should be all the time.

The next morning Gwen got us up and we proceeded to do our morning thing. Gayle and I went to dinning room table and sat down then Gwen brought us oatmeal for breakfast. I hate oatmeal, I really mean it. Gwen said, "Mine is special, I make it taste good. Just try it." Wow she was right. It had raisins in it and cinnamon and sugar with just a little bit of butter. She sat down with us and started to talk. "We are going to be doing something today together with your mom. It's going to be fun and tiring and I hope you two will try to help as much as you can without any emotional out bursts." I asked "What are we doing?" Gwen said, "We are going to make your Halloween costumes from scratch." I looked at my sister and back at Gwen. "I want to be a monster," Gayle said. 'I want to be a butterfly." Gwen said, "Okay, we can probably figure this out." Since it was Saturday, Gayle and I were allowed to watch cartoons on T.V.. While Gwen was cleaning the kitchen, we were watching cartoons. Mom woke up and came into the living room. I had to move out of her futon chair, so she can sit. She told me to get a cup of coffee for her. I hated that, Why couldn't she do it? Gwen heard her and she was already making it for me. Gwen whispered in my ear, "You are way too young to do this. Just pretend you are making it and stay in here with me." I looked at her in shock, so I was standing there watching then mom came in and asked "What's going on in here?" Gwen said "Oh nothing, just cleaning up a bit. You know how hard it is to clean oatmeal." I just smiled. Gwen said, "Tanya just go watch T.V. and I'll finish this for you. Sally we have to talk." I stood there and Gwen looked at me and moved her head indicating me to go. I smiled and left. I guess she was telling mom what we wanted to be for Halloween. Mom came back in and sat down; Gwen went to her room and got dressed. It was a very relaxing day, no arguing or fighting. I was happy. Gwen said "I'll be back and please don't start anything without me." I didn't notice the time at all and then Gwen was home. She had a bag of stuff. I ran to her while she started taking stuff out. Paint, paint brushes, news papers, felt, balloons and other things. She asked mom to get some hangers and the spare materials. Gwen went to the kitchen got a bowl of water and some flour. She mixed that together to make paste. Then she ripped the newspapers in long strips, had mom blow up a huge balloon to the size of my head and even a little bit bigger. Than we coated the pieces of paper with the flour and water concoction and put them on the balloon. While the balloon was drying, Gwen got some wire pliers and rearranged the hangers into separate large tear drops. She glued fabric around the tear drops and made a design in the middle of each one. Somehow she connected them together, making it look like butterfly wings. It was really pretty, well, to a 6 year old that is. My sister loved it, and so did I. The balloon finally dried so I got to pop the balloon. The weird thing is that it didn't make a loud pop. With the scissors, Gwen cut on the bottom of the balloon so my head can fit in it. Then the eyes out and then little holes for the nose. Gwen made ears for it and shaped the mouth. After everything was done and dried, Gayle and I tried them on and mom took a picture. I look at the picture every once in a while because it reminds me of a time where it was peaceful and I had fun, we as a family participating in an activity. When Halloween came, my sister wanted to be the monster. She said it looked better then hers. It didn't bother me, so I let her be it. In the middle of trick or treating she decided she wanted to change costumes. She said the monster was getting too heavy for her, so we went home and switched. I was able to wear both costumes. I have to say we had a lot of fun that Halloween.

Mom decided to open a day care in our home and Gwen was willing to help as long as she got paid for it. Everything seemed to go well. One day Gwen had to talk to mom in private. To this day, I still don't know why, but afterwards, Gwen came to us and said that she had to go somewhere and she'll be gone for a couple weeks. We started to cry because we didn't want her to leave, but she reassured us that she'll come back, so this meant that mom would have to do everything and she gets pretty upset over stuff easily. This is a part that I have trouble talking about and there are several more as well.

Mom didn't make us breakfast in the morning and she told us we were old enough now to know how, and she wouldn't make us lunch and told us the same thing. She told Gayle that she knew how to come home and she could do it by herself now. Mom started to show me how to cook and set the dinner table up. While doing so all she did was yell and I jumped all the time. I didn't like it.

Mom was babysitting this one kid; he only looked like he was 2 or 3. I remembered his mother saying something along the lines that he still doesn't like vegetables so don't force him to eat them. Mom smiled at her and said, "I have a secret way for children to eat their vegetables. If he doesn't eat them with me I won't force him." The mother smiled and left. Gayle and I both played with him until dinner. Mom put him in his high chair, gave him his dinner and told him to eat. Gayle and I started eating as well. After a few minutes, Mom got mad at the boy. He wouldn't eat his vegetables so Mom started to shove the vegetables in his mouth. He started crying and gagging. She yelled at him, "Oh stop your crying and eat your vegetables". Then he started choking, his face started to turn a gray color and his lips purple. Mom had to do CPR on him.

She looked at us and told us never to mention this to anyone or you'll get it. The mother came and picked him up about 11 pm when I heard the door knock. I got up from bed went the corner by the door so mom wouldn't see me and I listened in. Mom told the lady that her son seemed sick tonight and that she should watch him over night and see how he is in the morning. We didn't see him the next night, but the following night we did. He seemed fine now, and we went through the same routine but this time dinner was different. Mom gave him apple sauce instead. She wasn't mean to him this time. As a matter of fact, she wasn't mean to us either. While we ate, mom was making our lunch for the next day and getting everything cleaned up in the kitchen. I asked her why she wasn't eating with us tonight, and she said, "I wasn't hungry, and that I'll eat later". My sister and I helped clear off the table. The little boy went to the toy box and we followed after. We played until we had to go to bed. At 11pm we were waken up. Mom said that we had to take the boy home and pick up his mother because his mother's car wouldn't start. On the way there, Mom was complaining about how she was almost out of gas. The car started to make a noise and made jerking movements. Mom pulled over, looked at us and said, "I'm leaving you guys here. I'll lock the doors. I need to go get gas." She was gone for a while and a car came up to ours at first and I thought it was mom, but it was the lady and an officer. The lady knocked on the window then I rolled the window down. She asked if everything was alright and we nodded our heads yes. Beside us was her son asleep. She asked "Where's your mother?" I said "She went to get gas, she'll be right back." The lady said, "Okay, open the door so I can get my son." I did that. Then she said "We'll be in the car behind your until your mom comes back. Roll up your window so you don't get cold" Again I said, "Okay". My mom shows up and saw the car behind us. She looked in the car and saw us but not the boy. The woman and the officer came to the car. The lady was very upset and was yelling at mom. "How could you leave my son in your car without supervision? Why didn't you take him with you? What's wrong with you, how can you be so irresponsible?" Mom was quiet while she was talking, so I guess she didn't want us to hear. On the way home she started to blame us for what happened. She accused us of drawing attention to the car by moving and making shadows. I had no idea what she was talking about. When we got home mom yelled at us to go to bed. We cried ourselves to sleep. We never saw or heard from the boy again.

I heard the alarm go off in mom's room, got up and got Gayle up, went to mom's room and knocked on the door. Mom said rudely "You know what to do, so do it. Watch the time." So we did this for the two weeks Gwen was gone.

One day Gayle said she met someone on the way home from school and he wanted to meet me. I said, "Okay, we'll see him on the way to school tomorrow. We'll leave a few minutes early." My sister was excited all night. Mom kept on yelling at her to calm down and sit down. She was excited about me meeting her new friend.

On the way to school the next morning, Gayle was skipping and running ahead of me, yelling at me to hurry. I yelled back at her to come back here and I didn't feel like running. She started walking next to me and talking about her friend. "He said if I bring you there we would get free candy and cookies. He said he would write a note for us if we are late and he would walk us to school too." I said, "Mom told us not to talk to strangers." "Well, he's not really a stranger, when Gwen would walk me home he would be in the yard and he would wave and say and hi to us. He has a nice smile." "So, did Gwen talk to him?" " Yes, she would say hi back and smile back at him." "Okay, okay, we'll see." We got to his house, and the yard looked dead but so does everyone else's. His windows were covered in something dark and he didn't have a screen door or a doorbell. I told her, "If I said we have to go we will have to leave." Gayle said, "Okay." Gayle knocked on the door and he opened it a little to see who it was. He opened the door and looked outside and said, "Okay come in." Gayle was so excited and said, "Okay, I brought her. Can we please have the candy and cookies?" The guy said to hold on a moment. I told him that we couldn't stay long and we needed to go to school. "So will you please give her what you promised so we can go?" The guy was acting funny and said, "Let me find them first. I can't remember where I put them. " He was still acting weird. I told Gayle, "Let's go, he probably doesn't have anything." I sensed something was wrong, I told her I was leaving and you should too. Gayle said hold on a minute. I was almost at the door at that point then she dragged me to the kitchen. The guy said, "Gayle, come with me to that room. I think it's in there." I said, "Wait, don't go in there." She said, "Like what is he going to do when you're here?" I waited for like 20 seconds then yelled, "Let's go or you won't be able to come here again." She came out with a couple of cookies. The guy said, "Come back tomorrow, I must have eaten all the candy." I grabbed Gayle and dragged her out of the house and told her that we are late to school now. She shared the cookies with me on the way to school. I told her that I didn't trust him and that we wouldn't be going there anymore. She said, "Okay, but he'll be looking for us now that he knows what time we come this way." I said, "We'll have to change our route to avoid him." I told her it was my responsibility to make sure she was safe and not to talk to strange people again. We were only 5 minutes late thank God. I was worried about Gayle all day because she would have to walk home by herself. I couldn't concentrate on my school work at all. I figured out what time she would be home so I pretended I was sick and had to go to the Nurse's office. I asked the nurse if I can call home to see if mom was home. She said okay so I called home. Mom answered and I asked if Gayle made it home safely. She said, "Of course she did, and Gwen is back so she picked her up at school today." I thought to myself, "What a relief, I can relax now." God does work in mysterious ways. He sure was looking out for us. I said goodbye to mom and looked at the nurse and told her I felt better and went back to class. When I went home, Gwen and Mom were sitting in the dining room drinking coffee and Gayle was eating cookies and milk. Mom said, "Come here", and I thought to myself, "Oh God she found out. I'm in deep trouble now." "Gayle told us what happened this morning. Why did you go into that house without an adult? Some thing could have happened to you." I said, "Gayle told me that Gwen knew him and he was alright, so I believed her. At least she didn't go in alone." " Yes, that was very stupid on your part too. What if something happened to you and you couldn't get out to call for help?" "Mom, I thought he was okay." Gwen stepped in and said, "Look, I won't be here forever. You have to be smart and start doing stuff for yourself. We already took care of that guy. He won't bother you again. As a matter of fact, you won't see him at all. Don't talk to another stranger again. That means you too Gayle." Gwen continues to talk, "Okay now that's out of the way, I have something to say to you girls and you're not going to like it to well. I have to go to California to have surgery and I'm staying there for a long time. I will be having several surgeries, so I'm moving there." Gayle and I looked at each other and then to Gwen. We started to cry, "Why are you leaving us? What did we do wrong that you're leaving us? Please don't go, stay with us. We love you just the way you are." I went to hug her and so did my sister. Gwen said, "I'll be here for about 6 more weeks. Then I'm going to California. We will spend a lot of time with each other before we go. One day I'm hoping I can come and visit you. You two are wonderful children and I hope that someday I'll have children just like you." After dinner, we went to bed and cried ourselves to sleep. The next morning was back to "*normal*" as always. The time went by quick. Gayle and I forgot what Gwen said and the night before she left she told us her good byes and gave us kisses and great big hugs and we cried some more. The next day was hard on Gayle and I.

I'm not even sure how we survived what we went through. I haven't heard from her to this day. I'm not even sure she's still alive or what. She would be in her late 60's early 70's. If she's still around I hope she'll read my book and try to find me. I want to let her know that without her support in our life, we wouldn't know what happiness would have felt like and we very much still love her. She was the first nicest person we knew. She made our life easy for awhile, our guardian angel, sunshine in our lives. Of course being 5 and 6 we see things differently and it sticks to us in that point of view, but the feelings are still there. Writing this part of the story was hard to write about. I had all kinds of emotions going on. I had to stop a couple of times to collect myself so I can continue. I asked myself, "I hope I'm doing the right thing in writing about my experiences. I hope my family doesn't care what I write. Especially my favorite Uncle, I don't want him to get mad at me for writing about his sister like this." My heart is fluttering right now. I'm anxious and worried about it all. Hopefully he'll understand and for the rest of the family, I just don't care anymore.

Where Did the Time Go?....

Where did the time go? I've lost about two years of my life after Gwen left. I only remember a few things from the ages of 6 to 8. I guess life was bearable. I do remember getting chicken pocks again. Yes, I said it. <u>AGAIN</u>. I had chicken pocks at the age of 2. Well, that's what mom told me. I caught it from someone in daycare during summer break. I hated that day care. I couldn't do anything without permission and I was around all kinds of other children. None of them had anything in common with me. I had to take naps with everyone else, ate meals at the same time as everyone else, go outside with everyone else, and had activity time with everyone else. I hated it there. It smelled and was very noisy. There were some days we had to be there at night because mom had to work, I think. I couldn't say if my sister was there, I don't remember. Anyways, the chicken pocks made it hard for me to sleep. They were so itchy, mom tried to help by putting this pink cream on or to give me some sort of bath with stuff in it, to take the itch away. She taped socks on my hands to help keep me from scratching the red bumps, which was a nightmare because I still sucked on my fingers at bed time and I couldn't sleep without them.

Yes, I still sucked my fingers at the age of 7. It was the only way I knew how to handle stress in my life. Mom hated it and tried for years to get me to stop sucking on my fingers. Please don't judge me because of that. I had a hard time in school because of it. The kids teased me about it and bullied me as well.

A couple of days later, my sister got the chicken pocks. Talk about a double whammy.

Poor, poor mom, she had to take off work to take care of us. At first, she would just leave me home alone and write down things to do for my spots, but now she has to be home. I can see the aggravation in her face. My sister had a real hard time dealing with the itch. She cried all the time and mom would yell at us for scratching. I don't know how we ever managed to survive that.

So, when school started again, I had these scabs still on my face. I had to walk, alone by myself, to school and the kids looking at me like I was some kind of alien. I felt horrible. I wanted to turn around and go home. I sat next to the school door waiting for the bell to ring so I can go in. The other kids would walk by and laugh. I put my head down. I didn't want to see anyone. The bell rang and I ran in and went to the cafeteria to see who my teacher was. My teacher didn't have to call my name. She knew who I was because of my spots. She came up to me and introduced herself as Mrs. Detz. All the kids were gathered around us and then she said lets go. She grabbed my hand and the others followed.

She had everyone sit down. She told me to come to her desk and sit down in the chair. I looked outside when I was seated in her chair. "You can see all the play ground and if there were kids out side you can see them to." She bent down and whispered in my ear, "I saw everything this morning. I will take care of it right now". She turned to the class. "Everyone this is Tanya. She's recovering from chicken pocks. I know you remember what it was like to have them. I saw a few of you teasing her this morning. I don't like that at all. Just leave her alone if you don't have anything nice to say.

Tanya, you can go sit down in that desk there." Then she started teaching. At lunch time, I was the only one at the table. I could feel the tears swell up in my eyes and that feeling when you're about cry and the only way to get rid of that feeling is to cry. So that's what I did. Some one saw me crying, came up to me and told me to go to the nurse's office. She grabbed my lunch and I went there with her. The nurse gave me tissues and I sat there and finished my lunch. Second grade can be so brutal to sensitive kids. For about two weeks I had to eat in the nurse's office and then finally was able to go outside and play after lunch. My class mates stayed away from me.

The other kids would either ignore me or come up to me and asked if I was the pizza face girl or the pimple face girl and would say things like, "You must be the very ugly girl that everyone is talking about." Some girl named Theresa came up and started to yell and push the others away, shouting, "Leave her alone!" She sat down next to me and said, "Don't worry about them. They are meanies." For a while I had someone to eat lunch with and go to recess with. I started to relax and smile and have fun. One day she bought me a Popsicle. We went under the pavilion to get out of the sun. We were watching this boy pick on this girl so Theresa yelled at him to leave her alone. This girl had a Popsicle stick in her mouth and the boy shoved the stick into her throat. She started gagging and blood started coming out of her mouth. Theresa ran to get help while I just sat there in shock. The play ground monitors came running. One of them said, "Who did this?" Theresa pointed to the boy and the monitor grabbed him and left. The other monitor was holding the girl, and then I saw a lot of teachers coming out of the school. They were yelling at everyone to go to class and hurry. Theresa and I went to class. I was crying and I couldn't believe someone could do that. We heard sirens coming to school. Everyday I asked my teacher if the girl was okay. She told me not to worry about it and to get back to work. I never saw the boy or the girl again. To this day I still have no idea what happened to her. A few weeks went by and Theresa told me she was moving to New Mexico or Texas. I can't remember which state. I was very upset that my only friend is moving. I just didn't know what to do. I told her that there isn't anyone here to help me now. Once she's gone, everyone will tease me again. The last day she was there, we were hugging a lot and crying. I felt miserable. I gave her my address, but never received a letter from her. I haven't forgotten about her and I probably won't. After she left, I started hiding at recess. I didn't want others to tease me. I found a nice, warm area under the school window and I just sat there in the corner holding my legs. The way the sun hit the corner kept it nice and warm. I fell asleep there. The play ground monitor found me and told me I couldn't be there, so I went to the jungle bars to play for a little while. No one paid any attention to me. The school bell rang and I went inside. I kept to myself for the rest of the school year.

I don't understand why people, in this case children, would pick on others just because they are different. I mean, there's no logical reason for the way I was treated. So what if it seems like I was slow, shy, and different than you. I'm writing this part to the people, and you know who you are, that loved to pick on people that are not like you and you thought it was cool to do so. It's all wrong. I've kept quiet for many years and I've tried many times to forget the rude ways you treated me. I feel sorry for you. That only means back then you were insecure about yourself, had low self esteem, and were hoping that no one would notice if you treated others so badly. This is just a part of what happened to me and this was only first and second grade that this happened to me. I'm not the type of person to get back at people that hurt me. I would love revenge, but what's the use in that? Besides which, I don't even remember your names, and if I did, I wouldn't mention you in my book because your name just might corrupt my book and make it stink like a skunk. People are reading this book to understand me for once in my life. Someone is interested in me and not judging me. Back then if I had the guts to stand up for myself, I would have just walked away from you because you would be a waste of my time. I just wanted people to like me. This was a new world for me and I was only here for 7 to 8 years. Why couldn't you just leave things alone? You made me very unhappy, upset, and mad at you. I hated you, I hated school, and I hated the teachers. There wasn't any encouragement from the teachers at all. To this day I've been trying to figure out how I survived all this and continue with my life. You are so lucky!!!!!

After school ended I thought we would stay at home and relax, but no, we had chores and we had to help mom watch the kids she took care of. During play time, she would throw us outside and would lock the screen door so we couldn't come back in. One time I was thirsty and I needed to go to the bathroom. She wouldn't let me go in so I went to the bathroom behind the big tree and drank water from the hose. I let the other kids drink from it too. After a couple of hours, she decided to let us back in because it was nap time. She had cots in the living room for the other kids so they had a place to lay down on. We had to go to our room and wait for them to wake up before we could come out. A few days went by and Mom was on the phone talking to all the parents she was babysitting for. I heard her say that she had to go to South Dakota to visit my dad and for the kids to see him. She wouldn't be back for a few weeks. I ran to my room and told Gayle that we were going to see Dad and Grandma.

Gayle was happy and Mom called us out and told us all over again. I couldn't wait, I was so excited. We went to our room and started packing our things. Mom came in to make sure we were doing it right. "We must hurry, we are leaving as soon as possible." I didn't understand why we were rushing to go. Next thing I knew it, we where off on the road, it was the same situation as before; Traveling across the United States just to visit my family. Again, it was very hard for us. I hated sitting all the time, but at least this time she let us out of the car and run around at the rest stops to get our exercise. We got to South Dakota at night, and mom parked the car next to Grandma's house and just sat there for a few. I said, "Let's go. I want to see everyone." Mom yelled, "Hold on a minute." I looked at Gayle and we were anxious to get out of the car and go see Dad. Mom said, "Okay now, it's late and we have to be polite, so don't be loud." We got out of the car and walked to the front door. Mom knocked on the door and a few seconds later a light turns on in the house and then the porch light. The door opened and it was Dad. The excitement was unbelievable, I just looked, and I didn't know what to do. Mom said, "Here are your kids. I'll be back in about 3 weeks to take them back for school." Mom gave us kisses, said good bye, and left. Dad said, "Come on in but stay quiet. We don't want to wake anyone up yet." I was nervous and I think Gayle was too. Dad asked if were hungry and if we need something to drink. We said that we were a little thirsty so he told us to go to the bathroom and wash up. We went to do that and when we came back, he had something for us to drink and said that we would have to share a bed for the night. The bed was the couch in the living room, the hide away bed. I never did that before. Gayle was on one side, Dad was in the middle, and I was on the other side. I felt uncomfortable but I still fell a sleep. A few hours went by, I woke up, and I needed to go to the bathroom. I was scared to move. I just laid there for a little while to see if I could just ignore it, Not a chance, so I got up and tippy-toed to the hallway. I heard someone in the bathroom, so I knock a little bit, but there was no answer. So I whispered, "I need to go to the bathroom." Still nothing, but I saw a shadow moving in there. I cracked open the door to let who ever it was in there know to hurry. There was no one. I mean nothing. I rushed in, closed the door, and went. I almost didn't make it. What a mess that would have been. I ran back to the bed and in the morning, Grandma was in the kitchen cooking. I think I was the first one to wake up. I went in the kitchen to say hi to her. I shocked her, and she jumped and said, "You scared me dear. You're up early. How was your trip? Are you hungry?" I was very hungry. Then Gayle came in, we sat down at the small table by the back door, and Grandma brought us something to eat. I'm trying to remember what we had. It's on the tip of my tongue and I can't seem to write it down. She sat down next to us with a cup of coffee and started asking more questions. Like, "Where's your mom?" "What time did you get here?" "Why didn't your Dad wake me?" She didn't let us answer until she was done giving us questions, so I told her we didn't know where mom went, she just dropped us here and then left. We got here about 1am and Dad didn't want to wake anybody yet.

Every now and then, Grandma would take us to her work at the local laundry mat. Her job was to clean the machines out, take the coins out, sweep and mops the floors, clean the bathrooms vacuum the rugs, clean the windows, and does other peoples laundry. I was told she worked there for many years.

Dad worked at an air conditioning place. He worked on cars and other things. One day we had to go to his work and he was working on a table and chair set to take home with us. I stood there and watched him weld pieces of the table legs together and attach them to the table. After he was done, he put the table up. The top of the table was blue, my favorite color, which somehow Gayle would find a way to argue with me on who loved the color more, but I loved watching my Dad work. I never heard him curse or argue with anyone. He seemed to always be calm around others.

Well, Grandma came and took us back to the house. She made us lunch and after that we were able to go outside and play. I was amazed at what the back yard looked like. Everything was green; there weren't any fences between properties and all the neighbor's yards were kept up so we just ran from yard to yard to see if we could get anyone's attention and to see if there were any other kids around. We had so much fun at Grandma's. Dad came home and I ran to him so did my sister. We kind of tackled him down. He gave us a great big hug. He said, "Play for a little bit, I have to talk to ma." So we did. I don't remember what we were doing when he came in and sat down on the sofa and we followed. We watched T.V. with Dad for awhile and then Grandma said dinner was ready. We went to the kitchen, and there was corn, potato salad, pork chops with barbeque and some kind of green that I didn't recognize and I didn't care for that to much either, but I did eat everything else. She was shocked at how much we ate. She just looked at us and let us eat. Time went by so fast. Gayle and I had a lot of fun with Dad and Grandma. We went to a fair and I remember running to a show that Dad wanted to see, and he told us to hurry. It was our Uncle Doug; he was going to crash his car into others. I was very scared to watch it, but I did. Dad assured us it was just a show and to just enjoy it. There were about 15 cars out there, circling, hitting each other. Then one by one they started to quit working from all the hits they were taking. There were two cars left on the field working, one was my Uncle and the other was some one I didn't know. The whole entire time there I was holding onto Dad really tight. I didn't like watching people get hurt. This other guy somehow got enough energy to ram my Uncle in the side so hard that the car left the ground and flipped over on the roof. I jumped up and started crying. Dad said, "It's okay, he'll be ok. Just watch." Emergency people came out to the field because our Uncle wasn't getting out of the car. That's when Dad said, "Okay, now we'll have to go and see what's going on." So we left the bleachers and he picked up Gayle and we ran to the entrance to the field. By the time we got there, they were taking our Uncle out to the ambulance. Our Aunt was upset and crying and Dad said, "You know he'll be alright. He's tough." Dad took us home and had Grandma watch us and then he left. We sat there with her for a while. I knew she was worried but she wouldn't talk to us about it. Then she said it was time to go to bed. I asked her if we can stay up until Dad came home, but she said, "No, I don't know how long he'll be gone, but I'll sit in here until you two go to sleep." We woke to the noise of the door opening and it was dark in the living room. I saw a figure walk past our bed. I said, "Dad, how is he?" He said, "He's fine, just a broken arm and a beat up lip. He had to get stitches, now go back to sleep." I saw him go towards Grandma's room and I fell asleep again.

The next morning we woke up to the smell of bacon and eggs cooking. I jumped up out of bed and ran to the kitchen. Grandma said to go and wash up for breakfast. I woke Gayle up and we went to the bathroom. We got out went to the kitchen and sat down and looked at all the food on the table. Grandma opened the back door and yelled down to the basement, "Breakfast is ready."

A few minutes later, the door opened and it was Dad tucking in his shirt, and I started to giggle. The breakfast was really good; Eggs and bacon with toast and a glass of orange juice. It was nice, and I felt happy and safe for the first time in months. After breakfast, Gayle and I went to get dressed to go outside and play with whatever we can find to play with. When we were in the bathroom getting ready, the door bell rang. It was Mom, and she came to pick us up. Dad said "You're kind of early aren't you?"

Mom said, "Well, I would like to go home early and thought you would like me to take them now." We ran out of the bathroom and stood by Dad. I believe we were holding his legs. I saw Grandma getting our things together and I started to cry. "I don't want to go. I want to stay with you Dad, please?" My sister and I pleaded for him to keep us, but all he said was, "It's your mom's responsibility for you two not mine. You were here to visit not to stay." When we left him, we were crying and screaming really hard. I felt my heart breaking; it hurt so bad, sometimes it was hard for me to breath. That's the day I should have figured out that my Dad didn't want us anymore, but that didn't happen until later. Mom told us, "Shut up, I want you to meet someone before we go home, and I don't want him to see how upset you are." You know how hard it is to stop crying when you hurt so badly? It made it hurt more. We got there and she said to stay put and she'll come and get us. A few minutes went by and here she comes with this guy. He was tall and skinny with short brown hair and he wore glasses. He was wearing a white plaid shirt and dark brown pants. Mom opened the door and told us to get out. He looked at us and then he said something to mom that I didn't hear. He started walking to his place and mom followed with us tagging behind. We heard them arguing while we just stood there in the living room. Somehow we were at his semi truck checking it out and mom took a picture of it with us by it. I don't remember how we got there, but I thought it was cool and all my troubles disappeared for a while. Then mom told us it was time to go. We said bye to this guy and got into mom's car and waited. She came back crying and we asked her what's wrong. She said, "It's none of your business. Stop asking." The trip home was hard, we weren't supposed to talk, cry or argue. The only time we were supposed to talk was when mom asked questions. That was very rare. At night when mom was driving, I would just put my head on the arm rest on the door and look up at the stars and just pray in silence so no one could hear me. The stars were bright. I was hoping that this time God would hear me and do something to change the atmosphere or the quality of my life. I had a taste of it; wouldn't you think things were going to change for the better? I didn't hear anything from God and things didn't change. As a matter of fact, they got worst. I mean down right bad. We got home and mom told us to empty the car. I didn't want to, I wanted to go inside and rest for a while. I didn't feel like doing anything, but Mom made it very clear what we had to do.

She started yelling in our face, "If you know what's good for you, you better empty that car." We started to cry, and mom hit us on the side of our head, then there was a ringing in my ear and I held my head. "Now get going". It took us a while to do it. Do you remember what it felt like when you didn't feel like doing anything? It felt like it was hard to do and it didn't seem to be getting done at all. It just took too long. Well, that's what it felt like. I couldn't wait to get done. When we finally got done, we came in and shut the door and went to our room. Mom didn't say to put the stuff away so we didn't. It's a common thing for kids to assume. I was laying in bed and my sister was playing with something, then Mom comes barging in our room and started yelling at us. "Why is everything in the dinning room? Why didn't you put the things away?" She pulled me out of bed which was on the top. (we had bunk beds) I fell to the floor and she grabbed Gayle and dragged us to the dining room. She made us put the stuff away while yelling at us all the way, until we were done. Then she told us to go to our room. A few hours later, I came out to tell mom we were hungry. She didn't want to hear it. Go back to your room, now! Next thing I knew it, I woke up with my stomach growling and it was morning. I woke Gayle up and we went out to the living room. Mom wasn't there, so I went to the kitchen to find something to eat for both of us. I found that we had milk. I guess mom went to the store last night. I looked in the cupboard and there was cereal. It figures, the kind we didn't like, rice puffs I believe. There wasn't any flavor to them so we put sugar on them and then we ate. After breakfast, we put our dishes in the sink, went to the living room and watched some T.V. About noon, mom comes out, looked at us and went to the kitchen. I heard her banging things around and then I heard her on the phone. Then she comes out, sits down and told us to get dressed and go outside. We did what she said. I didn't want anymore yelling. Gayle told me she was hungry, so I opened the sliding screen door and peeked in. I said, "Mom, we are hungry. Can we please come in and get something to eat?" Mom said, "Is that all you think about? Food? Go ahead go find something to eat." At this point, I couldn't wait to go back to school. I really hated mom right now. We had peanut butter and jelly on crackers, since we haven't been to the store yet. Gayle and I were talking in the dining room just trying to have a little fun when mom yells at us to shut up. We just looked at each other. We had no idea what was going on with mom.

For awhile we were walking on egg shells, anything we did was wrong, anything we said was wrong. We spent most of our time in our room or outside away from mom.

School was starting soon. For the first time I was looking forward to school. I didn't want to be around mom. Besides, after coming home from my Dad's, everything was boring, nothing to do.

What's so strange is I don't remember my second grade at all. Maybe I was in some kind of mode to protect me; you know how kids can be with bullying. I have no idea. All I could remember was finding out mom was going to have another baby. Gayle and I didn't take it too well. We didn't want a brother or sister and we started to cry. Mom yelled at us, saying, "You two are the most selfish kids I have known. You're going to have a bother or sister no matter what so get use to it." After that I just looked out the window in dining room at the Catalina Mountains, looking at a white dot. Later finding out it was Kit Peak, the space observatory with a huge telescope.

One night mom brought home a guy for us to meet. Scampy our dog was very protective over us. He was a Lhasa Apso, had white and tan wavy hair, and didn't shed, but we did have to brush him a lot. We loved that dog. Anyways, Scampy started to bark and growl at him. Mom had to calm him down petting him and telling him that it was okay, but the guy knew right off the bat how to take care of Scampy. He held out his hand to him and Scampy came up to his hand and smelled it. Mom introduced the guy as Lee and told us he was a family friend and to be nice to him every time he came over. He seemed nice and he loved to play games with us. He treated us like we where apart of his family, in a nice way. It was kind of nice and relaxing to be able to let my guard down and live a little. He took us on hikes, camping, and fishing, you name it, we probably did it.

Mom finally found a babysitter, right down the street, approximately two houses down. Her name was Michelle. When mom went out at night, Michelle would come by and watch us. I remember one night there wasn't anything interesting to eat so she made noodles with milk, butter, salt and pepper. It was really good and it filled us up. I've tried to this day to replicate that recipe and I can't. I remember mom coming home while we were eating it and said, "What is that?" When Michelle told her, she said that wasn't good for us to eat. Michelle turned and said, "There isn't anything else to eat." Mom looked like she was embarrassed. Michelle proceeded to tell mom that her mom told her to make it. Mom stopped giving her problems and left again. Michelle told us she'll be right back, she has to go home for something. So Gayle and I sat there watching T.V waiting for Michelle to come back. She came back with a bag of chips and some sour cream and onion dip. We never had chips and dip before so it was our first experience. I loved the stuff and I couldn't seem to get enough of it, but Michelle said not to eat too much we would get a tummy ache. It was so good, but then she stepped in and said no more. That was one of the good memories I have of her. She always seemed to find stuff for us to do. She'd help with homework, let us watch T.V., and played with us outside and in our room. She'd even helped us clean our room once.

One day mom said we were moving to Lee's house because mom couldn't be alone anymore. Somehow she was able to pack all our stuff though. I don't know how, but she did. Lee lived in the desert part of Tucson.

We had to go to this strange school. It had these rooms not connected to buildings, I guess portable rooms. The kids didn't like me at all. Once again I was left alone. I didn't like that school. Everyday I would say to myself I hope we move again soon. I don't like it here.

I liked Lee's house, in the front there was this huge blue rock with bright streaks of green in it. I would sit on it, examine it because it looked pretty. I asked him about it. He said it was his favorite rock. He found it at work and he brought it home. He told me a little secret that this rock is worth a lot of money. If someone knows about how much this rock is really worth, they can steal it from me and then I would have to hunt them down and kill them. I just looked at him like I was scared of him. He'd just rubbed my hair and said, "But Tanya I would never harm you or your sister. You two are good kids." and went inside. The back yard was huge. Lee told me to be very careful out there, there are rattle snakes, scorpions, black widows, and all kinds of poisonous creatures and not to go beyond the yard line without him. His yard and the others weren't fenced in but that was okay, because I didn't care. I loved being in the desert because there was

43

no one to tell me what to do and how to do it. It was nice and calm and I can talk to God all day long without any interruptions. All my life that's all I did was to talk to God. I didn't go to church, I just knew about him/her. I like her because it's more personal that way. I never brought water with me to the desert. I never thought of it. If I got thirsty all I had to do is go home. One day Lee said, "Let's go rattle snake hunting." I looked at him like, "What? You want me to go?" I was shocked, that he said yes and let's go. He grabbed his gun off the top of the fridge and opened the sliding door and said, "Aren't you coming or what?" I said sure and off we went.

While we were out walking in the desert he was explaining to me where the snakes would be. He said, "Depending on the time of day is where the snakes are. This time of day, they are either on top of rocks to get warm or they are under bushes to get cooled off." The time of day was about 1pm, so he said, "If you hear a rattle stop and look. Don't move until you have located the noise. Movement makes the snakes jittery and they strike at anything that moves." I wasn't paying attention because I was happy I was doing something with him. He was so nice to me. He yelled, "Tanya stop!!!" So, I stopped. He said, "Carefully look down to your left." I looked and there was a rattler under a bush, curled up and it looked like it was getting ready to strike. I closed my eyes and then all of a sudden I heard this loud gun shot. It made me jump really high. I looked down to see if the snake saw me jump and it was dead. I ran to Lee and held him. I was never so scared to death in my entire life. He said, "Now you know why you have to be observant. You can't just assume I'll always be there to protect you or what ever else is going through your head." Lee's hobby was to kill rattlers and skin them for their skin and he would let them dry and then make belts, hair bands and anything else he set his mind to. He also knew how to make stuff out of wood. From that day on, I watched what I was doing a hell of a lot more carefully. One day when I came home from school, the house was locked. I didn't know why, but it worried me. They never locked the door, so I sat at the front door waiting. A few minutes later Lee drives up, gets out of the truck and walks up to me. "Your mom's in the hospital, she's having the baby." To myself, I was thinking, "Oh great, there goes my life." I don't remember where Gayle was; I guess I was so wrapped up in myself that I didn't pay attention. Lee said, "Let's go in and just wait now." I said, "Wait for what?" "Well, I'm waiting for someone to watch you so I can go back to the hospital." Wow, no one has ever done that before. Mom would just leave if the babysitter was running late. "Okay'"

I said, "Can't we just go with you?" "Oh no, your mother would just kill me." I don't remember who came to watch us, but before Lee left he said he would call no matter what time it was to let us know.

I woke up to go to school and I went to the kitchen to get something to eat. Lee was there drinking coffee and smoking a cigarette. "You're mom will be coming home today with your sister." I thought to myself, "A sister, great. I'll have to watch this one too." Lee's looked at me, "Why aren't you excited?" "What?" "Why aren't you happy you have a sister?" I looked at him and shrugged my shoulders. He said, "Tanya, no matter what she's your sister, you're her big sister now. It wasn't her choice to come into this world it was your mom's. Don't hate her because of that. She's going to look up to you and want to learn from you." I said, "Okay I guess." He said, "One day you'll see what I mean and you'll think to yourself, 'Lee was right after all'." I asked, "Can I go to school now?" He chuckled and said, "Okay, but remember from this day on, you're stuck with your sister." I said that I know.

Yes, I know, I was a very selfish little girl. All those years of being treated badly, I just wanted everything to be the way I wanted. I wanted everyone to pay attention to me, not this new baby that is here. I was finally happy and I didn't want that to go away. If only you can see it through my world, then you can understand what I was going through. I mean it to this day, I still have problems coping with the decisions I made back then. If I had only known what would happen, I would have done things differently. I would have treated my sister differently, but someone said, "We learn from our mistakes, even if it takes a life time." I wish I knew who said that, because it makes sense.

I came home from school and dropped my book bag in the living room and ran to Lee's room. Mom was in bed holding the baby. Mom said, "This is your sister, Shallon." I came closer to her and saw that she was small with yellow hair and she was wrapped up in a blanket. Mom didn't want me to hold her yet because I might drop her or something. I don't know.

After a few months have gone, things were comfortable and enjoyable. I met this boy down the street, I'll call him Rob.

I figure since I found someone to go out to the desert it'll be ok. We had fun exploring different things. We came across a giant stone that looked like it had a cave underneath it. Rob checked it to make sure there weren't any snakes. He yelled, "Wow! Look! A puddle of water with small toads!" I ran to look and they were so tiny, not even a quarter of an inch, and they were black. I never saw anything like it before. I ran home to get something to hold them in, because I wanted Lee to see them. I got to the back yard and I saw a black snake next to the sliding door, and boy was it big, so I stopped and thought about how I was going to get in the house to let Lee know. The snake wasn't moving so I went around the house and entered the house from the front. Lee was sitting down and watching T.V. and smoking and drinking coffee. He looked up at me and said "What?" "What is a big black snake called and is it dangerous?" He said, "King snake and yes it is dangerous, why?" I said it's in the back yard right under the sliding door. He jumped up grabbed his gun and ran out the front door. All I heard was one shot. He came back in holding a snake in his hand, his gun in is pants and a cigarette in his mouth. He looked at me and asked "Is this it?" I just stood there and said, "Uh huh." with a shocked expression on my face. He said, "Good. I'll skin it and clean it. I'll cook it up and we'll have snake for dinner." "Ewwwh, gross." He said, "Well then your mom and I will have it and you don't get any." I ran out the door with the coffee can to meet Rob at the giant rock and we put a couple of toads in the can. I told him what happened and that's why I was late. He just looked at me weird and said, "Oh that explains the gun shot." I didn't have a care to the world. Life seemed to going good for me. It was easy for me and I enjoyed it every second of the day. I didn't have to hear yelling or screaming or anything negative. Yep, life was good.

Well, I don't remember much after that. I guess I'm not supposed to. That's okay, it's best that I don't. There are certain things that are down right boring, but at least I was living I guess. No rush to go anywhere and the time I do remember with Lee will be stuck with me for the rest of my life. To me he saved my life.

Mom never talked to us about her personal life. She always would say, "Children are meant to be seen and not heard." Or, "You're a kid and you aren't supposed to know adult things." But, when it came to Lee, she said, "You have nothing to worry about." and she kept it that way.

This is what happened:

One day, I was walking home after the bus dropped me off at the corner, and I noticed a sheriff car out front of my home, so I ran to the house to see what was going on. I noticed the door was ripped off the hinges and put on the side. I walked in and asked what happened. The sheriff said just sit down on the couch with your sister, while your mom finishes packing. "What, why?" "Just sit down!!!" So I sat, watching everything. The sheriff looked at his watch and said, "You only have a few minutes. You don't want to be here when he returns." At this point I was scared and I started to cry. Mom came out with two big black bags with some of our things in it. She started walking outside, looked at us and said, "Let's go." She stuffed the bags in the car, told us to get in the car. She tried to go back in the house but the sheriff wouldn't let her. She came back to the car, got in it and started the car up. She was shaken, nervous, and crying at the same time. I asked if she was okay. She snapped and said, "I'll be fine." She started to drive the car. I asked what happened. She said it was none of our concern and not to worry about it, "Now be quiet while I think about what I'm going to do." I don't remember much after that. All I remember vaguely is that we were living in a studio apartment for a while with a bedroom, kitchen and a bathroom; our roommates were roaches all over the place. There was no TV and I had to deal with my mom, Gayle, and Shallon. The only entertainment was out side with just dirt and tumble weeds and a mesquite tree. I didn't like it there. Mom had the place dark at all times, and she would sleep all the time. We would sneak outside to get some fresh air which was hard to do, but it seemed like she just didn't care anymore. As a matter of fact, I don't even think we went back to school during our time at this place. Summer came quick and the place seemed to get hotter every day. Mom went out one day and told us to stay inside and keep the door locked until she came back. A few hours went by, and I was getting worried. I started looking out the window, and wondering if mom will ever come back. We started to cry and I guess we fell asleep, and the next thing I knew it, Mom is walking in with some food and a fan. Mom said that Grandma and Granddad where coming down soon to visit. I got excited about seeing them. I asked when and she said in a couple of weeks.

Lee passed away a few years ago, doing his job as a safety inspector for the giant machines at the mines. He was inspecting a machine and he wasn't paying attention when the wheels started to move, grabbed his foot and that was it. It just rolled right over him and no one had a chance to save him. Ironic, huh? Like I say, Things Happen for a Reason.….

During the first week of summer, Mom's parents came to visit. They stayed at the Tucson Inn. It was nice there. It had all kinds of plants and trees and it seemed to be cooler there because of that. Nana and Granddad were so happy to see us.

When mom needed to go to work one day, Nana and Granddad took care of us. So we didn't have to go to the daycare. We went swimming in the pool, ate lunch at the Inn and went to Randoff Park which is called today as Reid Park. Back then It was so nice, it had a big pond with an island in the middle with ducks and a couple of swans. There was a river with a water fall that was connected to the pond. My sister and I played in the river and splashed each other. Nana and Granddad sat at the near by bench and just watched. After a little while we went to the Park Zoo. We walked around it for a little while, found a snack bar and got something to drink and got cotton candy. We went back to the Inn and for the first time in a long time we actually took a nap from all the running around we did. Nana woke us up a couple hours later and said it was time to get ready for dinner and that mom was on her way. So we freshened up washed our faces and brushed our hair. We went to the Spaghetti house, a popular restaurant that made all kinds of spaghetti. It was one of my favorite places to eat. I loved the salad with homemade blue cheese dressing. I loved that dressing hoping mom would pay attention to me more. I did things that mom liked to show her how much I loved and cared for her. I don't even think she noticed. I loved their spaghetti too. It wasn't as good as mom's, but close. During dinner, Mom, Nana, and Granddad were talking about us. Nana came up with the idea of taking us for the rest of the summer, and if it worked out, they would take us every summer but only for a few weeks and the other weeks they would pay for camp so we would have something to do during the summer instead of being cooped up at a daycare all the time.

They asked us if we wanted to do that. I looked at my sister and she looked at me, but they couldn't take Shallon for some reason. We nodded our heads yes.

Summers with Nana and Granddad

Nana and Granddad lived in New York City in a gorgeous quiet apartment a few levels up. They had an outside patio with Japanese garden settings and a small water fountain. Gayle and I would play in the fountain to cool off and Nana let us. It was a nice area for us to play in.

As you walked in the apartment, on one side of the hallway there are closets and a bathroom. In the living room to the right was a small dining room with the only T.V. in the place. Off the dining room was a small kitchen. The living room had a big Japanese tub and it had fish in it with decorations. Nana told us in the old days they would use the tub to bathe in and heat the water over a fire to put in the tub. This particular tub was meant for a royal family member because of the detail work on it. The tub in its self had beautiful Japanese drawings inside and out. I would stare at it for what it would seem to be for hours. I even loved watching the fish. Nana would tell me to be careful because the fish were expensive. I don't know what they are called but I think I can describe them. They look like gold fish but with big bulging eyes and they came in all different colors, black, white, orange, and red. I guess they were saltwater fish because I've seen them put salt tablets in the water. Granddad said it was to help the fish stay healthy. I wish I had that tub.

On the wall there were two painted pictures of my mom and one of Uncle Will when they were kids. I enjoyed looking at them too.

When you first walk into the apartment and you make an immediate left, there's a hallway going to a bathroom, a den, and a bedroom. The den had a statue of a beautiful Asian woman with two demons one on each side of the woman. Granddad said she was a Dream Goddess with the two demons protecting her. On top of a book shelf there where paper puppets made from China or Japan (I can't remember). They looked mean and scary and I didn't care to look at them. When we visited, that's where Gayle and I slept; in the den. At night we had a night light which was the globe of the earth. We had it on because of the statue. That was like that for years.

(I wished I had it now. I sure do miss it. I don't even know what happened to it.) Nana and Granddad's bedroom was nice and bright all the time. They had two beds, two large dressers, two closets and a bathroom. It was a nice cozy apartment.

Well, the first week of summer, mom was with us, so she can spend some time with them too and to make sure we would adjust okay with our grandparents. We had no trouble what's so ever when it came to them. Mom was impressed or jealous at the fact that we behaved with them. We actually didn't see much of her. I guess she was out with her friends. Have no idea.

One day we went on a ferry ride with all of us. Granddad took a picture of mom and Gayle and I. Shallon wasn't in the picture. Nana was holding her and standing next to Granddad. I liked the ride, but didn't see what the big fuss was about. I just didn't care. I guess we went to see the statue of Liberty, didn't care. I was off doing my own thing. I had no problems with being on the ferry. I've heard about sea sickness but, it never got to me. Even years later, Mom said I had a knack for the sea. After the ferry trip, we went out to eat at this Japanese restaurant where you had to take off your shoes and you had to sit on pillows. The chef cooked for us at the table. It was so cool to watch someone cook for us. He was throwing the knives up in the air and catching them, chopping the food and throwing it up in the air. It was nice to see.

I ate so much to the point I wanted to fall asleep right there. After dinner we walked back to the apartment. We sat down on the couch and mom came to us and said that she was leaving tomorrow to go home and she'll see us later. She gave us a hug and said, "I'll be gone when you wake."

hoping maybe we would start to cry or something. We said, "Okay. Good bye mom."

We had no worries, we loved our Grandparents, and they were the most loving and caring people on this planet. We were the luckiest kids on this planet to have such wonderful Grandparents. I loved them with all my heart.

Mom left and went back to Tucson for some reason, I'll never knew why. There wasn't anything to go back to. We didn't really have a home or any solid ground to stand on. I was hoping that she would move back to New York, so we can be a big happy family but no. She went back to Tucson. I loved being able to see everyone and to enjoy their company.

We woke up the next morning excited about what we were going to do next. We went to the kitchen where Nana was making our breakfast of oat cereal and yogurt. We sat down at the table and started eating. Nana and Granddad sat with us having hot tea and toast with 3 minute eggs. Nana let me try some. They were talking to us about what we were going to do today. All I heard was that we were going to Reading, Connecticut to stay at their home there for a week. I looked up. "What? Another home?" Nana smiled, "Yes, and you were there before when Will got married." I was excited again. I can't wait to see what I might explore this time and I couldn't wait. Gayle and I had to pack up all our things and we had to make sure we didn't forget anything. Nana was packing their things and packing food for the other house. Granddad had to go somewhere, I think to the office, but I didn't care, we were going on a trip to another place, another town.

Granddad loved to drive. Watching them in front while we drove to Connecticut was entertaining. Nana would nod her head back in forth as if she was falling asleep. Granddad would step on the gas a little at a time to speed up a little. For some reason Nana would wake and say, "now Bill you're going to fast, you need to slow down." My sister and I just giggled a little. Granddad looked in his rear view mirror and smiled. Nana didn't like going to fast. It scared her.

When we got to the Reading home, we tried to help Nana and Granddad to unload the car. I look back and try to figure out how in the world did we do that? We were little. It just amazes me to this day what we could do and have done when we were little.

I was dragging my little suit case up the stairs, thinking I was doing a great job in helping. I didn't think I was having trouble doing it. All of a sudden Granddad grabs my suit case and said that he got it and off he went. I got to the top of the stairs and just looked. I fell in love at the way everything was in place. In the hallway there were tall windows with see through curtains. On the right side there was an elephant couch. Nana said, "They would put it on top of elephants for people to sit on and even sleep in them." It was beautiful, made out of some kind of red wood and had all kinds of pillows on it. I hopped on to see how it felt. It wasn't really comfortable. It was hard, and I guess that's why there were a lot of pillows on it. Nana came up to me and said, "Get off of it, it's not a toy and it's an antique", so I got off. Right beside the elephant couch there was this huge metal bowl the size of me on a pillow with this large wooden mallet with beautiful cushioned material on one end. You would bang the bowl with it and it would make a noise so soothing to the ear. I loved playing with it. To separate the hallway from the dinning room there were two wooden walls that you can see right through because they were cut out in a design pattern. In the dinning room there's a small wood stove, a hutch, a wooden dining table with eight chairs, a marble table with metal legs, and a sliding door to the outside. On the walls there were different patterns of plates, glasses, tea cups, and coffee cups. The floor was put together with Mexican tile, not smooth but rather bumpy and curved and the color was off white and tan. It was very cold tile, so I had to wear shoes to keep my feet from freezing. From the stairs to the left is the living room/ TV breakfast room. The living room had a large stone fireplace and on each side of the fireplace was a very large Chinese red wood chest that I could never open. On the far side of the room, there was a bookshelf full of books and next to that there was a small table that the Ming collection was on. I couldn't touch that either. The wall near the stairs was the phone area; a table, a phone, a chair and a small lamp. In the middle of the living room was this huge glass table and under it was four concrete creatures holding the glass up. On the glass were loads of books of art. On one end of the table was a bright green couch with some white small pillows.

My GrandDad sitting on the green couch.

On the other side of the table were two big wicker chairs that my Nana loved. Above the living room there are four large round paper lights with symbols on them. When you first walk into the living room, you would notice immediately a set of narrow stairs going up to the loft. On the right of the entrance there is a table with 6 chairs and a T.V. This was where we ate our breakfast and watched T.V. The kitchen had three ways to go in or out. One way was to go through the dining room, the second way through the breakfast and T.V. area, and the third through the sliding doors going outside. The Kitchen was long and small, at the end where the sliding doors where there were the washer and dryer with a small table with two chairs made out of red wood and above the washer and dryer was more cabinets. That's where we would eat our lunches at. On one side of the kitchen were two sinks and a dish washer. Over the sinks was a small window. On each side of the window were off white cabinets. On the other side of the kitchen was a small utility closet where all the cleaning supplies are stored, next to that were the stackable ovens, a small counter, the stove, and then more counter space. Above all, there where more cabinets. Outside the sliding doors was a wooden fenced in yard with a swimming pool, and a wooden porch near the house. On the other side of the pool was a Chinese or Japanese house which Granddad called the pool house. That's where everything was stored for the pool. On each side of the pool house there was another creature guarding it. On the deep end of the pool on the stone area there were two giant jugs with wooden lids on them. Granddad said he used them to put the stuff he gets out of the pool in them for compose used in Nana's little garden along side the fence. The jugs had decorations on them too. I could spend all my time to explain what this house looked like. There is so much to say and describe, but I'll leave that for right now. This house was like a museum, every where you looked it was something to study and to enjoy. I loved what they did to the house; well technically it was a barn before a house, but I looked forward to going there for the adventure of finding out information on things that caught my attention. Sometimes they wouldn't tell me because there were other things much more important to do or didn't have time to explain. I didn't mind. I was happy to be there.

Granddad had this little barn next to the Little forest. The lawn mower was there plus something else. One day he drove up to it with the truck and told me to stay put. He opened a door to the barn and there was a gas pump there. He filled his truck up, closed everything up, got back in the truck turned his head to me and said, "Shhh, this is illegal, no one knows about this, so don't tell anyone." I looked at him and asked what it was and he said, "Diesel fuel for my vehicles, I make it in the barn." I said, "Ohh, I won't say a thing." Oops I said something, but that was years and years ago. I don't know if its true or he was just making a little story for me, but I never told a soul until now. It was our little secret and I would keep it for him as long as he was alive. Granddad told me that the reason he got the place in Reading was because the river that went through the property. It was called the Little river. I believe it still is called that today. It was his name sake and he made it a home for Nana and him. He so much loved her, he use to call her Dinky. We weren't ever to call her by that, only Nana, but I never saw the sparkle in any else's eyes like I saw in them. Every time they looked at each other there was this sparkle of happiness between them. We never heard any arguing, yelling or even fighting with them. They kept that to themselves. When they needed to discuss something they would leave the room and go to their room and close the doors and talk to each other. They made sure we weren't involved in any disputes. It was easy and safe to be around them. I tried my best to obey and behave for them. I tried to be good so I can continue to see them. I didn't want to jeopardize what I had with them. The only problem I remember I didn't want to do was clean our room. I hated that, just because of what we had to go through earlier with mom, but I did it and took a while but it got done with no complaints. They would throw parties there. Nana would buy us nice looking outfits for us to wear. She said beautiful children always need to look lovely for others to see. One of the outfits was a dress. It was green and white checkered with a cut opened apple in the front. Oh, I didn't like to wear dresses, but somehow she persuaded me to wear it. There weren't any children at this party and we had to act like young adults, so that's what we did. To this day I still don't know what the party was for and all those people I didn't know, but they were nice to us and I had fun. I got to eat as much food as I wanted. No one telling us that's enough you'll get sick. I had a ball. As you can tell the food was the main thing that made me happy. We didn't have to go to bed at a certain time and were free to do anything we wanted as long as it wasn't bad to do.

I remember I was getting tired and I think my sister was too. Without saying anything we went to our room, put our pajamas on, and went to bed. I remember waking up and seeing Nana tucking us in and saying goodnight. Then she turned out the light. She made everything fun and happy. I will always miss her.

The next day was another exciting day. I looked forward to finding out what we were going to do next. I ran in the kitchen and Nana was making breakfast, the three-minute eggs with buttered toast and cranberry juice with orange juice mixed. I still don't know how she made it so good. I've tried so many times to figure that out, came close but there was something missing. She sat down with us and I asked where Granddad was and she said he had to go to New York for work and he'll be back tonight. Okay, something different. So I asked, "What are we going to do today?" She said "Well, you're going to be taught how to swim. I've hired a swim teacher to come and teach you how to swim. I even bought you swimming suits to match. Don't worry it will be fun, wait and see. In the mean time, you can do what ever you want just don't get hurt, lost or do something wrong". So, Gayle and I ran out side. We explored the whole property, four acres worth. Like I said earlier, I loved the Little forest, so I went there. Gayle followed but got bored after awhile. She took off somewhere. She yelled for me and I ran where I thought she was. I couldn't see her. I yelled, "Where are you? I can't see you." She jumped up from a field of wild flowers and tall grass and started laughing. We picked flowers for Nana and brought them to her.

She said, "Oh how did you know wild flowers are my favorite?" We just smiled. She got a vase and scissors and put some water in the vase. While she was doing that she said, "I'll teach you something about flowers so they won't die too quickly". She dropped an aspirin in the water and then started to cut the flowers. She said "Now you have to take the leaves off of the stem of the flower so it doesn't dirty the water. Then you cut the stem of the flower at an angle like this and immediately put it in water". She put the flowers in the middle of the dining room table where it had the most sunlight. She had a way to keep us focused and eager to learn new things. She was a very loving and caring soul. Why wasn't mom like that?

I couldn't tell Nana or Granddad what mom was really like and I don't think Gayle could either. It just didn't seem right somehow. At lunch she made these little sandwiches with different stuff in them. I didn't know what it was but it was good. It had butter on the bread and that's all I remember of the sandwich. She also gave us grapes with a sweet sauce with it. I know what the sauce was, but I'm not telling.

We sat at the table in the kitchen and Nana was doing laundry. She started to talk. "In an hour your teacher will be here to teach you how to swim. While you wait for her you can watch a little bit of T.V. and then go and change into your bathing suits. I'll let you know when she is here." Every minute passed slowly, I was excited to learn how to swim, and I wanted to be a pro at swimming. I couldn't wait.

Learning how to swim was so easy. We learned how to float on the back and on our stomach the first hour. Then we learned how to kick and move our arms. The teacher told us that once we learn the basic swimming techniques we can basically do anything. She was a good teacher. I didn't think I would need to remember her name until now. Sometimes I wish my Grandparents where still alive. The stuff they told me when I was younger would be great right about now. I would definitely put it in this book. She was patient with us and God knew she needed to be. We were wild and always fighting each other for others attention. We couldn't just take turns nicely. I would grab her hair to pull her back and try to run to the teacher before her. She'd come and jump on me to try to dunk me under the water. It seemed we were always fighting and angry with one another, and sometimes it felt that way too. So the teacher had us hold her water proof watch and told us to keep track of the time so we can take turns. I did my part and waited patiently. Now it's Gayle's time to hold the watch. The teacher looked at the watch to see what time it was and proceeded to teach me something new. It wasn't even five minutes and Gayle said it was her turn. The teacher stopped what she was doing and said okay it's your turn then. I took the watch and looked at the time and showed it to the teacher. I didn't think it was Gayle's turn yet. The teacher wasn't happy with Gayle and told her it was still my turn. Sometimes Gayle had to make things more difficult then what they can be. She started having a fit. I told the teacher I could wait and that I was in no hurry so I did my own thing. I picked up leaves from the bottom of the pool and put them on the sidewalk and I jumped out of the pool and jump back in. I kept myself busy. Then I heard the teacher tell Gayle that it was time for her to get out and take a break. It was my turn. While I was learning to move in the pool on my back Gayle was wrapped up in a big colorful towel sitting on the chair and had an evil look on her face, like she wanted to kill me. I just ignored it. After I learned to move on my back she took me to the deep end to teach me how to hold my breath and to dive down to touch the floor of the pool and push myself up. The first few times was hard. I had a hard time holding my breath that long. After a while it got easier and I was able to do it. Gayle came running to the side of the pool and asked if she can learn that. The teacher told her tomorrow. She just sat at the edge of the porch with a frown on her face. I was holding on to the edge of the pool and the teacher wanted to show me how to dive in to the pool to reach the bottom. She said it was a lot quicker, so I watched her. It was amazing watching her dive down and swim to the bottom and watching her swim back up. When she came up she swam to the edge where we where at and said, "The next time I'm here I hope you can do this." Then she said, "Gayle it will be your turn to learn something first and this time I hope you'll listen and share your time."

Before we learned how to swim, Nana and Granddad bought us two floating bubbles that you strap to your back. They were made of Styrofoam. We tried to swim with them. I couldn't go under the water with it and the only time I was allowed not to wear it was if I stayed in the shallow end. Did I tell you the pool was huge?

Granddad told me it was the size of Olympic pool. The shallow end was 3 feet deep and the deep end was 12 feet deep. It was what he needed to swim in. He used to swim professionally in high school and college. I use to just sit out on the porch and watch Granddad swim. He would do ten laps a night and when he was done he did some sort of exercise on the side of the pool with Nana. They taught us how to do them. They said it was like stretching after a good hard swim. It also felt good. By the end of summer my sister and I knew how to swim really well.

Every where I turned there was always something we were doing as a family. The only time we were alone was when Gayle and I went outside and played in the big yard or went fishing at the Little river. I recall Gayle and I fishing and catching crawdads, and we caught a whole bunch enough to have for dinner. Well that's what Nana said. To my surprise, Nana knew how to cook them. So we had crawdads with lemon and butter sauce. She was such an excellent cook. There was a whole bunch of crawdads and it looked like a lot more than what we caught, but I didn't complain. We didn't know how to eat them, we never had them before. Nana showed us how. We were having fun eating them one after another laughing, talking, smiling, just enjoying every minute at the dining table. Granddad just sat there watching. I think I over ate and I know my sister did. In the middle of the night she got really sick. Nana thought it was too much butter in her tummy, but Gayle said it was the crawdads.

Being apart of Nana and Granddad's life was an honor and privilege to be there. I felt as if they were VIP's, everyone was friends with them and when they had parties it seemed the whole world was invited. I loved my family in New York. They were always on my mind. When things got bad at home I thought of them. They're smiling warm faces looking at us, the hugs that I got endlessly throughout the day, the tickling and kisses, and games that normal families do. I just wished mom was like that. She always was upset with us or really mad. She hardly showed us any affection. I met Jeff, one of me uncles. He was so cute. I also met Uncle Don and he seemed really nice. Then there was Aunt Rity and Uncle Nelson. Aunt Rity was Nana's sister. She was always at the dinners in New York with Uncle Nelson. Aunt Rity didn't have children and every time she saw us, she had to pinch and kiss our cheeks and give us hugs. We didn't like it too much but we allowed it because she enjoyed it so much. Uncle Nelson had a gentle soul. He was very patient and did things one at a time. He use to be a architect and drew a lot. He had all kinds on drawing pens and different types of paper.

They had a small apartment and not much room to move so Gayle and I sat mostly. Uncle Nelson taught me how to make a garlic dressing for the salad. We ate there once. I don't remember what we ate but I did remember the salad. Aunt Rity would try to make conversations with us but we just didn't have anything to say mostly. I think she got frustrated with that. She seemed to be angry all the time. She hardly ever smiled, but she seemed to like the visits we made. We just noticed that she wasn't a very happy person, but Nana and Granddad always visited and never talked about her condition or why she was always like that. I really don't know much about them, but I had to say something about them. There's something about Uncle Nelson that always got my attention. He always seemed loving and caring and didn't have an angry part in his body. He always seemed to try to please Aunt Rity all the time. I think that's what drew me to him. He always tried to make her happy. Like I said earlier he had a gentle and loving soul.

Every year it felt like I was being ripped away from the people I loved. I cried just about every year when I had to leave.

For five years, that's what we did. We went to Nana and Granddads. We had so much fun with them. I don't think we experienced any major negativity with them. We would go to plays with them on Broadway, at least one play a year. I didn't care for the plays but I didn't care because I was spending time with my family. We went to different museums. My favorite to this day is the Metropolitan Museum on Fifth Ave. The Ming collection is there, it was donated to the museum by my Granddad before he passed away, but the main reason I liked the museum was because of the Egyptian display and the Japanese garden. One day I hope to go there again.

I just remembered something. One day Gayle and I were playing in the Little forest, just having fun. Nana called us in when it was dinner time. We ran in and washed up, got to the table, sat down, and were ready to eat. We were having her famous chicken and rice soup with sour cream. Nana put our plates down I started right off the bat eating. OH my God was it so good. By the time Nana got done serving everyone I was ready for seconds. She looked at me, took my dish and walked away shaking her head. She comes back puts the dish down and says, "Wait now for everyone to start". I looked at Granddad and he wasn't eating yet. I looked at Gayle and she wasn't eating yet. I just like felt ridiculous and embarrassed, so I just sat there with my hands in my lap and waited. Nana sat down pulled her chair in, put her napkin in her lap, took her spoon, and looked at Granddad. Granddad grabbed his spoon and started to eat. Then Nana looked at us and said, "Okay, you can eat now." She didn't once yell at me or hit me. All she did was talk to me. I believe I had about seven servings of her soup that night. I know there weren't any leftovers. The next morning I woke up itching something fierce. I woke Gayle up, and she had red spots all over her. I ran into Nana and Granddads room, I woke Nana up and said I'm itchy and my sister has spots. She looked at me, jumped out of bed, grabbed me and went to our room. She looked us over and said, "Well, it looks like you have a case of poison ivy. It doesn't look bad. Let's draw you a bath and I'll give you special soap to help with the itch." Nana had everything in that house. Calamine lotion for after the bath, the soap during the bath and she put something in the bath water. The poison ivy was gone in a couple of days. She was an amazing woman. It was like she was super woman or something. She knew exactly how to take care of us. No complaining, always showing her love to us and understanding. She was everything I wanted my mom to be. Why couldn't my mom be like her?

At the end of every visit it was hard for me to let them go. I wanted my life the way they showed me what my life should be like. I didn't want that to end. I didn't want to go back to the life that made it hard for me to enjoy. I will always cherish all the times I spent with my grandparents. They where my life jacket.

My Life with My Stepfather

The first summer at my Grandparents' went fast. I wasn't looking forward to going home. I didn't even know what home was anymore. We got off the plane, mom signed for us, and she gave us a hug and a kiss. We went to get our luggage and then we had to walk to the car. Mom said she had good news and had a new place to live. It was walking distance to the Club and right across the street from our new school we were going to go to. Things were looking up. I liked the idea of the school just across the street. I wouldn't have to walk that far. The house had three bedrooms. Gayle and I once again had to share a room. Shallon had her own room and so did mom. The only problem I had was there was only one bathroom but we can manage. Mom had food in the house we had TV and furniture, a laundry room and a big back yard.

We started school and it seemed to be easy. No one was picking on me here and I was getting along with everyone. I knew most of the teachers and I got free lunch at the school so I didn't have to make my lunch anymore. I felt like I was in a dream. Everything seemed really easy to deal with. Every morning I looked forward to school. I actually ran across the street to school. Kids taught me how to do acrobats on the bars and other stuff I had no idea that could be done. One activity was sitting on top of the bar and then flipping back and landing on your feet. They told me what it was called but can't remember now. Anyways, I was making friends, enjoying life, and getting to know the neighborhood. Life was good.

Mom became a member of PWP (Parents Without Partners) and did all kinds of activities with them. There were potluck dinners, dances, bingo, and camping trips. We went to almost all the events that were possible. I didn't like camping that much, but since my family was there I endured it. Once we even went to Mexico at the beach for a camp out. I taught Shallon how to wash dishes in the water like mom taught me. The water was very cold but I didn't mind. We found sand dollars and shells on the beach. I actually didn't want to leave the beach but mom said we had to go back to school. Maybe one day we'll be back. During these events everyone was nice and helpful. I was happy.

Just thinking about this part of my life makes my heart flutter. I'm trying to find the right words to start. It caused a lot of discomfort in my life and not just mine, but my sister's as well. Shallon doesn't remember thank God. Well that's what she told me anyways, but Gayle, that's another story. To this day I don't understand why her and not me and how come we couldn't do anything to change it.

One day after school, mom told me to baby sit and I would get paid for it. All I had to do was make sure the chores were done and we ate dinner and go to bed at a decent time. I told mom I'll be glad to help. I babysat often for her, I didn't mind. I was happy. I just didn't like the idea of changing Shallon's diaper. Shallon had some kind of food allergy and had messy diapers a lot. One time she made a very messy situation in her crib and we had to clean it up. Mom was nowhere to be found.

One night we were rudely awakened by mom yelling at us, and she had a wooden spoon in her hand. Mom hit the bed with the spoon and it sounded like she hit me. She started asking if she hurt me I said, "No, it didn't touch me." She asked, "Why we didn't do our chores and why is everything a mess?" "We were too tired to do anything." She said, "Well, you had some sleep now get up and do your chores." We had to get up, clean the kitchen, living room and our room. By 4am we were finally done. We went back to bed then Mom woke us up for school. I was still pretty tired. I had to change Shallon's diaper and feed her breakfast and eat breakfast myself and get dressed then go to school.

After school I was reluctant to go home. I didn't know what to expect. I got home and mom was in the living room with someone I didn't know. She introduced us, "Honey this is Mark, my new boyfriend. I met him at

PWP and I thought it was time for you to meet him." At that moment I had a feeling he wasn't going to be a good person. I said hi and went to the dining room table to do my home work. Shallon came to me and started to bug me. I told her to stay away from me and that I have things to do. Mom said, "Don't treat your sister like that." I said whatever and then Mark jumped up from the couch and started towards me. Mom said, "Mark, I can handle this. These are my children not yours." Mark sat back down.

Things were moving pretty quickly. One moment we just met and the next he was sleeping over. One morning, I was arguing with my sister Gayle. She didn't want to take care of Shallon and it was her turn. I guess we were too loud and woke up Mark. He came out naked and yelling at us. That stopped us immediately. My mouth dropped I looked away and I was totally embarrassed. All I can remember what happened and what he said. He grabbed my arm and yelled, "You two need to stop arguing. You just woke us up with your bickering." He let go of my arm and went back to the room.

Gayle and I both got Shallon taken care of. I heard mom talking to Mark telling him that we never saw a guy before and he shouldn't have went out there undressed. Gayle and I were in shock and couldn't believe a person can do something like that.

We went to school as if nothing happened and had a regular day. We came home and mom said that we had to watch Shallon while she went out. She did this several times. Eventually, we ran out of food. We left mom notes before we went to bed hoping she would turn around and go and get some food for us. I looked forward to going to school to eat lunch. I constantly looked at the clock waiting to go to lunch. I didn't pay much attention to school work when I was starving. After lunch I had energy and was much happier. It was Friday and the whole day I was worried there wouldn't be food for us this weekend. When I got home, no car was in the driveway. Maybe mom went to get food because Shallon wasn't there either. I got my homework done, sat down on the couch and watched some TV. I like the TV, for a few hours a day I didn't have to worry or interact with anyone. It got dark out, but still no mom or Shallon. The phone rang and it was mom saying that she wasn't coming home tonight and Shallon was with her. I said, "Mom, there isn't any food for us to eat. I was hoping you where at the store getting us food." Mom said, "I'll get some tomorrow, I promise.

There must be something you can eat go and check." All I saw was pickles, rice and a can of tuna. I hated tuna, so I made pickle soup. The recipe to this soup is water, a cup of rice, ¼ cup of sliced pickles, and salt and pepper. I wasn't taught how to make rice so I improvised on how to cook it. I put water in a pot, put the rice in it, waited for the water to boil and I would stir it for awhile it seemed. I had to put more water in it because the water would vaporize and the rice wasn't done yet. After awhile the rice was done, so I put the pickles in it with a little bit of pickle juice plus the salt and pepper. I served it in bowls and sat down to eat. Gayle and I together put the spoon in the soup and at the same time put the soup in our mouth. The face my sister made was unforgettable. If you can imagine what it tasted like, you can imagine what her face looked like. We had no choice but to eat it. She was still hungry, so I opened the can of tuna and gave it to her. She ate it. "How can anyone eat tuna?" I thought to myself. It was late so I made sure all the doors where locked. The back door wouldn't close and lock so I had to tie a rope around the knob and to the wall. When we went to bed, I locked our door just in case. I didn't like being home without my mom. She did this to us several times. We woke and found there was still no food in the house. As a matter of fact, no mom either. I started getting worried. I tried not to show it with Gayle, but she knew. We had to find things to do to keep us busy so we weren't worrying to much. By lunch time, mom wasn't home yet. I was so hungry and so was my sister. We couldn't leave the house or anything or mom would get mad at us, but I decided to go in the back yard to keep my mind off of my hunger. Gayle had a mouse (it was black and white) and she brought it outside too. I told her it wasn't a good idea, "It might run off and then you'll be upset." It was getting hot out so we went to the other part of the house that was in the shade, I turned on the water to make mud so we can make a little maze and house for the mouse. At this point I felt weak and my mind was fuzzy like. I couldn't concentrate. Gayle put the mouse in the so called maze. I fell back against the house because I lost my balance. Got up and asked where her mouse was. We looked all over the place. I moved and found it was under my foot. I crushed her mouse. It was still alive with its guts out of its stomach. It was gasping for air. I thought if I put the guts back in, it would get better, but that didn't happen. When it finally passed away, my sister was crying, I tried to say sorry but she didn't want to hear it. She started hitting me and kicking me. I didn't know what to do. All I could say was, "Let's bury it." We did that but she was still crying. I felt very bad about what happened. It was an accident I didn't mean to do that. She still reminds me of it every now and then. I went inside to get cleaned up because of the blood and guts. I came back outside and my sister wasn't anywhere to be found. I started to worry and got nervous. All I can think was that she ran away again. What was I supposed to do? I heard talking and laughing from my neighbor's house next door. I yelled, "Is my sister over there." A voice answered back "Who?" I said, "My sister Gayle." "Oh yeah, she's here. Come on over." "How?" Then I saw a part of the fence open and my sister poked her head in. I went over and went through. There were three kids and a woman. The lady said, "How would you like to have lunch with us?" I said, "We aren't supposed to leave our yard and I don't know when mom will be home. So, I don't know." She said, "We'll make it quick and then you can go home." I said okay. She made tuna sandwiches with her special ingredients. I said, "I really don't like tuna." She said, "You'll like mine. I make it really good." I tried it and it was either really good, or I was just starving and anything would taste good. We hurried up and ate and afterwards, my sister and I said thank you and left. We went back home, hoping mom wasn't home yet. Thank God she wasn't. I was tired of being outside so we went back inside. I cleaned the kitchen which I hated to do. I tried to clean the laundry room but it was a total mess and there wasn't a way to clean it unless I threw away all the clothes. Mom didn't teach me how to do the laundry yet. I sat down in the living room and watched some TV. At about two in the afternoon, the living room door opened and the bright light from outside blinded me. I put my arm up to cover my eyes from the light. I saw a figure in the light. My sister Shallon ran to me and jumped on me. I threw her off onto the couch. Mom said, "I'm just dropping off Shallon, I can't stay long." I said, "Mom we need food." She went to the kitchen and looked in the freezer and the cupboards and said, "Okay, I'll be right back with something for you to eat for dinner, but I have to make it quick." Gayle asked, "Can I come with?" Mom said, "Okay but we have to make it quick." Not even five minutes went by and mom came back with hamburger meat and a loaf of bread. She started yelling at me about the mouse I killed. I told her that I didn't mean to do it. Mom said, "We'll talk about this later. I have to go." That night we had hamburgers for dinner, but we still didn't have stuff for breakfast except for oatmeal which I hated as well. It was Sunday and mom wasn't home again. I got up woken up Gayle and we both took care of Shallon. I made her breakfast and my sister Gayle fed her. I asked Gayle if she wanted oatmeal and she said no and so we had no breakfast again. At lunch we had rice and some hamburger with soy sauce and we had that for dinner too. By bed time mom wasn't home again. She called to say good night to us. I asked, "When will you be home?" "I'll be home in the morning I promise." I said "We don't have food mom". Mom said, "I'll get some tomorrow. Now don't forget to set the alarm for school." I said goodnight and hung up the phone.

The alarm went off in the morning and I got up along with Gayle. It was strange Shallon wasn't up yet. I peeked in to see if she was okay. I saw her stir and put her head up to look. She had her pacifier in her mouth which meant she must have been up for awhile. I grabbed her and changed her stinky diaper. There wasn't anything to eat, not even something for Shallon. We just gave her a bottle with formula and prayed that mom would come home with food. We had to go to school and we didn't know who would watch Shallon. Five minutes before we had to be at school, mom came home. I told her that we didn't eat breakfast yet and that there isn't any food. She said, "Just go to school and when you come home there will be food. Now go and I'll take care of your sister." Well at recess I saw that mom's car wasn't at the house. I smiled and thought to myself, "She's getting food." I went straight home after school, and mom wasn't home yet. I couldn't wait for her to come home. I got my home work done fed the fish that we had, guppies. I sat there and waited for mom to come home. I heard a honk and ran out to the car and helped mom take the food in. Shallon was left alone in the car. All of a sudden we heard a long honk mom ran to the door and yelled, "Oh My God!" and ran out the door. Mom's car was in the middle of the road. It rolled down from the driveway which was at a angle. Mom got Shallon out of the car and started spanking her, like she could feel that through the diaper. She was yelling, "Get your ass in that house." and she went back to the car to drive it back onto the driveway. Can you imagine what would have happened if a car was driving past our driveway and hit our car? While mom was outside, I could only laugh at the idea. Shallon put the car in reverse without even trying. The funny thing was that the car wasn't even on, so it really wasn't Shallon's fault. All I did was laugh. Mom came in fuming. I thought that any moment she's going to start throwing things and start hitting. I ran to my room with my sisters and after a few minutes everything was quiet. I opened the door and went out. Mom said, "Please put the groceries away." While I put the food away, mom went to my room, I guess to check on Shallon. Shallon ran to Gayle and held on. Mom said to her to come here and Shallon was reluctant to do that so mom grabbed her and took her to the living room. Mom said sorry to Shallon for snapping like that and that she shouldn't have spanked her for what had happened. It could have been anyone who did that. She gave Shallon a hug and a kiss and asked if she's okay. Shallon nodded her head yes. Mom put her down and Shallon ran to Gayle. Mom got up went to the kitchen and started making dinner. I went to the living room and put the TV on. Shallon and Gayle came out and sat on the couch and Shallon was still clinging to Gayle. After a while, she loosened her grip on Gayle and sat next to us.

We were sitting at the dining room table eating and heard a knock at the door. Mom got up and said that it was Mark and he came in and asked mom if she wanted to go out tonight. She said, "Yes, just wait a moment. I need to freshen up." He sat down on the couch and we just stayed quiet at the dining table. He turned around and asked how we were doing and we just shrugged our shoulders. Mom came out, grabbed Mark, and hurried out the door. While she was shutting the door she said, "Now be good. Do your chores and go to bed on time." I spent my time crying on and off. I just couldn't believe she would leave us like that. The next morning I looked out the window and saw that Mark was here so I told my sister to be quiet and to help with Shallon. I didn't want to see him again. By now I was hoping that mom would be in a different relationship.

I have no memory at all about Thanksgiving. I called my sister and she didn't remember. Maybe we just had a regular dinner and watched TV. I don't know. Christmas was another story. Mom didn't feel like cooking so Mark invited her and us with his family to The Wall, a Chinese restaurant for Christmas Eve dinner. Mom accepted. I have never seen so many kids in my entire life. I was in complete shock. He had five kids. I didn't say anything I was just in amazement at how many. The dinner went well and I enjoyed the meal and sometimes even laughed at something that someone did. I found out they were Jewish, but that was about it. I tried shark fin and it wasn't bad, kind of chewy but good. My favorite of all was sizzling fried rice soup. To this day I can't find it anywhere. Boy, was that good. I know I had to wait for everyone to get some, but I couldn't and I had another serving. It had all kinds of veggies, shrimp, pork, beef, chicken, and of course the white fried rice. They would put the very hot fried rice in the soup once the soup arrived at the table. The sizzling of the rice is what astonished me. I'm still trying to figure that out.

At the end of the night, I was exhausted. I couldn't wait to go to bed. When we got home, there were two bags of groceries, a gallon of milk, and a couple of stuffed animals. Mom opened the door, told us to grab a bag and she grabbed the rest. Then she proceeded to ask us, "Which one of us told someone about having no food in the house?" I had no clue and neither did Gayle. Mom got very mad at us. On Christmas Eve why? She said she didn't like liars and we weren't going to have Christmas if we didn't tell. All we could say was we had no idea. Mom sent us to bed and we cried ourselves to sleep. The next morning I didn't want to get up. I didn't want to see an empty tree, so Gayle and I stayed in the bedroom. I heard Shallon waking up and just pretended not to hear. Mom came in our room with Shallon in her arms and said, "Merry Christmas, sweeties. Now get dressed in your nice clothes. I'll take care of Shallon." I didn't know what to expect. I was crying and wasn't happy at all. We came out and saw there were gifts under the tree. Mark was there. "Great, make my day even more memorable." Mom said, "What's with all the long faces. It's Christmas cheer up." I looked at mom and said, "You said weren't having Christmas this year." "Oh Tanya, I didn't mean it. I just wanted answers and realized that you didn't have them. Now cheer up." The most memorable gift I got that year was a Mickey Mouse watch. I wore it every single day until I lost it.

During breakfast, mom and Mark sat there and started talking to us. "We are planning to move in together into a big house that will fit all of us. The house has a garage and it will be turned into two bedrooms and an office so there will be enough bedrooms for everyone. Tomorrow we'll go look at it." I just looked at Gayle and thought to myself, "Oh boy. I hate Mark; there is something wrong with this man. What does mom see in him?" I just couldn't figure it out. The rest of the day went well. I actually enjoyed playing with Shallon and Gayle. What a miracle….

The next day I was hoping to sleep in but nope, that didn't happen. Mom came in with Mark and said, "Wake up sleepy heads, it's time to get up." I just laid there trying to figure out what was up with mom. It was strange that the breakfast was on the table all ready for us. We had eggs, bacon, toast and orange juice. She never did that for us. "Now hurry up we have to leave soon to go see the house." I didn't like that idea. I liked where we were at. Why did we have to move?

We left after breakfast. I asked how far away it is and Mom said, "Not too far, just wait and you'll see." As I watched from the car window, I noticed we were getting further and further away from our house and school. We turned and I now longer saw my house or school. We pasted a stop light, and then another, and then we turned right. I said, "It's to far from the school. How far away is this?" Mom said, "Just be patient, we'll get there soon." I started to worry. I didn't want to move away from this school and my friends. I was finally happy where I was at. It was a twenty minute drive. I asked, "Mom, will I be going to the same school?" Mom said, "Uhm, no honey, you'll be going to a different school." I said "Then I'm not getting out, I don't like it and it's too far away from my school." Mom said, "Just come in and take a look, you just might like it."

I sat there for a while and I asked God, "What was I supposed to do now?" All I could here was, "You're curious, go inside, it won't hurt to see."

The outside of the house had a big yard with huge bushes up against one side of the house on the other side were rose bushes. Mark said that those roses where strictly for my mom. I rolled my eyes and thought to myself, "Whatever, who cares?" I walked in. The living room was first, and it had a nice carpet and tile around the front door. There were two walk ways. The left side lead me down to three bedrooms, and a bathroom with a tub and shower. The other pathway lead right into the kitchen, dining room and family room. It was bigger than what I was use to. The sink was up against the wall with cabinets above on the left of the sink up and against the wall were the stove and a lot of cabinets and counter space. If you turn around, and there's a hole in the wall with counter space and more cabinets. You turn again to leave and the fridge is right there against another wall, you have to walk past it every time you move to another part of the house. I liked that set up. When you're leaving the kitchen instead of making a right turn, you make a left turn. The dining room is connected to the family room and had tile on the floor with this huge built in table that is connected to the wall with the hole. Under the table was more cabinet space to store stuff in. The family room seemed dark. There was a fireplace in the corner and I liked that. The carpet was different shades of brown and had a furry texture. I liked that. Then they opened the garage door that was right off the family room. I looked in there and it didn't seem to be big enough for two bedrooms and an office. Mom reassured me that it was. On the other side of the dining room table there was the laundry room and the entrance to my mom's and Marks room. It was huge with a nice sized window and walk-in closet with a private bathroom. All together it was a nice house, but I just didn't want to move in with him and his family. I didn't trust him. On the way home, mom was asking questions. "Well, what do you think? Do you think you'll love it there?" I said, "I like the house, just not the location and I don't want to move." Gayle just said she like the house. When we got home the phone was ringing and mom answered it. It was Dad, and he wanted to talk to us. I got the phone first then I started crying. I told him everything and that I didn't want to move again. Dad didn't like to hear me cry and he said, "If I can work something out, do you want to live with me for a while?" I said yes, and I was so excited and all the sadness went away and the next thing I knew it, I was smiling again. He said, "Let me talk to your mom." I handed the phone to mom and she said to go to our rooms. I looked at her like, "What are you talking about?" She pointed to our room and said, "Take Shallon with you." I couldn't quite hear what she was saying on the phone. I heard muffled sounds, and then I heard the phone hang up. I ran away from the door and pretended that I was playing with my sisters. Gayle said, "So, what did you hear?" I said, "I couldn't hear anything." Then the door opened and mom and Mark were there. Mom came in sat on my bed and said, "Tanya, you are going to your Dad's to live for awhile." I jumped up, I looked at Gayle, and said, "What about Gayle?" Mom said that Dad couldn't afford both of us at once. He could only take one and told me I'm leaving in two weeks. I was so excited, I couldn't wait; I was finally going to live with my Dad. Gayle looked like she was being abandoned and Shallon was way too young to understand. Mom said, "Now we have a lot of work to do. I have to call the school to let them know you're moving to South Dakota and all that." I didn't care, all I could think about was getting away from Mark and Mom's stupid mistakes she is making or have made in the upbringing of my life, of my sister's lives. I could only change mine at the moment and one day I would change theirs too. All I could do was change my life right now.

I don't remember how I got to Dad's, I only remember being there going to school. I remember parts of the school and the neighborhood and the house that we lived at. After school, I was left home alone until Dad got home, but I was used to that. He let me watch T.V. before he got home. I was allowed outside. I practically was able to do anything I wanted as long as I behaved. I was in band class so Dad rented me a violin so I can learn how to play that. I loved learning how to play musical instruments. They were even teaching me how to play the piano. I looked forward to music class once a week. Come to think of it, the music class is just about all I could remember about the school. I don't remember the teachers, the kids, or anything. I was happy, enjoying the time with my Dad, Grandma, my aunts and uncles, and my cousins. We had a lot of family gatherings and there were tons of food. I didn't starve at all when I was with Dad. He didn't keep me from eating or drinking anything. He said, "You're only a kid once." I didn't like coffee so that was the one thing I didn't drink.

I remember snooping around the house and was scared that I would get in trouble for going through things that weren't mine.

I went in my Dad's closet and there were piles upon piles of magazines. I picked one up and it said Play Boy. I started looking inside because I had no idea what it was. I saw a girl on the front cover, and she was dressed like Daisy Duke but with less clothing. What I saw it, I got so embarrassed, I just quickly put it back and shut the closet door. I went in the living room and turned on the T.V. and was blushing for a while. When Dad got home, all I could do was smile and I was so quiet. At dinner, Dad asked if I was all right. I said, "I'm fine, I just had a weird day." Then he asked me how my day was. I just looked at him and said that I had a great day. After dinner, Dad made a Gin and tonic drink and sat in his chair to watch the news. A few minutes later, he moaned and got up to go to the bathroom, usually he takes his drink with him but not this time. I wanted to try it, so I took a sip. He didn't have much left but I was curious about what it tasted like. It wasn't bad. It tasted like it had a lemon in it or something with a certain pizzazz. Dad came back in, sat down picked up his drink, swirled it like he was trying to measure the weight of the glass, then he looked at me. I pretended I didn't notice. Two minutes later he got up and made another cup. After that I never took another sip. It's not for me.

One day I got bored and decided to sit outside with my violin to practice, hoping maybe I can draw some attention to me but no one was outside. I practiced for an half an hour then went and in put the violin away and went back outside. Dad wasn't going to be home for a while so I decided to go for a walk in the neighborhood to explore since I like doing that. I came across some walnut trees, and at the time I didn't know what type of trees they were. The trees had these green and yellow balls so pick some up along with a leaf and took them home to ask Dad what they were. Dad got home and before he had a chance to relax or do anything I had to know what it was. Dad said, "Geeze, I just got home and you couldn't wait for a few minutes? Okay, well it looks like walnuts before they are ripe. It's a fruit too, so you can eat the fruit part too, but not too much because it could give you a tummy ache. You don't want them too yellow or have brown or black spots on them because that's too late and it's almost time for the walnut." I tried it, and I've never tasted something like that before. It had a mild sweet taste with a little tangy bite. You have to take the outer skin of first. You can't eat the skin. That's the part that could give you tummy ache. Plus the texture of it could make you puke if you ate too much. I found something to do after school. I'd go pick the walnuts from my neighbors' yards. After a few days, I had my fill and got bored.

For the longest time I felt safe and happy with my Dad. We didn't do anything out of the ordinary like go to the movies or go camping. I guess my Dad didn't like that. However, from time to time we would go out to eat. Once we went out to McDonald's because that was what I asked for. Dad asked me what I wanted. I was shy and scared and asked if I could have a Big Mac and French fries with a soda. Dad asked, "Is that all, and are you sure that you can eat all that? Do you want a pie or anything else?"

I said no. He said, "Okay then." I looked at him and said, "Are you sure? Mom told me it was adult food and I wasn't allowed to have it." Dad just looked at me and shook his head. "Well you're going to get what you want then." The Big Mac was so delicious. How can a mother keep this away from anyone? It was like heaven. For the first time I had something that I really wanted and it was delicious. From that night on it, seemed we were getting to know each other. I loved his attention. He was always home when he said he was and if he was going to be late, he would call and let me know. I really didn't have to do anything except keep my room clean and do my homework. He did the rest or he had one of his "friends" do it for him. I never experienced something like that before except at Nana's and Granddad's. I started thinking about the way mom treated us and I started telling Dad. Dad told me, "Mom just needed the guidance in her life and sometimes she chooses the wrong one. Sometimes it affects everyone in her life. Don't worry you are here with me right now. I'll protect you for now."

A couple of weeks went by and it was time for report cards. I was looking forward to seeing it. When I was with mom she told us not to look at them without her, because she wanted to be the first one to see it. She'd threaten us if we did. So, I waited to see my report card. I watched TV, ate a snack, played the violin, went outside, and came back inside. I was anxious. I wanted to see my report card. I thought to myself, "Oh God, hurry up Dad, get here soon. The suspense is killing me." I was looking outside the window when I saw my Dad drive up, and I ran out with my report card in my hand to greet him. He got out and said, "I guess you didn't see your report card?" I said, "Nope, I waited for you, like my mom taught me too." He said, "Let's go inside we have much to talk about." I ran inside and sat down at the table in the kitchen. Dad said, "You're school called me at work to talk about your report card." I said, "Oh, okay." He told me to open up my report card so I did. There were D's and F's and one C. I started to cry because I was afraid Dad would hit me or yell at me. I thought I was doing well in school. No one, not even the teacher told me. Dad got up, kneeled next to me, put his arm around me and said, "It's not your fault, we should have figured this would happen. Changing schools in the middle like that. The principal said that they would have to hold you back a year so you can adjust to their way of teaching or you can go back to your mom's so this won't happen. Here, there isn't the right kind of education for you. They don't have the extra help to teach you. You should go back to your mom for now." I just started crying even more. "Dad, I don't want to go back home. Her boyfriend is mean and I don't trust him." Dad said, "We have no choice." I asked if I could keep the violin and he said, "No, it was just a renter, I'l have to return it." He said he would talk to mom to get her to get me one so I can continue to learn so I had no choice or say in this matter. Dad called mom and told her everything and she agreed to take me back. I guess I was so upset that I don't remember going home but I do remember showing up at the new house. Everyone was waiting in the living room to see me. It was a little too much for me to handle. I couldn't see why everyone would be so happy to see me. I don't know them and they don't know me. I felt like going under a rock or something to get away from everyone. I loved the idea of being left alone, but there was no chance of that. Everyone hugged me and welcomed me back and I just pretended to enjoy it and accept it. Afterwards everyone met at the dining room table to talk to me about the rules and chores of this house hold. Oh My God, I just want to be left alone! I wanted to know where my room was and I just sat there. Mark brought in the chore sheet. It had all our names on it with a color next to each name, and a list of chores with the days. Talk about confusion. I believe my color was orange. I hated that color and they wouldn't change it. All the kids were happy and smiling at me. One of them said they were happy the chores where less. All I could think was, "I was born to do something else not to do other peoples chores." I just shook my head in astonishment. I couldn't believe what I was hearing. At the end, Mark said, "If the chores aren't done everyday you will get punished. I believe in spankings, so I'm just warning you, do your chores." Mom just sat there, didn't say or do anything. I basically tried to keep to myself while being around and in that house. I didn't talk to anyone. I tried to do my chores to the best of my abilities and even though I seemed slow and incoherent, I had some idea of how things are supposed to be. I remember Shell and Elisabeth trying to get me to their chores and saying it was my turn to do them. I didn't trust them so I left. They yelled and said if it's not done you'll get it. I got mom and brought her to the chore sheet and asked her to tell me what I'm supposed to do. She showed me, and they weren't what the girls told me. Mom looked at them and said, "How dare you try to pull one on Tanya. You do your own damn chores." For a while mom wrote me notes telling me what I needed to do. The girls didn't like that, because I always did my chores and tried to keep from being noticed. I just wanted to be left alone.

One day, I came home from school and found that mom and Mark were sitting in the living room. Mark said, "We have something to talk to you about, but we have to wait for everyone to come home so we won't be interrupted." I just sat down in a chair and waited, playing with my hands and thinking to myself, "What did I do wrong this time?" We were all waiting on Shell to come home. The others kept on coming into the room and leaving, trying to see or hear anything. Ed the little one came in trying to get his dad's attention and he yelled at Elisabeth to come and get him. He told everyone to leave and go to their rooms and that it's none of their business. Shell walked in and her dad said, "Go and leave us alone." She asked, "Why? What's wrong?" Now I'm getting scared. He just looked at her and she left. Mom started to talk. "You're not in trouble, so calm down." Mark said, "We are getting you a puppy because you earned it, but before we do that, we wanted to know if you would like it. You will have to take care of it, train it, and feed it." I said, "Okay, I can do that." I was happy and excited. Mark yells out everyone come in since you guys want to know what's going on and told them everything. All of a sudden everyone yelled, "That isn't fair. Why does she get a dog and we don't?" Mom said, "Look, she hasn't done anything wrong at all while she has been here. She's done her chores and has kept from playing head games and she hasn't lied to me. She deserves this. I'm not mentioning any names, but you guys need to stop playing games and trying to cause trouble for Tanya. She hasn't done anything to you." I couldn't believe it. I was getting a puppy. A week went by when I came home from school and in the living room was a puppy. It was a very hyper, 6 month-old, light blue eyed and white and grey colored Siberian husky. She was on a leash and jumping everywhere. The guy, whom I have no idea who he was, said, "I'm going to train you with Shatzi. You'll be responsible for her. She will only obey to you." I was so excited that I dropped my books on the chair and went to Shatzi. I sat on the floor and she came to me, well, jumped on me and started licking my face. The guy jerked the leash and she backed off. He said, "See how she responded to me? You'll be able to do that too."

Mom walked in and said, "Oh! You're home! Why didn't you come and get me?" I looked at her, got up, ran to her, and gave her a big hug. "Mom, she's beautiful." Mom said, "Well, I thought you might like her. We have another dog too. Her name is Pepper, and she's already been trained as a watch dog. She'll protect us from any robbers and she'll be working at the store mostly, once she gets use to us that is." They introduced me to her and she started licking me. I looked at mom and said, "She doesn't seem mean to me. How is she going to protect us?" My trainer took Pepper and he was in some kind of pillow outfit, and then took her outside. Everyone was watching through the living room window and he showed us how she is if she has to be. I was so amazed at what I saw. She attacked him several times, trying to tear him apart. He said a word and she stopped and sat down and started panting to get an appraise from him. It was like she was two different dogs at once.

For the next three weeks, I hurried to get my chores and homework done. The trainer came every other day to show me what to do. Shatzi seemed to be very happy with me, but some of the methods he was using for her I didn't care for because it seemed to hurt her. I was afraid to tell him so I just kept it to myself and after he was gone I apologized to her, pet her, and gave her hugs. I think she knew that I didn't want to hurt her. It was strange though, she obeyed me just fine but if someone else tried to control her she wouldn't. One night Mark came in from the back yard and started yelling at me. I was so confused at what he was saying. Mom came out of her room and grabbed Mark and said to him to calm down. Mark took a few breaths and said, "Control your dog. She won't stop chewing on my wood." I was so scared, and I didn't know what to do. He grabbed my arm and dragged me outside with him. He said, "Now pick up the wood she chewed up." I just stood there stunned at all that happened. I didn't do anything wrong, yet he was treating me like it was my entire fault. While I was picking up the wood, I cried and Shatzi would come up to me and lick my face. I shoved her away but she wouldn't stop coming to me. I got so mad at her. Why couldn't she just see I was mad at her and I was cleaning up her mess?

A couple of days later, we had a family meeting. It was at night, of course, since everyone was at home at that time. We all sat in the family room. I sat next to mom and Gayle sat on the other side of her. Mark was in the middle of the room and I started getting a headache. I told mom and she said she'll give me something after the meeting. Mark started talking. "We've lived under this roof for a few months now and since it's very busy and noisy sometimes. Sally and I are going away for the weekend to Las Vegas. The only person that will be able to get a hold of us is Shell since she is the oldest. I don't want to get any calls that anyone is misbehaving and he looked at Gayle and I. I told mom, "I didn't like that idea, you guys are going to get married there and it's not going to be good. Please don't go. He's not right for you." I started crying. Mark just said, "We are not getting married. We just need a few days off." I thought to myself, "Yeah right, you lying son of a bitch." Mark said, "We will call the moment we get to where we are at. I want you guys to make sure the chores are kept up or you know what will happen. Shell will be in charge with everything." I just couldn't believe what I just heard.

"Mom, please don't marry him. He's bad, he's not good. Once he gets what he wants he'll ruin everything. He will hurt us."

Mom just looked at me and said, "Non-sense, we aren't getting married and if we were, we would do it as a family. He's not bad at all Tanya. He's strict but he's a good man." Mom called that night and of course Shell answered the phone. I couldn't touch it. She would snap at me and give me a dirty look if I did. Mom gave her the number and asked to speak with me. Shell handed the phone to me. Mom said, "Get a pen and a piece of paper so I can give you the number too. I want you to have it as well because you are my oldest." I put the phone down and went to get the pen and paper. By the time I got to the phone it was hung up. I looked at Shell and asked, "What happened? Why is the phone hung up?" I was getting mad at this point. She said, "Oh I'm sorry I thought you where done and forgot to hang it up." The phone rang again I went to answer it and Shell pushes me away. She answered it, and then handed the phone to me. Mom asked, "What happened?" I told her what happened and that Shell wouldn't let me answer the phone. Mom gave me the number and told me not to lose it and if I had any concerns to call. She said she would like to hear from me at least once a day. I told her that I still had a headache. She said, "It'll go away soon. Now let me talk to Shell." I said, "I love you mom, don't marry Mark." She said, "I love you too and don't worry, I won't." I handed the phone to Shell then went to the family room to try to get rid of this headache. I guess I fell asleep because Shell came in and rudely woke me up saying it was dinner time. I was still having problems with my headache and I just sat at the table hardly touching my food. I ate a few bites and that was about it. After dinner, I called mom and let her know. She told me to go to bed and rest this weekend and she'll find someone to do my chores for me. Again I handed Shell the phone. I listened in this time. I guess mom told her she would have to make sure my chores were done because I didn't feel well. I heard Shell say, "That isn't fair. She should be responsible for her own chores." Then I heard Shell say, "Okay, fine, but I won't do it again." and she hung up the phone. I went to my room and slept. No one bugged me or checked on me. I guess I didn't eat either. The night that mom was coming back, Gayle came and woke me up and said that I should go to family room and that mom will be home soon. I said, "I know and I know what she did." Gayle looked at me like with a puzzled face. I said, "She got married to Mark without our permission and she lied to me. This is why I have a bad headache. She's going to ruin our lives because she didn't listen to me." I went to the family room and lay down on the couch and fell asleep again. Shell came in and rudely nudged me and told me to get up now. I said, "I can't and leave me alone." She left and a few minutes later I heard the front door open and all the commotion that came with it. Mom yelled, "Come in the living room Tanya, we have something to say." Shell said in an arrogant and rude way, "She's asleep in the family room claiming she still has that headache." Next thing I knew it, mom is there kneeling down to check on me. I started crying, I mean really hard. She felt my forehead, got up and scooted under my head and yelled at Shell to get some water and Tylenol. I couldn't stop crying. I finally yelled, "You got married to him. I told you what will happen. He's going to abuse us." And that's when they announced it to us. Mom said, "Don't worry, he promises to take good care of you and he promises never to lay a finger on you." I said, "He lied, just like you did when you told me you weren't marrying him. Just wait mom, you'll see." Then she said, "We are also going to have a baby." At this point my head felt like it was about to fall off. All I did was pray. I couldn't believe what I was hearing. What's wrong with her? I warned her. It was like a bad dream and I was hoping I would wake up at any moment.

My mom walked me to my room, helped me into bed and sat down beside me. "Tanya, don't worry. I have everything under control. Our lives will change for the better. I'll protect you." I just looked at her with a skeptical expression.

A couple of weeks went by, and everything seemed fine. One night, Mark and Mom went out for awhile. First they went to dinner and then to the Alano Club. They told us not to call unless it was a complete emergency. I was just sitting in the family room watching TV. I heard all kinds of commotion in the back yard. I got up and looked outside. Shatzi was by the door sitting and whining for help. I slapped my knees and asked her to come. She couldn't move and she was whining a lot. The other dogs knew something was wrong because they wouldn't leave her alone. I said, "I have to call mom," Shell said that it wasn't an emergency. "We are not bugging them." I'm so glad I know the number, because when Shell went back to her room, I ran to the phone and called the Club. Thankfully mom was there. I told her what was happening and said, "I think she is very sick." Mom said that they would be home shortly to take a look at Shatzi. A half an hour later they were home. Shell came out of her room and said, "You guys are home early." Mom looked at her and said, "Shatzi's in trouble, didn't you know that?" Shell said, "Well, yeah, but I didn't want to disturb you two." Mom just glared at her. Mom and Mark went to take a look at Shatzi, and at this point she was lying down by the sliding door. She didn't look too good. Mark picked her up and she was yelping. Mom said, "We are going to take her to the doctors because he needs help." I said, "Okay, let me know." I stayed up all night waiting. I was pacing back and forth because I was so worried about Shatzi. At about 12:30 am, Mom and Mark came home and without Shatzi. I asked "Where is she?" Mom said,

"Sit down sweetie, we have to tell you something." Mark had a pissed off expression on his face like he was about to kill someone. Mom said "Shatzi didn't make it. She had eaten some wood and the splinters punctured holes in her stomach. She got poisoned by it." I started crying, I couldn't believe it. Mark started blaming me for her death, saying, "If you had kept more control over her and didn't allow her to chew my wood she'd be fine now." I cried even more and ran to my room. Mom told Mark, "That was enough, she's just a little girl." Mom came to my room and told me everything was going to be just fine. I said, "Mark poisoned the wood. She chewed on the wood before and she didn't get sick." Mark heard what I said, and he came in to my room. He said, "I put some chemicals on the wood hoping to teach her a lesson, but she didn't learn. It's still your fault." Mom looked at Mark angrily and pointed to the door and so he left. Mom tried to comfort me, but nothing she did could bring my dog back. I told her that I'll be fine and it was okay for her to leave.

For the longest time I blamed my step dad for what happened to my dog. I couldn't believe a human being would go down that far to hurt something or someone. I still didn't talk about my feelings and mom started getting worried about me. She took me to see a psychologist to help me express my feelings. I was so annoyed being there. Mom told her what happened, and then I got up and went to the window and stared out. I didn't want to be here. I just wanted to be left alone. I was getting angry. I started banging my head against the window. The psychologist told me to stop because she didn't want me to break the window, so I stopped, turned around and yelled at mom. "I told you, bad things will happen with this marriage. It's just the start. He'll find other things to do to torment us." The lady asked, "What is she talking about?" Mom said, "Oh, she doesn't like my husband, she thinks he's mean and doesn't care about her and her sisters." The lady said, "Oh. Well our session was up." and mom made another appointment to go back. We never went back because mom was afraid I'll say something else to embarrass her. I hated my step dad. I started having a reoccurring dream about me stabbing him to death in his bed with mom's favorite cooking knife: I was walking to the kitchen, opened the utensil draw and picked up mom's knife. It was about ten inches long, the handle was wood, and the blade was the shape of isosceles triangle. The blade alone was about seven inches long. Mom got it as a wedding gift from her first marriage to my dad from her parents. It was the middle of the night. No one was a wake. I started walking towards their room. I walked around the dining room table, walked into the laundry room, slowly opened the door to my mom's room, and tip-toed my way around their water bed. I stood next to Mark and just started stabbing him over and over again. He didn't move at all. I ran out of mom's room, closed mom's door quietly, grabbed the bleach from the laundry room, went to the kitchen and cleaned the knife. I put the knife and the bleach away and went back to my room. I woke up with night sweats.

This dream wouldn't stop. I started thinking about whether or not this would work or if mom would be blamed for his death. From the moment my dog died, all I did was go to school, came home, did my chores and home work, ate my dinner and went to bed.

Mom wasn't feeling well. Mark took her to the doctors. When she came home, sat down at the dining table, lit a cigarette and called me over. I sat next to her as the sun from outside was coming in through the sliding door. It was really bright and I squinted my eyes so that I could see her. She took a couple of puffs and said, "I have to be in bed for a few weeks, I'll need you to help me. This pregnancy is hard on me and the baby." I replied, "I will help as much as I can mom, everything will be just fine." I didn't feel or see anything to make me think of anything else. She smiled, got up, and went to her room. I followed her in to make sure she was fine.

During this time life was a little bit easier, and I was starting to think that maybe I was wrong. Mark was a coach for a soccer team and enrolled Gayle in it. She seemed to like it. He got me into coins and stamps, and I really enjoyed the stamps. I thought they were fascinating. I started getting used to having this big family. I let my guard down, but I shouldn't have.

One day Elizabeth and Ed told me they made a fort outside and was wondering if Gayle and I would like to check it out. We went outside, and it was nice to see a fort again and we went in. Elizabeth and Ed came in too. Elizabeth pulled out a cigarette from her dress and asked, "You want to try this? I promise I won't tell. I'll even try it myself." I looked at her and Ed. Ed said, "I'll try it too." I said, "I'm afraid your dad will find out and then all hell will break lose." "Don't worry, no one will know," Elizabeth said. I took the cigarette and she said, "I'll be right back. I forgot the matches." Ed left too. Next thing I knew it, she's back but no Ed. I started getting antsy and said that we shouldn't do it. Elizabeth got mad at me and said, "Oh come on, you won't get into trouble. You know you want too." I finally said okay. Once I took a puff which I didn't inhale, there was Mark. He was yelling at me and he grabbed me and my sister, dragged us to the house, and made us sit in the family room. I was so scared and crying. All I was thinking is, "Elizabeth wasn't my sister or my friend at this point. She's a back stabbing two faced bitch." Mark wouldn't even let me talk. Mom heard all the commotion and came out. Mark told her what he thought happened. She sat down on the couch as Mark continued to talk to us. I said, "Gayle and I weren't the only ones trying the cigarette. Elizabeth and Ed are the ones that gave us the cigarette." Mark looked at the two and asked if that was true and, "Not to lie because you know what will happen if I catch you in a lie." Elizabeth said no and Ed said yes. Mark looked at Elizabeth and said, "You have a chance to change your answer and then I will beat it out of you." Elizabeth sai yes and at the point, all four of us were crying. I alone was shaking, I didn't know what to expect. I looked at mom and she seemed mad at me. Mark said, "You four stay here, I'm getting your punishment." I just sat there. I didn't trust anyone anymore. He came back with a box of cigars. He said, "Everyone has to smoke these cigars until they are all gone or someone pukes." It didn't last long. He still had a half of box of cigars left. My sister Gayle puked. She ran to the bathroom and Shell followed to make sure she wasn't faking it. Shell came back and said she threw up. I only had a few puffs. The burning in my chest is something I will never forget. It was like the time I drowned. He shouldn't have done that. After he made us smoke the cigars, I started seriously smoking cigarettes. Mom got me MORE, a cigarette brand that was menthol and long and skinny. I smoked when I got home from school, after dinner, and all that. So did my sister.

At this point I didn't know who to trust. I kept to myself. Again I just wanted to left alone. School wasn't helpful either. No one wanted to be friends with me and I really didn't want friends anyways. I didn't want them to know my family because of the drama there was. It was easier to be by myself. Every morning, I would get off the bus, walk into the front doors to the school and the Principal would greet me and say, "Good morning Tonya Tucker, how is my favorite person doing today?" I just smiled and said fine. He would say, "I sure do love your smile." I smiled again and went to my room. That's the only time I looked forward to going to school and of course to get away from that so called family of mine. I came home, did my homework and my chores. Mark started yelling, "Who took the last banana and didn't put it on the grocery list?" Elizabeth said, "Tanya did." "What? I'm doing my homework. I didn't eat anything." Mark grabbed me and Elizabeth and started interrogating us. "Which one of you is lying?' I said to Mark, "In the past, haven't you learned that I do not lie?" Elizabeth said, "It wasn't me dad I swear." Mom came out of her room and asked what the commotion was about this time. I struggled to get away from Mark and I ran to mom and held her. Mark said, "Someone ate the last banana and didn't write it down. I'm just trying to find out who did." Mom said, "Not like that." Mark said, "Well then these two will be grounded until someone tells me the truth." I just looked at Elizabeth in a pissed off way. Mom looked at me and saw I was mad. She said, "Tanya just go to your room and don't worry, she'll confess." I looked at mom like I was expecting her to do more. I just couldn't believe it.

That night, no dinner and finally she confessed. Mom told Shell to make me something to eat. She didn't like that either. I had a sandwich and some chips with an apple. I went to mom and gave here a good night's hug and kiss and just glared at Mark. He said, "You'll stop staring at me like that if you know what's good for you." On the way out of their room, I was grinding my teeth to keep me from screaming. Elizabeth tried to say sorry in our room, but I just ignored her. The next morning I woke up late because Elizabeth didn't wake me up. I hurried to get my clothes on, got my books together, went to the kitchen to grab a piece of toast to eat. Shell said, "It's your turn to make the coffee." I told her that I was running late for school and I didn't have time to. She disappeared and then Mark came into the kitchen and yelled, "Where is the coffee? Whose turn is it to make the coffee?" He looked on the chore sheet and it was me. He stood there looking at me while I was eating my breakfast and than said, "It's your turn to make the coffee so get up and make it." I looked at him and said, "I'm running late for school and the bus will be here any moment." He grabbed me and said, "How dare you talk back at me? Now pull down your pants and underwear so I can give you a whipping." I started screaming for mom and he said she couldn't help me right now. He pulled the pants and underwear off for me and threw me over his lap and started hitting me with his belt. I started screaming and crying for mom when she finally came out and saw what Mark was doing. She yelled, "STOP NOW!!!!!" I got up, still crying hysterically, and pulled up my clothes, barely able to walk and went to mom. She held me and shouted, "What did you do?! I never hit my kids in that manor." She looked at me and asked if I was alright then looked out the front window and saw the bus was there. "No, go to school, I'll take care of this. Try to stop crying, okay?" I just looked at her with disbelief. I ran to the door and the bus was just about to leave when he saw me coming out of the house. I was still crying but the bus driver didn't ask if I was alright or anything.

I couldn't sit. I was holding on to the seat like my life depended on it. The bus stopped at the school, and I knew the principal was going to look for me like he always does, but I came in quickly beside someone so he didn't see me. I tried to sit at my desk, still crying because I couldn't stop. I was lying on top of my desk. The teacher noticed something was wrong, and she came to me and asked. While I was crying, I said, "I was spanked by my step dad with a belt and my mom sent me to school anyways. I can't stop crying it hurts so much." She had one of the girls take me to the Nurse's office and the principal was waiting for me there. He said, "I missed our greeting today." He saw the distress in my face and he asked what happened. I told him everything. He was upset and furious at the same time. "I'll take care of this. Go and lay down." The nurse helped me. "I have to make a few phone calls." Next thing I knew it, mom's here with somebody else. I have no idea who he was. I ran to mom. She held me away from her and said, "I didn't realize he hurt you that bad. I'm sorry I didn't see." Then she held me. The guy said we have to look at her bottom to make sure there isn't any broken skin. I started freaking out. I didn't want any body to see my bottom. That's embarrassing enough as it is. Mom said, "How about me? Let me look sweetie, then I'll tell him." I agreed to that. My bottom was all red and hot to the touch but no broken skin. In order to prove that, I had to give my underwear to the guy so he could examine them.

The principal said, "She can go home if she wants. Take a day off so she can recover. I won't mark her absent." I looked at him and at mom and said, "I'd rather stay here. I don't want to be around him right now." "Okay, well it's lunch time now. Do you have a lunch?" I said no, I didn't have time to make it this morning. The principal took me to the lunch room and had them give me a platter of food. I just looked at him and smiled. He said, "Awwwh, there's that smile I was looking forward to." He gave me a hug and told me that everything will be fine now and not to worry about anything. "I'll be here if you need me." He smiled back at me. I sat down at a table very slowly. Lisa, the girl who took me to the nurse, sat next to me. She started talking to me. "Are you all right?" I nodded my head. "What happened?" I just looked at her and said I don't feel like talking about it. "Okay, can I eat with you and keep you company?" I nodded my head again. After lunch I started to walk outside and Lisa was right beside me. A boy came running past us and he turned around and yelled at me, "You're such a cry baby." Lisa yelled at him, "You'll get yours." I sat on a bench under an olive tree. The principal walked up to me and asked how I was doing. I said much better now. Lisa told the principal about the boy that said the remark and pointed to him. The principal went to him and then both of them left the play ground. The rest of recess the kids in my class asked if I wanted to play with them. I just told them no. Lisa just sat with me. She just wanted to be around me. I guess she felt sorry for me or something. I didn't look forward to going home so I went to the principal to see if I could go home with him but he wasn't anywhere to be found. I had no choice but to go home and face the mad mob. My heart was beating fast and I was shaking. I was so scared to death. Mom was waiting for me outside. She never did that before. She gave me a hug and asked me how I was doing. I said, "I guess I'm fine. I really don't want to be here." She said , "Well, come on in." Everyone once again was in the living room waiting for me. I walked past them and went to my room. Mom yelled, "Hey they want to say something to you." I yelled back, "I don't care anymore, now if we aren't leaving this place I have nothing else to talk about." I slammed the door. Mark never apologized to me and of course I wouldn't accept it. He doesn't deserve acceptance from me. He abused me and for the rest of my life I will never forget it. One night I woke up after that dream that I kept on having. This time I was going to go do it. I got up, tip-toed out of my room as to not to wake Elisabeth and sneaked through the hallway to make sure I didn't wake the boys up. I tripped over the step into the family room. I proceeded into the kitchen, opened the drawer that held mom's favorite knife. I continued to walk out of the kitchen, into the dining room, and around the table. I got to the laundry room and stood right in front of their door. I stood there for a few seconds thinking and hearing my heart beat really fast. I started shaking. I was thinking, "If I do this, mom will probably get blamed for it because it's her knife. She'll be put away for the rest of her life. Lose custody over us and we wouldn't have a mother anymore." I couldn't go through with it. It would be totally wrong and I know that God would take care of us. I hurried back into the kitchen and put the knife back into the drawer before anyone woke up and sees me with a knife in my hand. After I put that knife away, I made a great big sigh and went back to my room.

The following weekend Mark and Gayle had a soccer tournament. Everyone had to pack into the van to go to the field so we can support and cheer for the team. I was the last one going into the van and Mark was at the sliding door. I didn't trust him so I got in backwards watching him. I was in so I put my right hand on the van frame to turn around so I can sit in a seat. I saw Marks face, the face that said I got you now, that he was up to something, and then he slammed the door on my hand. I started screaming, "Open the door!" Mom turned around and looked at me. She said, "What's wrong?" "He slammed the door on my hand mom!" I yelled again' "OPEN THE DOOR!" He was just standing there smiling. Mom said, "Hold on," as she jumped out to open it, but couldn't because it was locked. Mom said, "Unlock the door." I couldn't, I was holding my arm with my hand and crying. The pain was unbearable. Ed got up and unlocked the door. Mark opened the door and Mom grabbed me then said, "Let me see." I was shaking and afraid of what Mark would do now. I said, "It hurts so badly." She went to move my fingers and I yelled, "Don't move them, they hurt." There was a cut and it started to bleed. Mom yelled at Elizabeth and Shell to go get ice and towels. The bleeding wasn't stopping. Mom said to Mark, "Just go without us. I'm taking Tanya to the hospital. Her hand doesn't look good." Mom helped me get in her car and put my seat belt on. By the time we got to the hospital, my right hand was swollen and I couldn't move my fingers. It took a few minutes for the hospital to see me. They took x-rays of my hand. The doctor came is and said, "The good news is it isn't broken. Your hand is swollen due to inflammation of the muscles and tissues surrounding your bones. You are very lucky Tanya. I've seen cases where people have lost the use of their hand due to broken knuckles and torn ligaments along the fingers. You'll heal just fine. Let me take care of that cut." I looked away. Whatever he did stung like someone was burning me. I jerked my hand and he said, "You have to be still, I'm almost done. There." I looked and there weren't any stitches. I asked, "What did you do?" He said, "I glued it shut. The cut wasn't big enough for stitches." He put a band aid on it and wrapped my hand. He said, "Now don't write with it for a few days or do any activities with it. You'll be just fine after." I said, "I'm left handed." He looked surprised and said, "Then you won't have any problems." He smiled and left the room. After we left the hospital, I said, "Mom, Mark did it on purpose. He knew my hand was there. I don't feel safe anymore. I don't want to go home." She said, "Now knock it off Tanya. You're still upset at the fact that we are a family now and you don't like it. He didn't do that on purpose." I said, "Mom, you should have seen his eyes and his little smile. He's crazy. I don't trust him and I will not trust him for the rest of my life. I can't wait for the day you finally open your eyes and see what type of person he really is." Mom said, "That is enough young lady. Don't say anymore." We got home and no one was there. It gave me a few minutes to be by myself before everyone came rushing in. Mom gave me some Tylenol for the pain. She actually gave me a Tab. She never gave us her soda before. I smiled and said, "Thank you." She smiled back. I had an hour to myself. Mom was in the kitchen cooking dinner. We were having goulash. I couldn't wait, I was starving.

Everyone came rushing into the house at once. Gayle came to me and said, "I saw what happened, he did that to you on purpose." I said "I know, I tried to tell mom but she told me it was nonsense and to forget about it."

My mom had a baby boy in September. Three days after he was born, he had his Briss. A Rabi circumcised him. I wanted to be there, but Mark told me it was for the men and besides, it wasn't my religion, but Shell and everyone else was there. When I got home from school, I ran to my brother to see how he was doing. Mom told me everything they did. She knew how I was, curious about learning interesting stuff that caught my interest. Things seemed to quiet down. My brother was the center of attention but I didn't mind as long it was kept off me. He seemed to cry all the time and everyone tried to calm him down. I said, "Let me try." Shell said, "You are too young to take care of our brother." Mom stepped in and said, "You have no right to tell that to my daughter. She is old enough." Mom took my brother from Shell's hands and placed him in my arms. Immediately, he stopped crying, and his dark eyes were fixed on me as if he was studying me. Mom looked at Shell and said, "See she is a natural for taking care of babies. Don't go between them." My job from then on was to calm my brother every time he cried and wouldn't stop. I didn't mind that, because I knew he was interested in me and wanted to be near me. I sensed he was quite happy being around me.

My birthday was coming soon, so I made a small list and gave it to mom. She looked at it and then at me. "What's this?" I said, "The things I would like for my birthday." She said, "Oh, I thought it was for Christmas." I said,

"Nope. I'm still working on that list." She said, "You might as well put this on your Christmas list because we can't afford your birthday this year." "Why? You took care of everyone else's birthday without a problem." She said, "Yours comes too close to Christmas and Hanukkah." I just couldn't believe what I was just hearing. She called me selfish in the past but, I had every right to be pissed off at her and everyone around me. I yelled, "THIS ISN'T FAIR." and stormed off to my room. She was right. All I got for my birthday were three lousy gifts. Things I didn't want and on top of that, I had to sit there and observe Hanukkah and participate in it. I didn't mind it. I like learning new stuff, but when it came to the gift part of it, my sisters and I didn't get a gift. Mark said it was because we weren't Jewish, so I kept my mouth shut. I didn't care anymore. Christmas came, and guess what? His kids got gifts, I mean a lot more than what my sisters and I got. I looked at mom and said, "They are not Christians so why do they get gifts?" Mom said, "They have a Christian mother." and kept it at that. I was just shaking my head. My heart broke because I didn't feel I was wanted anymore. I cried most of the day.

I didn't see the point in Christmas anymore or any holiday that is dealt with gift giving. I felt like I had nothing. At dinner, mom noticed how red my eyes and face were. She told me to follow her. We went to the living room. She said, "Stop being selfish, this is our first holiday together as a family. Now go and wash your face and join the family." I went to the bathroom but took my time. I didn't want to have any part of this so called family. Someone knocked on the door and said, "Hurry up, dinner is getting cold." I yelled, "I'll be right there." I opened the door with this ugly face on and walked into the dining room everyone was looking at me. I just didn't care anymore. I sat down when Mark stood up and said, "Before we have dinner, I have something to tell you guys." I'm going, "Here we go again," and rolled my eyes in disgust. He continues. "We are going to California for a vacation to visit your grandparents." Everyone started making noises. He said, "Now, now, hold on there's more." Again I wasn't impressed. He continues, "We are also going to Disney Land and Water World." Everyone was so excited. I just sat there. How nice. I just couldn't wait to eat. Everyone was eating and talking about the trip. I just kept to myself. I didn't care like always. I didn't see the purpose in going. We left the next day. The drive there was okay I guess, but I don't remember it at all. When we got to his parents house, we just sat around and did nothing. I noticed the air felt heavy and it was hard for me to breath. Mom said it was because of the smug. Mark came in with a camera and told us to smile, but of course I didn't. He said, "You better smile if you know what's good for you." I don't remember much our so called vacation. I wasn't interested in it at all. The next day we went to Disney Land. Mark gave me and my sister Gayle an all day ride pass. He looked at me and said, "Now don't lose yours. This is the only one you'll get and if you lose it you'll get another spanking from me." I don't think mom heard him say that. He told everyone to meet in the same place in two hours to check in. I had my Mickey Mouse watch on, checked the time, and off we went. Gayle and I were going on rides and running around the park. We got autographs from her favorite characters. As long as I was with her I was fine. The last ride were on, I left my pass on it. At the time I didn't realize it. We got to the spot and no one was there yet. I looked for my pass and realized I didn't have it. I started to shake and was so scared. Gayle said, "Mom won't let anything happen to you. Don't worry." I started to cry. She was rubbing my back like good sisters do. Mom and Mark got there before anybody else did. I told mom what happened and then Mark started yelling at me. "I knew you would lose it. You're not good at keeping things that are important. How could you lose that?" He grabbed me and started shaking me. I was crying really hard and I saw people walking by and just looking at us. He said, "Look you are embarrassing me in front of all these people, now what are you going to do to fix this?" I said, "I'll go back to the last ride I was on and see if they have the pass." He said, "That's a good. Start now go." My sister went with me. All that went though my mind was, "I hope it's still there." When we got to the ride, I asked the guy and he noticed how stressed I was and said, "Sorry, I didn't see anything." Then he points to the sign. It said. "WE ARE NOT RESPONIBLE FOR YOUR LOST ITEMS." I just started balling again. I'm dead. I won't be able to enjoy Disney Land now. We walked back at the spot. I saw mom sitting at the water fountain with my baby brother and we went over to her. She said, "Well, did you find it?" I had my head down and said "No, and they aren't responsible for lost items." Mom said, "Here have mine. Now, don't lose this one." Mark came back with a pass and handed it to my mom and just glared at me. Mom said, "Now hurry and enjoy yourselves. We are leaving in an hour and a half." Gayle grabbed me and we ran to the next ride. After that ride, I looked at the time and we only had a half an hour left. Gayle wanted to go to the Magic Mountain before we went back. I told her we don't have enough time to go on that ride. She started to pout. We walked back to our mom. We were the first ones to return. Mom asked if we had fun and I said yes, but Gayle said, "No not really, I didn't get to go on a ride that I wanted to." Mom looked at me and frowned. Shell came back with Shallon. Mom said, "Shell will you please take Gayle to Magic Mountain so she can have a ride?" Shell said okay. I sat next to mom and Shallon sat next to me. A few minutes went by and everyone else showed up. All we were waiting for now is Shell and Gayle. Mark was pacing and chewing his nails. I've never seen that happen before. Mom said, "Dear relax, they'll be back soon." Mark said, "I really want to go now, so we can eat and get plenty of sleep for tomorrow." Twenty minutes went by and Shell and Gayle showed up. Mark replied, "What took so long?" Mom stepped in and said, "You know what took so long. Now stop."

The next day we went to Water World. I stayed with mom this time. I didn't want to be blamed for something I didn't do. I actually loved Water World. When you first walked in, there was a small aquarium with star fish and sea cucumbers and just about all the little sea life there is. Mom, my little brother, and I stayed there for a while. I was able to pick up a starfish. It felt weird, with little fingers tickling my hand. The top was rough and bumpy and on the bottom was smooth and slimey. I put it back before I got into trouble. In the next small aquarium there were dolphins. I didn't get to go and see them. Mom said that we had to go to a show so we had to hurry. Mark made sure we sat in the second row right in the middle. He was smiling and he said, "We have a big surprise for all of you. You'll have to wait to find out." All during the show I kept on looking at mom and Mark. Then I saw mom pick up my baby bother and cover him up with a blanket. I was watching the show with walruses. The trainer signaled it to do something. Next thing I knew it, I got sprayed in the face with water and it felt like someone punched me in the face. I heard my brother crying. I looked and I saw mom hit Mark. I got up and went to mom. Mom said, "Hold your brother for me. I have to get out a dry blanket for him before he gets sick." After the show, we walked around looking at stuff. I wanted a keepsake and mom said we couldn't afford it. "Just try to remember today and the good stuff." Another show was about to start and we rushed to go and see that. Thank God we were higher up. The setting was castaways, I believe. Dolphins, seals, and small whales were swimming in the same pool. The trainers were telling them to do stuff, like flip in the air and jump high in the air to get the fish. The seals where throwing to each other a beach ball and catching it. I was nice to see. It was a very peaceful day. I think it was because I was with mom. She always tried to keep the peace and keep Mark from blowing up. It was getting late and we had a long ride home. I slept most of the way home. That's all I could do.

One day I came home from school and no one was at home. It was strange that I was home alone. For the first time I felt happy. I got my chores done and that day I didn't have homework, so I went into the family room, turned on the TV, found something to watch and sat down on the couch. I lit a cigarette and began to relax. Then I started thinking. "Things seemed to be easy today. There's something bad going to happen I can feel it." All I could do was sit there and watch TV and pray that mom would get home soon. The front door opened and I cringed at the thought that I might be yelled at so I just stayed put. Mark, Shell, my baby sister, baby brother, and Gayle came in. I looked at Gayle and she seemed stressed. I asked, "What's wrong?" Mark sat next to me and I moved to the corner of the couch holding my legs and stared at him. He said, "Your mother is at a health resort. She'll be there for three to six weeks. She had a mental breakdown and needs the help." I started crying. He tried to comfort me all I did was shove him away. He got up, motioned his arm and hand like he gave up on me, and left. Shell sat down and said, "Dad was trying to be nice to you. You didn't have to do that." I looked at her and said, "I will never show him any affection after what he put me through. He didn't have the right to do in the first place." She got up and left. Gayle sat down and gave me a hug. We held each other for a few minutes and then Mark yelled for Gayle get her chores done.

I was not looking forward to three to six weeks without mom. I didn't trust Mark or his family. They liked to play head games and tried to get my sister and I into trouble. It was one of the most difficult times in my life that I had to deal with. My mom wouldn't be there to protect us. I was scared, upset, and sad at the same time. I didn't know what to do or who to trust. I didn't trust anyone, so everyday I did what I did before. There were arguments between us kids and I got used to them. I learned how to play their games well enough that I got out of most of their lies. I learned to have evidence on most of the stuff that they threw me. I didn't like them and they didn't like me, so I protected myself as much as possible. My sister Gayle didn't need that much help. She was friends with Shell and Shell handled her situations.

Three nights into mom not being there, the phone rang and Mark answered it. It was mom checking in. I ran to him and bugged him asking him for me to talk to her. He wouldn't let me. I heard him say, "Everything is fine here. No one has tried to kill each other. Your kids are doing fine. Yes dear I'll let them know, you sure you don't want to talk to them? Okay, honey, I love you. Talk to you soon. Bye." Then he hangs up the phone. I looked at him in disgust and said, "I wanted to talk to her." He looked at me and said, "Did I tell you that you could talk?" and he gave me a facial expression that scared the crap out of me. "She will call later to talk to you. Not right now. Let her relax first." I left and went to bed.

I was rudely woken up by Elizabeth, yelling at me to get up or I was going to miss the bus. I looked at the time and looked at her. She was already dressed and ready for school, but she didn't wake me up. I jumped up, got my clothes on, grabbed my brush, and started running down the hallway brushing my hair the same time. I put my shoes on and as I was walking in the kitchen I looked out the living room window and the bus was there. I grabbed my books and ran out the door. On the way to school, I was thinking, "Oh here we go again. Why in the hell did she do this to me? Why didn't my sister come and see if I was awake yet? Elizabeth and I shared a room. I didn't hear the alarm go off. What did she do? Stay up all night so I wouldn't hear it? Why was she being so conniving right now towards me?" All I could do is ride it out. I got to school and went to the principal and asked him if he had anything for me to eat because I didn't have time again to eat breakfast. I told him what happened. He gave me his banana and said, "I hope this ties you over for lunch." Then he asked, "Did you at least pack lunch?" I just shook my head. He said, "I'll take care of that too." He smiled at me and I smiled back.

When I got home from school, I did my homework and my chores. Gayle came home and I told her what Elizabeth did. She said, "She'll wake me up for now on until mom comes home." I thought to myself, "Oh Thank God," and gave her a big hug. I sat in the family room and lit a cigarette when Elizabeth came walking in the front door. She went to the chore sheet and started complaining about how she had to clean the dogs mess out side again. Her father came to the chore sheet and said, "Well change with someone." I sat there and rolled my eyes. She said, "Dad, look, Tanya doesn't have it all this week so can I switch with her?" He said yes. I got up and said, "I already have my chores done for today. How is she going to switch with me?" He said, "She'll just have to do one of your chores tomorrow then." "That isn't fair." He said, "Nothing is ever fair and one of these days you'll realize it. You chose which chore she'll do for you." I had the dinner mess and the kitchen to do and made her switch with me. I went outside and took care of all the dog's messes and changed their water and put food in their dishes. I went back in to find Elizabeth sitting there smiling. I was so pissed off I was seeing red. I didn't say a word to her for the rest of the night. I still felt like something was up. I was waiting patiently to see what it was. Thank God there wasn't school the next day, I was planning to sleep in and get some extra sleep. About seven in the morning I was rudely woken by Mark banging on the door. I jumped out of bed and opened the door. He said, "How many times do I have to tell you not to lock the door." I looked at him with a confused face. I didn't lock the door. Elizabeth wasn't in the room she was up already. I said, "Ask your daughter. She got up before I did." He said, "She's the one that told me that you locked it to get some extra sleep and you didn't want to be disturbed." "I did no such thing." He grabbed my arm, dragged me to the office, threw me in and said, "How dare you talk back at me. You are to stay in here until you have picked everything up in here." I just looked around and there where tons of papers on the floor, on the desk and everywhere. He shut the door and locked it. I didn't get a chance to eat breakfast or get dressed. I wanted mom, and then it dawned on me the phone was in there. I called my dad in Roswell, New Mexico. I told him what just happened. I heard the door open and it was Mark. My heart was jumping, I was shaking and I was very scared. He yelled, "Who the hell are you talking to now?" I looked at him and said, "It's my dad." He grabbed the phone out of my hand and listened. Than he said, "Who is this?" My Dad said his name. I never saw Marks face turn white before and inside I was jumping up and down with joy. My dad said something to him and then Mark handed the phone to me. "Please don't take to long you have to get your chores done." Mark left but the door was still opened so I shut it and started talking again. "What did you tell him dad?" He said, "I just told him to watch himself if he knows what's best. Sweetie I know it's hard for you. I'll come down and visit soon I promise. How about next weekend?" I said, "Okay. I love you dad." "I love you too Tanya" "Good bye." I hung up the phone and got to work in the office. Most of the papers were picked off the floor when Mark came back in and said that's enough you can go now. Elizabeth will finish since she was the one that instigated the whole situation. I left when it was twelve noon so I went to my room, got dressed, and went to get something to eat. After lunch I went to look at the chore sheet to get started on my chores. Everything was crossed off with Elizabeth's name on it. Shell came to me and I pointed to the chores sheet, and said, "I don't have chores today?" She said, "Let me check with my dad." She came back and said, "Yep, Elizabeth has to do your chores on top of hers." I was on cloud nine. Still I just couldn't shake that bad feeling way. Something else was going to happen and I don't want it to. I'm so tired and stressed at this I just don't want to go through anymore of it. I prayed to God all the time for help, asking her to take me away from this. "Why would you allow this to happen to me?"

I didn't want to be apart of anything anymore. I thought to myself that one day mom will realize that being married to Mark was a bad idea and we will leave and never look back. I looked forward to that day. I just didn't know when it was.

Mom Came Home

My mom came home and everyone, I mean everyone, hovered over her sat next to her, holding her. I just stood there watching everyone and thinking, "This isn't your mother why are you doing this? Why can't I spend anytime with her, she's my mother?' For a few minutes I was just there, looking upset and mad and jealous at the same time and no one cared about me. Mom was smiling a lot and holding my baby brother. All of a sudden she looked at me, "What are you just standing there for? Come here and let me hold you for a while. I've missed you so much." I went to her and sat down, and Gayle was on the other side. Mark finally said, "Okay kids, let Sally spend some time with her own kids now." I waited for Mark to leave and then everything just rushed out of me like a rapid river. I was crying so hard and I couldn't stop. I finally was able to say, "Don't leave me like that again!" and just continued to cry. Mom said, "I had to go, I had to find out who I really am and fix what ever was wrong. What happened when I was gone?" I just said, "Nothing I couldn't handle." Gayle just stayed quiet while holding mom. She was just happy she was home.

Everything was quiet for a while, no one picked on me, and mom came and woke me up every morning, and gave me my list of chores to do. What was so strange is that I never made coffee again. I was happy about that. One morning Elizabeth told mom, "I can wake her up for now on, I promise." Mom looked at her and said, "We already tried that Elizabeth. I will do it for now on. When I feel you guys won't pick on my kids anymore is when I'll let you do stuff to help out." I was smiling inside. My mom was actually standing up for me and taking care of me. I got up, got dressed and started walking out the bedroom when Elizabeth stopped me. "I was just doing what I was told from my sister. I didn't mean to be mean to you." I looked at her and then left. I did what I did everyday. I ate breakfast, cleaned my dishes, got my backpack and went outside to wait for the bus.

My sister Gayle always beat me home from school. I always wished I could have at least once beaten her home so I can rub it in. She always had her chores done before I got home and it just irritated me. One day I got home, and it was a strangely quiet in the house. When I walked in the door, I saw Shell walk towards her room. I went to my room and put my things on the bed. I went to the dining room where I usually saw my sister doing her homework. All I saw were her books on the table. I looked at my chores and then went to Shell's room and asked if Gayle was in there with her and she said no. Then I asked, "Where is she then?" Shell yelled at me, and said, "Why don't you look in the laundry room? It's her turn to do the laundry." I said that she wasn't there. Shell yelled, "Go look again." I went to the dining room and looked at the laundry room and no one was there. Mom's door was closed, but her car wasn't home, so I went to knock on the door, because I knew something was wrong. Mark yelled, "Who is it now?" I just stood there. He opened the door, and I saw that he didn't have a shirt on and only his underwear on. As he was yelling at me I saw my sister on the bed, upset and crying. I looked up at him and said, "I'm going to tell mom if you hurt her." He started yelling at me, but I didn't care. He said, "I will do the same to you as I'm doing to your sister if you don't leave us alone." I heard Gayle say, "Please help me." I left and sat down in the living room all of a sudden the door opened and it was my mom's girlfriend. I said, "Mark is doing something to Gayle and he won't stop. He doesn't have any clothes on and she's on the bed. Shell won't even do anything." Mom's friend said, "I don't have time for this. Your mom needed me to get something for her out of her room." "Well, you won't be able to go in there because Mark and Gayle are in there." She went and knocked on the door. Mark said, "For God's sake, who is it now? It better not be Tanya again." Mary said, "It's only me, Sally needs me to get her cigarettes. She ran out." He said, "Hold on a moment." A minute or two went by and Mary said, "Come on. I have to get going." Then Mark opened the door and handed her 2 packs of cigarettes. Mary tried to look in the room but I guess she couldn't find anything, so she turned around and started walking towards the dining room. I said, "Where is she?" Mary just shrugged her shoulders and then I saw Mark behind her. He is so easy to hide. He's really short. I started to shake. He walked by me and stopped, grabbed my arm and said, "You're next when I come back. I looked at Mary with a worried look on my face. They continued to walk towards the door. I ran to mom's room, but Gayle wasn't there. I whispered, "Where are you?" I looked in the bathroom, nothing. Then I noticed the closet door was shut so I went and knocked on the door when I heard Gayle whimpering and crying. I opened the door and Gayle jumped back. When she realized it was me, she gave me a big hug. At the moment I didn't know mom was in the car outside. I was hoping that Mary would come back. Instead mom came walking in like she was worried and Mark followed behind her. Mark saw us and he gave us an evil look. Gayle ran to mom hysterically crying and mom looked at me and I pointed to Mark. Mary was in the kitchen on the way into the dining room. I ran past Mark, he tried to grab me but missed. I went right to Mary and hid behind her, holding her waist. Mark tried to get to me but Mary wouldn't let it happen. All of a sudden, mom was coming towards me, punched Mark in the face while holding Gayle in one hand and proceeded to walk towards the door while yelling for Shell, "Where is my son?" Shell came out holding my baby brother and mom took him from her, I grabbed the diaper bag and we left. Mom was crying really hard asking questions to Gayle, "Are you sure he was about to? You better not be lying to me if you know what's good for you." Gayle crying, "I'm sure, I wouldn't lie to you about this." I reassured her too. I said, "I saw him mom. Please believe her." Mom started to cry. She just couldn't believe he would do something like that. I heard her say out loud. "What kind of man did I marry?" For a few days I didn't remember where we were before we got our own house. The next thing I knew it, we were at our new home not too far from where we used to be. I didn't like that the fact that we were going to the same school as Mark's children, but I guess it was alright because I liked my school.

Shallon, Gayle and I called our new home termite house because of all the termite tunnels we find hanging down from the ceiling, but we liked the house. It was located on the corner of a street. The front had a huge tree in the middle of a grassy yard. Up against the house were some bushes blocking the bedroom windows to keep it cool during the summer. There was a little porch connected to the house and an open garage for a car and other areas to park other cars. On the side of the house was a room where a motor home can park. Before the back yard fence, there was a pomegranate tree where I used to get my pomegranates free. I loved the taste of pomegranates. In the back yard there are bushes along the left side of the fence when you first walk outside. There were two fruit trees in the middle of the yard, one was a lemon tree and the other was an orange tree. On the right side of the house there was a brick fence and a gate to go out to the front. I used to use the brick fence to climb up onto the roof. Mom didn't like that but I did it anyways. There was nothing else to do. I also would jump off the roof into the front yard since there was grass and the ground was soft there. I even attempted to fix the air conditioner several times to save money for mom. I remember the repair guy showing up and I was up on the roof before him and had things opened up for him. He looked at me like, "Who is this person?" I just continued to play up there. The guy said, "Why don't you get down now? I don't need anymore help." I guess it was because I might have made him nervous or something; to this day I have no clue. My next door neighbor's house was full of bushes and trees. I guess to help keep it cool during the summer. We only saw her every once in awhile when she felt like coming out. She would only come out during the evenings.

One night mom had to work and asked me to watch my sisters and brother. I said, "Sure, I won't mind." She told me what to do and gave me a number to call if there was an emergency but to first call 911. My sister and I sat down on the couch and my baby brother was in the play pen sleeping. We were watching "Alligator" the movie on the TV. We heard a big banging noise from the door. I asked, "Who is it?" Mark said, "It's me, open the door. I want to take your brother for a little while." I said, "I have to call mom first. I can't open the door to you. She's not here." He said, "You know me now open the door." and he kicked the door. I ran to the phone and called mom. She said, "Don't let him take him. Tell him you'll call the police if he doesn't leave." So I told him. He yelled, "I won't leave until I get him." Mom said to me, "Hang up and call the police. Call me when they show up. Don't forget to tell Mark you're doing it." I hung up the phone, and yelled out, "I'm calling the police." He said, "Good I want them here anyways." I was on the phone with the police for a few minutes. Everything was quiet and the officer on the phone said, "They should be there now. When you hear the door knock open it. It's only them." The door knocked and I opened the door. I told the police what happened. One officer stayed with us and the other one went to Mark. I watched and I couldn't figure out what he was doing over there. I looked at the officer who was with us and asked, "What he was doing to Mark?" He said, "Uhm, he's reading his first rights. This means if he comes here again without us we can arrest him without any questions asked." After a few minutes, the other officer came back to us. He started asking me questions. "Is that guy your step dad?" I said, "Well, uhm, yeah in a way." He said, "You are too young to watch your brother. How old are you?" "I'm old enough, I've watched him since he was born and I'm 12 years old will be 13. He's lying. Mom wouldn't leave my sibling alone with me if I was too young. Besides I baby sit my neighbor's children too." I pointed to the house across the street. "Why don't you go ask her? She's home." The officer said, "No that's ok, I believe you. Where is your mom now?" I said, "I believe she's at work." "Will you please call her so I can talk to her?" I dialed the number and handed him the phone. "Mrs. Swanson, your husband is here. He wants to take your son saying that Tanya is too young to watch him." All I heard was the officer saying, "Huh, okay. Um aw ha , yep. Alrighty then, we'll take care of it for you. We suggest you find someway to cover your shift and come home for the night. Your children need you right now." Then he hung up the phone and gave it to me. The officer told me to shut the door and don't answer unless it was them and if Mark came back to call them and they will come and arrest him for trespassing and disturbing the peace. "Your mom should be here soon and will take care of everything later." I said, "Okay, I guess, but I know mom won't come home, she never does." The officers looked at me and said, "Don't worry, everything is fine now. He won't scare you anymore. We won't leave until you shut the door and lock it." I did what they said, still very much scared to death. I was shaking badly. I looked out the window and watched. I saw Mark leave and then the officers. The phone rang and it was mom. "How are you doing?" I said, "We are pretty upset and scared here mom. You should come home." Mom said, "You're fine now. I'll be home later." I hung up the phone, sat down on the couch and cried. "How can mom be like this? Doesn't she love us anymore or even care about us? I don't understand why she has to be like this." Gayle, Shallon and I were holding each other on the couch watching TV, but I don't think either of us was even paying attention to it. It was just something to keep us distracted and thinking about what just happened. The phone rang and we all jumped up. Gayle looked at me and said, "Well, are you going to answer the phone?" I said, "No you answer the phone. I'm tired of it all." Gayle answered the phone, "Hello? Oh hi mom. Yeah okay, hold on." She hands the phone to me. "Hello?" Mom said, "Pack up all your brother's things. Mark is coming to pick him up." I said, "What, why? He doesn't know how to take care of him right, I do. We will never see him again. What are you doing mom?" "Don't talk back at me young lady and do what I tell you to do." "If you do that, he won't stop bugging us." I said, "All I have to do is call the police and they will come here and arrest him." Mom said, "We don't want to do that. Let's just make this easy on us." "So, you just want to give up and let him win?" Mom said, "Just do it, he'll be there in a few minutes." I hung up the phone and proceeded to put my brother's things outside along with his play pen, then just sat there waiting for the door to ring. It did and said, "Hold on." I called mom before I answer the door and she said to answer the door. I opened the door to find Mark and his daughter Shell was there. I had the phone up to my ear and heard mom say, "Now hand him your brother." I did what she said. Mark said, "Is that your mother on the phone?" Mom said, "Just tell him it's the police." I did and he gave me this terrible look that made my heart beat really fast. "Then tell your mom to call me so we can talk about what we are doing next." I said fine then shut the door. I said, "How can you make me do this? I hate the man, he scares me and you made me deal with him tonight." Mom said, "You and your sisters did really well tonight. Don't worry you won't have to deal with him anymore. Now get ready for bed and I'll see you tomorrow." I got off the phone and just about lost it. "Why didn't she just come home? Why couldn't she stand up for us and keep our brother here with us?" I was so mad at mom and so scared for the safety of my brother. Mom couldn't see that.

The next day was just another day. I woke up to find mom wasn't home once again. Shallon was in the living room watching He-Man the cartoon. She really loved that cartoon. I asked if she ate breakfast, and she said no. I said, "Let's eat some of that yummy cereal that we love so much.' Thank God mom had brown sugar in the house because it made it taste better. We had rice puff cereal, and like I said before, had no taste at all. We gobbled that down in a matter of seconds. We sat down in the living room and watched some more cartoons. She had this blanket she always carried with her and snuggled with. We had a quiet Saturday morning. Gayle woke up at about noon, came out and asked if mom was home. I said, "Nope. I don't think she came home yet." Gayle seemed upset and angry at the same time. She went back to our room, got dressed and went to the bathroom. The door opened and finally it was mom walking in the house with a bag of groceries. "Sorry I didn't come home last night, I just couldn't come home." I just sat there upset at her. She put the bag on the kitchen table, and asked Gayle to put them away then asked her to make her a cup of coffee. Mom went to her room and a few minutes later mom came out and went to the bathroom. I heard the shower start. The door opened again and mom came out in a towel and went to the kitchen to get her coffee. She ran back to the bathroom. The shower wasn't on that long. I asked Gayle, "Should we ask mom what we should have for dinner or should we just wait to see what she is up too?" Gayle said, "Wait, I don't feel like making dinner or anything." We just sat there waiting for mom to get out of the bathroom. Mom came out went to the kitchen and back into the living room grabbed her purse and headed to the door. I said, "Mom, what's for dinner and where are you going?" Mom looked at us and said, "I don't care what you make for dinner as long as it's good for you and I'm going out. I need a break. Be good and behave. Don't fight with each other." Then she left and I was upset again. We had macaroni and cheese with green beans for dinner. Nothing special. Gayle disappeared into our room with the phone and in a few minutes she came out and put the phone back where it belongs and went to the bathroom. A few minutes went by, and she came out all dressed up and ready to go out herself. I said, "Where are you going? You have to stay and help with Shallon and mom would get very pissed off at you if you went out without her knowing." Gayle looked at me and said, "What mom doesn't know won't hurt her. Besides, I'll be back before she comes home. Don't tell mom if she calls. Just tell her I went to bed." "Okay, what if she comes home before you do." She said, "Just tell her you don't know where I'm at, which is the truth anyways." I just shook my head. At nine pm mom calls to check up on us like she always does and Gayle wasn't home yet. I was scared, when Mom asked, "How is everything going?" I said, "Just fine, when are you coming home?" Mom said, "That's none of your business." I said, "Okay, but are you coming home tonight or not?" Mom snapped at me and said, "Why are you asking me all these questions? You're not supposed to question your mother. Let me say good night to Shallon and put her to bed then you and Gayle go to bed too." I handed Shallon the phone and the front door opened. I put my finger to my mouth to suggest Gayle to be quiet. Gayle said, "Shallon, let me talk to mom before you get off." Shallon hung up the phone and all hell broke lose. Gayle started yelling at Shallon for not listening to her. Shallon said, "Mom didn't want to talk to you." I asked Gayle where she went and she said, "It's none of your business." I helped Shallon into bed and I went to bed, not even thinking of Gayle at this point. Next thing I knew it, I was rudely woken up by my mom asking where Gayle was. I was so confused that I said, "I left her in the living room." Mom yelled, "She's not home!"

I sat up in my bed and said, "What? Of course she is. What time is it?" Mom said. "It's 1 am." I said, "I don't know where she is, she doesn't tell me anything." Mom finally said, "Fine, since you don't know anything just go back to bed. I'll handle this." I went back to sleep in an instant. Again I was rudely woken, this time with a lot of yelling and things being thrown. I just laid there in bed waiting to see what will happen next. I looked at the time and it was 1:48 in the morning. I was scared to death and didn't know what to expect. Mom came barging into my room and turned on the light. "Tanya," she yelled, "Gayle said you knew she was out and that you said it was okay as long she came home before I did!" "What?! I never said that! She was home when I went to bed. I don't even know what's happening right now." Mom turned off the light slammed the door and I lay back down to bed. Waiting….

This time I didn't fall back to sleep. I didn't want to be rudely woken up again. It quieted down and the door opened and it was Gayle. I said, "Why did you lie, especially to mom? Why did you get me involved with your problems when I had nothing to do with it?" Gayle said, "I was hoping you would support me in going out." I said, "No way. You're too young to go out. I don't even go out." She said, "You don't have friends, you're too ugly and you don't know how to make friends in the first place." That hurt my feelings. I said, "So what happened?" "Oh, well mom grounded me for 3 months but you know I won't listen." I said, "Where do go when you go out?" She said, "I just hang out with my friends." "Doing what?" She said, "That's none of your business, now go back to sleep snoop." I just laid there trying to figure out how much I was in trouble.

The next morning was Sunday, and Mom came in and woke us up. Gayle didn't want to wake up but mom made her.

Mom made us sit at the kitchen table. She made us a breakfast composed of French toast, pancakes, scrambled eggs and burnt bacon. I looked at her in a puzzling way while she was finishing the bacon. She noticed and said, "Don't be staring at me like that." I kept quiet. After the burnt bacon was done, mom grabbed the plate and sat down at the kitchen table with us like she was going to spend some quality time with us. The only time she does this was if there was something she had to talk to us about and needed our full attention. What was so strange was that her coffee was already at the table along with an ash tray and her cigarettes so she was prepared for a long talk with us. I didn't care anymore, she really messed things up with marrying Mark, so I don't think she would ever listen to me again. Mom put the food on Shallon's plate this time. Usually she asks one of us to do it. Mom was acting stranger by the minute. I felt like I was sitting on pins and needles. I was waiting for the ball to drop any moment now. I hated the waiting game, the anticipation of what she was going to say or do next. Finally she starts. "Gayle, you can't go out like that again, you are twelve years old. You're not aloud to date until you are sixteen years old. You need to stop." Gayle just had her head down. "Gayle, you are grounded for three months, you are to come right home after school, you can't use the phone or watch TV, and you have to clean the house everyday after your homework is done. The stunt you did last night could cost this family. I can lose all of you. Do you understand?" Gayle said, "Yes, but it isn't fair." Mom said "I called your dad about it. He agrees with me about how old you should be to be allowed out. This summer after Nana and Granddad's, you two are going to your dads. I'm hoping this will help you understand the importance of what being a kid is all about. Gayle you need to learn to be responsible. Now Tanya, you need to learn how to have a back bone. You're too soft, and you have to learn take charge of a situation. Don't let Gayle bully you into anything. If she does something wrong you need to call me." Mom put a piece of bacon in her mouth and throws the rest back on her plate like she was disgusted with it. "Tanya, stop being afraid of everything and stand up for yourself." I'm thinking to myself, "Yeah right, if only you were in my shoes you would have a better understanding of me." I'm rolling my eyes at this point. Where does she get off telling me how to change? She hasn't been apart of us for a couple of years now and as a matter of fact hardly ever. She's never home, never takes care of us, and doesn't even know what happens when she isn't here. What type of mother is she? Mom continues, "Gayle, if I don't see any improvements with you, I will have to send you away to get help. If you can't behave, this is what will happen. You will go to a girl's camp for the help you need. This place is a lot harder than here and I suggest you listen to me." I'm thinking to myself, "Trying to scare her won't help, it will just make things worse." "Now we have six months before summer gets here so Gayle, you have six months to straighten up your act or else.' After breakfast mom got up and said, "That's all I have to say. Please clean up the breakfast mess and get your chores done." Shallon left the table and sat down on the couch to watch cartoons again. I just sat there listening to Gayle. Gayle responded, "Well, I won't allow this to happen. She's not the boss of me. How dare her to say that to me. Just wait, she'll be sorry." I asked, "What are you talking about?" "I don't like to be confined, and I want to go out and have fun." "You're only twelve years old, like mom said you are way too young to go out on your own. I don't understand where you are coming from." I picked up my dishes and put them in the sink, walked into the living room, and sat down with Shallon. Mom came out of her room all dressed up again and said, 'I'm going to the club to play cards and to go to a couple of meetings. Please have everything cleaned up before dinner." I just sat there and said in an annoyed voice, "Okay mom, what ever you say." Gayle picked up her dishes and put them in the sink. Mom yells, "Now Gayle, remember, no TV or phone calls. I'll check in often." No answer from Gayle. Mom yells, "Did you hear me?" Then finally Gayle said, "Yes mother." and Mom left.

I went to the kitchen, hoping I can help Gayle with the dishes. I figured that's where she was when mom was talking to her. She wasn't there. I looked in the laundry room and there she was standing in the middle of the room and standing towards the laundry room. I said, "Gayle." She jumped and turned around, "What?" I said, "Do you need help with the dishes, I'll help if you want. The sooner we get them done the sooner we can do other things." Gayle looked around in a daze. "Ok, sure." We went back into the kitchen and did the dishes and it took a while to clean the bacon pan. Mom really did a doozey on that one and we laughed about it. I asked her why she was just standing in the middle of the room like that and she snapped at me and said, "I don't know and stop questioning me." "Okay." After the dishes where done, Gayle said that she was going to clean the bathroom and the living room. I said, "I'll start the laundry then.: The phone rang, but I didn't see Gayle run to it like she use to, she was still in the bathroom so I answered the phone. It was mom, "How is everything?" I said, "Fine, we are doing chores right now. The kitchen is clean, the laundry is started, and Gayle is cleaning the bath room. Oh yeah, Shallon is still watching TV." Mom just laughed at that. "Well, I'll be home for dinner, so I'll see you in a few hours." "Okay mom, good bye." Gayle peeked her head out of the bathroom and said, "Well, what did she want? Was she checking on me?" I said, "No, she was checking on all of us if you didn't hear my part in the conversation." Next thing I knew it, Gayle's head was back in the bathroom. I sat down with Shallon and watched TV with her. We were watching this old Chinese movie with martial arts and the voice didn't match the lips. I wish I knew the title of it. One day I suppose I will find out. It was just fascinating to watch and sometimes it made me giggle because some of the moves weren't logical. Shallon just watched. After the movie I said to Shallon, "You should go outside for awhile and get some fresh air and sun." Shallon went to her room, got dressed, and went outside and I went outside with her. I sat down on the frame that was holding up the roof of the house and watched Shallon ride her bike. Then after a while I got bored just sitting there and I jumped off and started walking around the property line, keeping my balance. I thought it was just a few minutes so I went back inside. We were outside for almost an hour. I noticed Gayle sitting on the couch, and she looked like she was sleeping straight up or something. She didn't respond to me saying her name. She just sat there. I went back outside, and yelled for Shallon to come back. We went back in and Gayle was getting up from the couch to go check the laundry, well that's what I thought anyways. Shallon went to her room to play I guess. I went to laundry room and Gayle was doing the laundry. I was so afraid I would see her just standing there again. I asked her if she needed help and Gayle yelled, "No, I don't need help, just leave me alone." I went to the bathroom and noticed nothing was done.

I came out and asked Gayle why she didn't lean the bathroom and she yelled at me saying she did and I saw her cleaning it. She went right to the bathroom and saw it was the same as it was in the morning. I said, "Look, let's both clean it really fast before mom comes home so that way we won't get into trouble." I looked at her and asked, "Why didn't you ask me for help? I would have helped you in the first place." Gayle said, "I seriously thought I cleaned this bathroom!!!!!" "Okay," I said, "I believe you. Right now I'm just worried that we won't have everything done before mom comes home, so let's hurry." Shallon comes walking in and says, "I need the bathroom." I told her to make it quick. Minutes went by o I knocked on the door. "Are you done yet?" Shallon said, "No, I'm not. Leave me alone." Gayle and I were up against the wall in the hallway waiting for Shallon to get done. I'm tapping on the wall with my fingers and Gayle was banging her hands against the wall. Then we started shoving and pushing each other to see which one would fall first. Neither of us fell, but we did have fun for a little while. While we were doing that, Shallon opened the door and just looked at us and went right back into her room and shut the door. Gayle and I both at the same time tried to get in the bathroom. She punched me in the arm and I said ouch, and she beat me into the bathroom. We got the bathroom done right as mom walked in. That one was close. She bought us dinner from Wishbone. We didn't have to wait for mom to burn our food this time. We had a family night and I liked it. Mom stayed home for once and we watched TV together. Shallon was practically sitting on mom. Gayle had her back turned against us doing her homework at the kitchen table. Mom said, "Gayle, if you get your homework done soon, you can come in here and watch some TV with us." Gayle perked up and rushed to get her homework done. She came and sat with me. We watched a Disney movie that came on every Sunday called Old Yeller. It was a very sad movie at the end. Before the Disney movie the show was a nature program that came on too. I loved the fact that mom showed us some kind attention during show night. It felt like we were a family. I cherished those nights.

Something happened that just made things confusing to me. Mom sent my sister Gayle away to a girl's camp. She said it was because Gayle was hard to control and she needed the help. What kind of mother would put her own child away like that? All she needed was a mom. She was only there for a couple of weeks. Those two weeks went by fast. I went to school, came home, and took care of the chores and Shallon. Mom took me to the club a couple of times to play canasta with her and the girls. That was a fun game. Shallon just played with her toys and kept to herself. Shallon knew how to behave well. One night, Gayle escaped from the place and walked to the nearest road and hitched a ride from a trucker into town. She showed up at home a few nights later. I was so happy to see her, but Mom got really upset at her. She was yelling at her telling her that she needed to go back to finish her time there. Gayle said, "Hell no, that place isn't helping. It's like a prison there." I said, "Mom, she won't do anything bad anymore, let her stay home." What got mom so upset is the place never called mom to let her know that Gayle was gone. Mom asked how long ago did she leave the place and Gayle said about a week ago. Mom called the place and started yelling at them, asking them why they didn't call her and she wanted her money back and on and on. Gayle didn't really say much to me about what happened to her. All she said was they made her get up at 4:30 in the morning and she couldn't smoke and she had chores to do all day long. She escaped through the window in their bedroom. The place said she wouldn't be able escape, but she proved them wrong. Mom finally got off the phone with them, looked at Gayle, and said, "I don't know what we are going to do with you. I've tried everything for you to get the help you need. Maybe one of my friends can help with you. I'll call her tomorrow. Now go to bed both of you."

I woke up like I normally did, dressed, and brushed my hair. I didn't eat breakfast anymore, it made my stomach upset. I made my lunch, which wasn't much because I didn't like to do it. I left the house and went to the bus stop. I was in Junior High now. Lisa wasn't in that school. Her Grandparents put her in private school, so I had to be in Junior High all by myself. I didn't have anyone to protect me and I was so scared and I had every right to be. The kids at school were so mean to me. They would bump into me in the hallways, then yell at me, "Watch it Yoda," or, "Watch it pizza face," "Look where you're going fish lips." One of them always slammed my locker door almost on me, so I stopped going to my locker and just carried everything with me. The adults didn't do anything. The principal said I was a big girl now and I should stand up from myself so I just kept to myself once again. That's the only way I could protect myself. In Junior High I didn't have any friends at all. Every day someone picked on me. I had a couple of classes that I liked and enjoyed and it kept my attention to my work. One was art class. The teacher liked me because I had the skills of an artist. I did everything she put in front of me without a struggle. I didn't ask questions, I just did it. One of my projects was to draw a picture of something that I liked. I decided to draw a picture from National Geographic of two adult bold eagles in a nest full of hatchlings on a ledge of a cliff. I worked on it for three weeks. It was amazing what I did and I couldn't wait to find out what my grade was and to take it home to show mom. My teacher told me I got an A on it and she was going to enter it into a contest. I had to sign a piece of paper giving her permission to do so. I should have read it, but I trusted her. I never heard of anything and never got my picture back. The next project was a lot of fun too. I was going to make Kermit the Frog out of paste, paper and paint. It's called Paper Mache. This time the teacher wanted me to give it up so she can put that into a contest. I told her, "No, this is for my mom for her birthday. Besides, I need to show her my work somehow." The Kermit looked so real. I did an excellent job. The teacher gave me an A for it. I was so proud of myself and I couldn't wait to give it to my mom. Mom's birthday came I had her gift wrapped up. I even made her a card. Gayle made her breakfast and her coffee. Shallon just made her a picture. We knocked on her door and opened it, and saw there was a guy in her bed. We closed the door real quick. We knocked louder, then said, "Mom, wake up. We have something for you." Mom said, "Okay, you can come in now." We opened the door again and saw that she was sitting up. All three of us said Happy Birthday at once. Gayle handed her the breakfast and Shallon and I gave her the gifts. She opened mine and just about cried at what she got. I said, "I made it in art class." She said, "I love Kermit the frog and you did an awesome job." She put it on her table and she looked at Shallon's picture and gave Shallon a kiss and a hug with thanks. Then she looked at my card, and she gave me a kiss and a hug too. She thanked Gayle for breakfast and gave her a hug and a kiss too. The guy just sat there. He didn't say a word. Mom said, "Okay kiddos. Leave me, shut the door. I'll be out in a few." We left and closed the door.

The phone rang and Gayle answered it. It was Dad. She smiled and started talking to him. Mom came out of the room and asked who was on the phone. I told her. Mom motioned Gayle that she would like to talk to him. Gayle told him and handed the phone to her then Mom left the room. She told me there's a chance she would be living with Dad but mom and him had to work out the kinks yet. I said, "That isn't fair. I want to go too." Gayle said, "You already tried living with Dad, it's my turn." Mom came in as said, "Well young lady, you're going to live with your dad. You are leaving next week." I just looked at her like she was lucky. "Start packing your things. You're dad is sending the bus ticket." Gayle was relieved and happy. I was upset that my sister wasn't going to be here so I can talk to her about the problems I have at school or with mom. We always had each other to work out of problems. I cried the day Gayle left and I also was relieved she was gone. I didn't have to worry about her anymore. Now I had my own room.

I still had problems at school, and no one was nice at all. I started to feel left out, like I was invisible or something. They ignored me at recess and basically every where else. I couldn't play any games with anyone. I tried one day to play basket ball with a group but they left when I tried to join in so I did hoops by myself. The next day I wanted to play flag football but no one wanted me in the game. I found a quiet area to sit and pout until recess was over.

Things seemed to calm down in school. I was able to go to class without being picked on. At lunch no one picked on me there either. I was able to do some hoops on the court at recess. The bell rang and I went back in without a problem. I was thinking maybe everyone is getting use to me and found it a little boring to pick on me now. I was smiling for the first time since I started at this school. I left the school smiling with my head up. I was finally happy. I got on the bus and went to my seat. One of the boys in my class was sitting in the seat in front of me and his name was Tom. He had some sort of Down syndrome, but he didn't have it that bad. Anyways, one of the other boys on the bus came up to me and said that Tom had a crush on me. I looked at Tom and said, "No way." The boy said, "Yes he does, go and ask him." I tapped Tom's head, he turned around. I asked, "Is it true you have a crush on me?" Tom nodded his head. I just couldn't believe what I was hearing. The boy that told me said, "See I told you. I dare you to kiss him, and if you kiss him we won't pick on you anymore. If you don't we will make your life a living hell." I didn't like the idea of kissing Tom. I didn't feel anything for him, but I didn't like it when they picked on me either, so I kissed him. It was the biggest mistake I have ever made. Everyone one the bus was teasing me. They were singing the K-I-S-S-I-N-G song to us. I felt very bad. They even told Tom we were together now. I didn't know what to do at this point. I couldn't wait to go home. I felt sick to my stomach. I hated them. They tricked me. The bus stopped and I ran off of it as fast as I could. I called mom and told her what happened. She didn't seem to care. All she said was, "You're old enough to handle these situations by yourself." All I can think was, "OH MY GOD, what am I going to do now?" I could just forget about it and see if others forgot about it. Why would I put myself through the humiliation again? How will I keep others from noticing me the next day? I was trying to think of a way to go through school without being noticed and to get on the bus without being noticed. I had an idea, but I would have to go to school to get it started and to see if it worked out. I just can't believe mom didn't help me fix my little problem. Sometimes I just really hated her.

The next day, I was sitting there waiting for the bus and I already regretted going to school. I didn't want to be bothered by them anymore and I hated the fact that Tom was getting hurt by them as well. Tom wasn't on the bus going to school and I noticed the others were getting antsy and there was a lot of whispering and laughing going on. I just sat back on the seat and slid down a little so I didn't have to see them talk amongst themselves about me. I sat there looking out the window praying Tom didn't show up to school today. Some days his mom drops him off to school because he had a hard time getting ready for school. The bus stopped right in front of the school. I looked out and didn't see Tom there, so I waited for awhile, waiting for the others to leave the bus. I didn't want to be in that group when getting off the bus. The bus driver saw me just sitting there and he said, "Let's go young lady, you don't want to be late for school." I just looked at him in a worried look and put up one finger. He nodded his head like he understood. I watched the last boy leave the bus than I got up and got off the bus. I quietly walked into the school ran up the stairs and went right into class. Tom was there. I sat at my desk and bent over and said, "I'm sorry about yesterday. I didn't know what else to do." He looked at me and said, "I wanted you to kiss me. They just helped you do it." I just looked at him, like how can you do that. Then I said, "I thought you to be a better person. I didn't expect you to be the bullying type, a person who likes to hurt others." He just chuckled a little and went back to what he was doing. Of all the people, you wouldn't have thought it to be possible. It took all I had not to cry. Once more I felt really alone and had no one to turn too. Tom motioned to me to get my attention. I looked at him in anger and said, "WHAT?" He said, "You're very pretty when you want to be." I said, "Thanks," then turned back around and continued to do my work. Lunch time came and I ate my lunch out side under a tree. I sat up against the trunk looking up in the sky and all around me, trying to keep my thoughts from running away with me. I didn't want to think about what happened yesterday anymore. It was a very peaceful day, the birds where flying and singing. The air had a gentle breeze, it was refreshing. The children were playing and laughing. I had a helpful lunch. I guess God does answer some prayers.

The bell rang and I went back to class. I told Tom that we will never kiss again because it was very wrong in the first place. I said, "At least you got my very first kiss, so I hope you'll remember it and enjoy it for the rest of your life."

The bell rang, school was over. I ran out the door, ran down the stairs, and to the bus. I got on. I said to the bus driver, "There are some boys that will try to bug me. Please help me with them." He said, "I noticed something yesterday, but didn't know what it was." I told him everything before the others came on the bus. He said, "I will keep things calm." I said thanks and went to my seat with a smile and sat down with a sigh. I saw the boys by the bus driver, and they were smiling and laughing. They sat down in their seats. One of them said, "Are you going to hold hands with Tom and give him another kiss?" I said, "Hell no. We are not going to be doing that." The boy said, "Oh yes you are, if I have to make you." I yelled at the bus driver. The bus driver told the boys to come to the front and sit down. That boy that caused all the problems started saying he wasn't doing anything wrong and why does he have to move. The bus driver said, "If you don't come up here, I will throw you out then you will have to find another way home." All the boys that gave me a problem went up to the front. For the first time in a while I felt safe and calm. My bus stop came up, so I got up and started walking to the exit. One of the boys tripped me. The bus driver saw it, grabbed his pink slips and started writing it out. He asked my name and I gave it to him and than he asked his. He gave the boy his copy of the pink slip and he put the other in his folder. The boy was kicked off the bus for a few weeks. That's okay because once I got my bike I started riding my bike to school, I didn't have to deal with them anymore. I walked into my house and immediately called my friend Lisa to tell her what happened. She was so proud of me. She said she wished she was there to see it. After I got off the phone with her I called my mom and told her. She was sort of proud of me too. She said, "See you can work out your own problems without me."

For the rest of the school year and the following school year, no one bothered me again. I passed Junior High and I was very proud of myself.

I went to Dads for summer break. My sister was so happy to see me. Dad had another girlfriend and she lived with him. Her name was Carol. When Dad and Carol went to work, Gayle and I watched TV, went outside, and took turns riding her bike.

It was the same routine as I remembered. Next to Dad's trailer there was a field of corn. I didn't pay any attention to it all too much. Just that it was green and tall. I forgot how boring it can be at Dad's. I had to find things to do and thank God, this part of my life was easier to deal with. Dad was always easy being around because he didn't ask much, but Carol, that was different story. Gayle told me stories on how Carol would tell dad in their bedroom while she was in her bedroom that she didn't like Gayle and she wanted her out of their lives. "Are you sure she said that?" She said, "She also told Dad she didn't like children period." I was so shocked to hear that. Dad wouldn't date someone like that, would he? This visit was only for two weeks and I had to make the most of it. Only two weeks away from the hell hole that I grew up in. Usually when we are gone for the summer, mom finds someone to move in with us. Because of that, I wasn't in a rush to get home. Gayle continued to tell me that Carol was a total bitch and once I get to know her, I'll see what she means. Carol had this giant gold and white cat. I never saw a cat that huge before. He came almost up to my knees and he weighed about 24 pounds. The poor thing was declawed, but he was the sweetest thing around. He mostly slept but I always went and bugged him. He loved to be petted. Gayle told me that he sleeps with her at night. My dad came home for lunch. His work was just down the street and if he wanted to, all he had to do was stand outside his work and look at his trailer to see if he noticed us.

For lunch he made us bologna and cheese with mayo sandwiches with chips, and some salad with my favorite salad dressing, which is ranch. It was strange to have him make my lunch, I looked at Gayle and Gayle put her finger on her mouth to keep me quiet. I just shook my head in my mind and smiled. I can't believe she was playing them like that. Dad didn't say much, he just sat there and ate. I said, "How's work coming along today?" He just snickered and continued to eat. I said, "What? Can't I ask you that question?" He said, "There's nothing going on at work today. All I'm doing is cleaning the garage out." "See, I think that's interesting." He just looked at me weird and continued eating. I said, "Well, we just sat here and watched some TV and went outside to ride Gayle's bike. Oh yeah we sort of played with the cat." He snickered at me again. "I'm trying to find something to talk about." He said, "We have all the time to talk when I get home from work." "Okay, fine dad. I'll see when you come home from work." Dad went to the fridge and took out something out of the freezer and asked me to put the meat back in when it defrosted. I said, "Sure, anything to help you out." He continued to the door shaking his head. I guess he just didn't understand us kids. I know he was smiling when he left. I felt it, even though I never saw it. My dad and I always had that kind of connection. Gayle just looked at me. I said, "What?" She said, "Nothing." We cleaned up the lunch mess and went back to watching TV. About 3 pm I checked the meat and it was defrosted so I put it back in the fridge. Dad had a built in bar, so I was snooping around in it. I saw a couple of purses. I looked through them. I saw a two dollar bill in it, tucked away like it was in a safe place. I just left it alone. I went back to the living room and sat down. Five o'clock came and two minutes later my dad came walking in. I jumped up ran to him and asked, "How was your day Dad?" He just smiled at me and went to the kitchen. I followed and showed him the mail. He turned around and said, "What's up with you? I know that's the mail." I said, "I'm just happy to see you. Trying to find things to say and do for you so I can have memories to keep me smiling." He just shook his head. I asked, "When is Carol going to be here?" He said, "Not until dinner. She stops at a bar and has a couple of drinks before coming home." I said, "Oh, I didn't know she drank like that." Dad said, "She only does that when she's stressed." I said, "I guess she gets stressed a lot then." "I don't like it when she drinks all the time, but I can't change that." Dad continued to make dinner and I set the table for him. Gayle was somewhere, probably still watching TV. Six pm came and in comes Carol. She walked right by me and I smelled the alcohol on her. I didn't like the smell either. Carol looked at me and said, "Do you mind? I'd like to a word with your father in private." I left the kitchen and went into my room, grabbing Gayle on the way. Gayle asked, "What? What are you doing?" "Carol's talking to Dad and she doesn't want us to hear." Gayle said, "Oh, yeah I forgot about those. They happen every time, even when she comes home." Dad called us out by saying dinner is ready and I ran to the table. Carol was already sitting there eating her dinner. We had barbeque pork chops, scallop potatoes, and green beans. Dad always made barbeque pork chops whenever I'm around. I think he likes them. While everyone was eating, Dad started talking. "Tomorrow we are going to go on a hot air balloon ride. Have you ever been on one?" I said no and so did my sister. He said, "Great, it's your first ride then. You're going to like it." All I can think of is, "What if the balloon pops?"

My heart was beating fast and I was afraid. I didn't know what to expect. Dad continued to talk. "We'll be waking up at six am and meeting our friends. They will be working to get the balloon filled with hot air. Then they will take you two up in the air and Carol and I will follow with the truck so when the balloon lands they'll have a truck to load the balloon on. Don't worry, they know what they are doing and won't let anything happen to you." I was excited and anxious about the whole thing. I had trouble going to sleep. Morning came quick, and dad came in and woke us up. I jumped up and got dressed, went to the bathroom, and brushed my teeth and my hair. I was ready in record time. Dad didn't even finish making his coffee yet. I said, "Where is Carol?" He said she changed her mind. "She's not coming with us today." I thought to myself, "That just means more of my dad to us." I was smiling even bigger. Gayle came out and we both sat down and ate some toast before we took off. Dad disappeared for a couple of minutes back to his room. Gayle and I stood there in front of the door waiting for Dad. He finally came out and off we went. We drove for about fifteen minutes then he pointed to the balloon in the middle of the field. It was huge, was rainbow colored, and had vertical stripes. It was beautiful, but it wasn't up in the air yet. It was still laying flat. Dad parked the car, and we got out and walked to the balloon. I was curious on how they did it. I saw flames shooting into the balloon. There was so much space in there. It was just amazing how fire and air just made the balloon rise into the sky like that. Dad told his friends that we never flew in the air with a hot air balloon. Both of them yelled, "Well then, we must have a ceremony when the ride is done." I just looked at Gayle and said, "What are we in for?" Gayle shrugged her shoulders. Dad just laughed. It took about forty five minutes for the balloon to be ready to go up in the air. I looked at Dad and told him, "I changed my mind. I don't want to go up." Dad said, "It's too late now get in." Someone helped me and my sister in the balloon. They told us to sit on the floor of the basket until we got into the air. That way it was easier to deal with if we got air sick. Once we were up, I calmed down a little. I got up to look over the side. It didn't seem that far up until they pointed to the truck that was following us. It was beautiful being up in the air like that. It wasn't that breezy that I felt but someone said there was a breeze and had to compensate for the change. We were only up for fifteen minutes. It went quick. On the way down we had to hold on to the one of the basket poles until we landed and then shift to a different part of the basket when it started to pull from the wind and the heat of the air. It was a very smooth landing and we didn't get hurt. They knew exactly how to handle the balloon and were very professional. We got out of the basket and the lady said, "Get the Pepsi, we have to do the ceremony now." "Oh great, now what?" The lady came up and said, "You thought we would forget." I just looked at her and said, "I have no idea what you're talking about." She said, "You both kneel down on one leg and put your arm on your knee and bow your head." She did some kind of prayer and poured Pepsi over our heads. Then she said, "Congratulations, you are now a part of the sky." We got up and immediately got sticky for the Pepsi. The lady said we usually use wine or champagne but you are too young for that. Gayle and I watched how they got the air out of the balloon. There was a window on it and they pulled a string and it opened. The air began to release. Someone took hold of a rope and guided the balloon back that way when it fell down it would be easier to fold. Once the balloon was deflated they were able to detach the basket from it. I watched them load the basket into the truck and then watched them fold the balloon. It took four people to carry the balloon to the truck. Gayle and I and two others sat in the back with the balloon and basket and the adults sat inside the truck and we drove to where we parked at. I jumped out of the truck and waited for my sister to get off and for Dad to get out of the truck. Everyone circled us. I said, "Thanks for an awesome ride, I had fun. I hope I can do it again some day." I saw Dad give the man something, but I brushed it off. The whole experience took until lunch time. I was very hungry and couldn't wait to eat. Dad took us to his favorite diner and we ate to our heart's content, even though we were sticky. I thanked Dad for a wonderful day and told him I would never forget. He just smiled.

We got home and Carol was no where to be found. Dad went to his room and changed his clothes. Gayle and I went to our room and got a fresh change of clothes. Instead of fighting with her on who got in the shower first I just let her go. I sat in the living room and fell asleep in front of the TV. Dad came in and nudged me. "I'm going out to find Carol, I'll be back soon." I said, "Okay, Gayle and I will rest a bit. I'm not use to getting up that early." A few minutes went by and Gayle came into the living room woke me up and I went to take a shower. I got out dried off and got dressed and went to the living room. Gayle asked where Dad went I said to go find Carol. She rolled her eyes. I said, "What's up?" "Carol will be drunk by the time Dad finds her. She gets angry and starts fighting if she doesn't get her way." I said, "Oh great." I was still exhausted from the day's activity and was about to shut my eyes when I heard doors slamming and in walks Carol cursing and yelling at Dad and then she saw us and walked straight to their room and Dad followed her. I heard some yelling. I couldn't believe that Dad can yell because that was my first time hearing him. After a while if became quiet again. Then I heard the door open, and Dad came out. He asked us what we wanted for dinner. We didn't care, just something to eat. He made macaroni and cheese and fed us it. Dad sat in his chair watching TV, the news, and drank his gin and tonic. We finished dinner and told Dad we were very tired and we were going to bed. I gave him a kiss and a hug and Gayle did the same and we both went to bed.

The next morning I smelled bacon cooking. I got up and started walking to the kitchen. Dad was making breakfast. I asked, "Where's Carol?" and he said, "She's still asleep. She'll be that way for a while." Then Dad said,

"Do you always wake up when you smell food cooking?" I said, "Only when bacon is cooking, that's about it." He laughed at my response. I'm glad I could make him smile. He told me to go wake up Gayle so I did. She tried to kick me. I sat down with my Dad at the table and asked him what we where going to do today. He said, "Well, we can work on the car or you can go swimming at the park first." I said, "What are we doing to the car?" He said, "I was thinking about changing the oil." I said, "Oh that sounds like fun." Gayle came out and sat down. I said, "Dad wants me to help with the oil change or we can go swimming." Gayle perked up and said, "I want to go swimming." I looked at Dad, I wanted to please him. He said, "Fine, you two can go swimming. We can change the oil some other time." After breakfast Gayle and I went to get our swim suits on. Dad took us to the park and told us to call him when we got tired of swimming. I said, "Are you sure? We can swim all day.? Gayle nudged me again. I turned to her and said, "What? I'm just making sure." Dad looked at us and said, "What do you mean you can swim all day?" "Well, you said to call you when we get tired of swimming. You shouldn't have said it that way. Gayle and I can swim all day if we can get away with it." Dad chuckled and said, "Okay, well, you're not swimming all day then. I'll come and pick you two up at one pm so we can have lunch." That'll give us a couple of hours then. I never was at this pool before so I didn't know what to expect. It was surrounded by huge trees to help with shade and of course you can't forget the fence. The building was white. They had a snack bar and bathrooms in the building. The swimming pool was huge and it had the tallest diving board I've ever seen. Dad told me the colleges have those types of diving boards. I loved the idea of swimming all day. The first thing I did was get use to the coolness of the water. That took a few minutes. Gayle dared me to jump off the tallest diving board. I couldn't resist her dare so I did it. It was very scary. My stomach tickled all the way down and couldn't but help to laugh. I had to hold my breath right when I hit the water. I couldn't stop giggling and I had to get my head out of water before I drowned myself. I reach the top and I continued to laugh. That was so much fun. I had to do it again, but you know what it wasn't the same as the first, I still enjoyed myself though. Gayle and I could have stayed all day but Dad picked us up and we went back home. Carol wasn't around again. This time I didn't say anything. Dad already had lunch made. We ate everything in our sight. Dad went and sat down in his chair, put his legs up and watched TV. After we got done eating we took turns taking a shower and got dressed. Dad looked at me an asked if I was interested on working on his car with him. I said, "Sure, I don't mind. I like doing things with you." He got up and motioned for me to follow. We went outside, and he popped the hood to his car. I tried to open the hood, but it was really heavy. Dad came up to it and opened it for me. His engine was so dusty and dirty. I said,

"Gross dad, your engine is dirty." He giggled and said it's normal for that to happen. He went in his shed and came out with a box full of oil, an oil filter, air filter, a pan, a wrench, and a oil filter wrench. I had no idea what we where going to do. Dad said, "Well, you're small enough to drain the oil out of the car." I said, "Huh?" He said, "I'll go under and loosen up the bolt and you do the rest." I said, "Okay, I guess. I've never done this before." He said, "Aww, its simple, don't worry. I'll talk you through it." He got out from under the car and said, "There, now it's your turn, don't forget the pan you'll need that." He handed me the wrench for the bolt. I slid under the car. It was neat looking how pipes coming from one part of the car went to the next. Brackets holding things up, and wire harness all through the car. Dad said, "Okay, now look carefully. You'll see a bolt with a drop of oil coming from it." I looked and there it was. I scudded right under it. He said, "Now have the pan go underneath the bolt so when you open the bolt the oil can go into it." I had the pan right next to my head and continued to loosen the bolt. I took it off and all of a sudden the oil started running out of the hole and got all over my head and hair. I started crying and Dad said, "What's wrong?" I put the pan right under the flow of oil scudded back out from under the car and Dad started laughing. I told him it wasn't funny. He had a rag and started to wipe my face with it. He said, "Well at least you learned how to change the oil."

We went back in the trailer and I took another shower. When I got out, Dad was inside and told Gayle everything. She was laughing at me. I went up to her and hit her really hard in the shoulder and she said, "Ow." I said, "It serves you right."

Carol came home only to pick up a few things, gave Dad a kiss, and left. I was thinking to myself, wow she really does hate children. Dad went back outside and finished doing the oil change. This time I watched him do the rest because I didn't want anymore surprises. He showed me where the air filter goes. That was pretty simple. It goes on top of the engine in the middle. The PCV filter was in the same compartment and he took that out to see how dirty it was. It was filled with oil. He said, "Great, I need a PCV filter and a new PCV." He looked at me and asked if I would like to go to the parts store with him. I said, "Sure. It's something for me to do." He finished the rest of what needed to be done. He got under the car, put the bolt back in, and took the old oil filter off and asked me for the new one. I handed it to him, and in a matter of seconds he was out. He got up, went to the engine, and pulled out a long metal wand. He told me it's called dip stick to measure the oil. He put a funnel in where the dip stick was and he poured the oil into it. That's all there is to changing the oil. I was so relieved. I didn't realize how fun working on cars was until I did it. Dad got me into cars and I guess he didn't expect that. We went to the parts store and I looked around and didn't pay attention to what Dad was saying to the clerk but we were out in a matter of minutes. We got back to the trailer, and he popped open the hood. He turned to me and said, "We have to wait a few for the engine to cool. We don't want to burn ourselves." I said okay. We went back inside and he said, "Since you guys like to go swimming, I could pick you up at lunch time tomorrow and take you to the pool and then pick you up when I get out of work." I looked at Gayle and we both jumped up and down with excitement. Dad said, "I guess that's a yes?"

When dad and Gayle where busy doing something I went to the bar and went through Carols purse and got the two dollar bill because I knew we were going to need stuff while we where at the pool. I didn't think to ask Dad because I thought he was the same way with money as mom. I didn't see any harm to my action at that moment. We had dinner, watched some TV and then went to bed. Dad was gone to work by the time we woke up, which I was thankful for the extra sleep. It was 10 am when I looked at the clock, so I ate some cereal and watched some TV. At noon I started getting lunch stuff out so Dad didn't have to do it himself. We started making our lunch. Dad walked in and looks at the kitchen table and was shocked that we started without him. He said, "Oh I see you guys can do stuff." I looked at Gayle like, "What is he talking about?" She just looked back. Gayle and I put the stuff away while Dad ate. He was still in shock. He got up, put his plate in the sink, and said "Let's go." Gayle and I were smiling all the way to the pool. Dad stopped the car and we got out, waved to him and said, "See you later Dad." and he left. As I was walking into the pool I told Gayle what I did. She said, "Really? You have money?" I said, "Yes, but I took it from Carol's purse." She said, "I looked there several times

117

and never found any." I showed her the two dollar bill. She snatched it of my hand and just looked at it. We never saw a two dollar bill before. Gayle said, "Let's go and get something now." I said, "No, let's wait for about two hours to get something. That way it'll tie us over until Dad comes and picks us up." Gayle agreed. It was still bugging me. I couldn't believe I did something like that. Gayle said, "Don't worry about it. Carol probably already forgot about it. It was still in her purse that she wasn't using right?" I said, "I guess, but I still feel bad about it." The two hours went by slowly and Gayle finally said, "Okay, let's go to the snack bar to get something to drink and to eat." We got two sodas, two bags of chips and a couple of pieces of candy. I didn't enjoy them at all, but Gayle did. Four thirty came and Dad picked us up. I was exhausted from all the swimming I did. We got a little bit sun burned too. On the way home Dad said Carol was at the trailer and she was going to stay until I went home which is in 3 days. All I thought was, "I hope Carol didn't notice her money gone." Dad asked me if there was something wrong and I said, "Nope, I'm just very tired." The rest of the ride home was quiet and I nodded my head a couple of times to make it seem like I was falling a sleep. We got home and Carol was making dinner, but I wasn't that hungry. After dinner I went to my room trying to find stuff to do. All of a sudden Carol came in and started ranting and raving at us, yelling, "Which one of you little devils took my money?" I was in complete shock. I never saw her face turn so red. Carol storms off and I heard yelling between her and Dad. I turned to Gayle and said, "See, I shouldn't have taken it. I should have left it alone. Now I have to confess and accept my punishment." I asked Gayle if Dad ever hit or spanked her. She said, "No, I don't think he does that." Carol came back and said, "That two dollar bill was given to me by someone special. I've had it for many years. How could you?" And she stormed off again. Dad came in. "Who was it?" He looked directly at Gayle. I said, "I did it Dad. I didn't think anyone would miss it. We needed it for something to drink and to snack on at the pool." Carol heard and came back in and just stood there. Dad said, "All you had to do was ask for some money we would have given it to you. You didn't have to steal it." I started crying. I felt really bad. I told him that mom never gave us money so we would hunt all over the house to find some. I found the money in an empty purse, and I thought Carol forgot it. Dad said, "Still, you stole from her." I said, "We can go back to the pool tomorrow to see if they have the two dollar bill and exchange it and then she'll have her two dollar bill back." Carol said, "It's no use. That money is long gone by now." She left the room. I saw dads face. I never saw him so disappointed in me in my entire life. The next day I didn't feel like getting out of bed, I didn't feel like getting out of my room period. I was so upset with myself that I didn't want to be around anymore. Gayle came in and said Dad left a note on the table. I said to give it here. I read it and it said, 'You girls are going to the pool today. Tanya, you will have to ask about the two dollar bill. I'll pick you guys up at lunch time." Gayle and I got ready, although I didn't really want to go. I would've rather stayed home, but I knew that it was my responsibility to get the money back. Dad came in made lunch, gave me the silent treatment and just sat there and ate his lunch. I couldn't even look at him that's how pissed off at myself I was. I wouldn't be surprised if he hated me know. Dad got up, put his dish in the sink and said, "Let's go." We got up and followed him to the car and got in. Dad handed Gayle a five dollar bill. "This is to be used to get the money back. What ever is left you guys could use it to buy a snack. If you can't get the two dollar bill back don't, spend the three dollars from the money I gave you, just give it back to me and I'll go get another two dollar bill from the bank." The first thing I did when I got there was run to the snack bar and talked to the person who took care of us. I was so hoping that the money was still there. The person said the money from yesterday is already gone. "We can't help you get the two dollar bill back." I started to cry even more now. I don't like the fact that Daddy was mad at me an was giving me the silent treatment. It just about broke my heart. The person saw how upset I was and she went to get the manager. He came out and asked what the problem was, so I told him the whole story. He said, "Oh, I have that two dollar bill, give me the two dollars and I'll give it to you." I perked up and was relieved that the guy still had it, but I still felt bad for what I have done. I gave the guy a hug, which he didn't expect at all and Gayle put the bill in a safe place. Dad picked us up with a hopeful expression on his face. Gayle jumped in and I sat in the back. Gayle handed him the bill. Dad gave a sigh of relief and started driving off.

Still Dad didn't talk to me as much as he used to, but I was getting used to it. I still had that empty feeling and I still felt horrible. I'm leaving tomorrow and things didn't go back to normal yet. All the while, I thought to myself, "I bet Gayle is happy that finally I screwed up and got into trouble. I bet she's smiling inside and having a party." Carol never came back or even showed up to see me off. Who cares? She didn't like me anyways. Dad said, "In time I'll forgive you but not right now. You did the unthinkable." I said, "I know Daddy and I love you." I gave him a hug and started crying. I just shoved Gayle goodbye. It took 11 hours to get home and mom was waiting for me at the bus station with some guy I didn't know again. I rolled my eyes at the idea.

Mom gave me a hug and the guy took my bags. Mom said, "This is Jack, he'll be living with us for awhile until he gets back on his feet. He used to live at the halfway house." I said to myself oh great another one. Mom continued, "I moved you to the laundry room so you can have your privacy." Again, thinking to myself, "You moved me there to keep me from hear your two from making noise at night." I giggled at that. Mom said, "What's so funny?" I said, "Nothing." We continued to walk out to the car. He seemed okay at this point. He didn't start telling me new rules or anything. Again thinking to myself, "Maybe he has potential after all." We got home, the lawn was mowed and the yard looked nice. It was a while since I've seen it look that nice. I walked in and saw that the house was cleaned up. I walked all the way to the back. Mom put up wall to separate my room from the laundry room. It was nice. I could lie on my bed and look out the windows to stare at the sky. I turned to mom and gave her a big hug and said, "Thanks, I love it." Mom said, "I thought you might." After about a week of being home Jack finally said something at dinner. "I've let you settle down and now it's time to tell you a few rules." I looked at mom and then at Jack. Mom said, "Jack, Tanya isn't the problem don't say anything to her. The one you have to worry about is Gayle and she isn't here at the moment." I just sighed. I was starting high school this year and I was sort of excited about that. In a week I get to go get used to the school, get my books and my schedule. I was happy to hear my friend Lisa was going to the same High School so I wouldn't be going through this by myself.

High School was easier. I still had my problems with the other students but not as bad as before. I thought I was making friends with the help of Lisa. She was in the same classes I was except for science and history. Most of ours were learning disabilities anyways so we couldn't avoid each other if we tried. English was the happening class. We had fun there but our teacher told us we had to act like we were learning something. There were these three girls that used to cause trouble between Lisa and I. Most of the time it worked, but Lisa always came back to me when she found out things that weren't true. I kept on telling her, "I never talk about you and I mostly keep to myself, so why would you believe what they say anyways?"

I still prayed to God almost all day long, but it seemed to be easier to deal with probably because it was the same old stuff as before.

The learning disability coordinator made an appointment for my mom. She needed to talk to her about my grades and progress and it was very important that she showed. I was only in school for two weeks. What would be so important at this early in the school year? I gave mom the note. Mom looked at me and said, "What did you do now?" I said, "Nothing."

Mom said, "Do you want to come to the meeting too?" "She just wants you to go." Mom said, "It has to do something with you, you have every right to be there. Meet me in front of the school a few minutes before the meeting. I'll write a note so you can. I did what mom said and we went to the room together. The coordinator was shocked to see me there. "Mrs. Swanson, Tanya doesn't need to be here for this meeting. We just have a few concerns to talk to about." Mom looked at her and said, "We are going to be talk about Tanya, she has every right to be here. So start talking." She grabbed a folder and opened it up. "Well, Tanya is failing Science so we have to take her out and put her in another class." Mom said, "Okay." "We feel she hasn't progressed well enough in school." Mom said, "What? How can you say that?" "Well, Mrs. Swanson, we don't have any other class to put her in except study hall and that's not a learning class. Tanya needs credits and the study hall doesn't give out credits." Mom looked at me and said, "Is there anything you would like to learn here?" I said, "I saw an auto shop here. I would love to try that." The coordinator said, "We wouldn't recommend that. We don't think she'll do well at that. Mrs. Swanson, we feel she won't amount to anything. She won't succeed at anything she puts her mind to." Mom snapped, "You don't know my daughter as well as you thought. She worked with her dad this summer on cars. And how dare you say that about her?" The lady said, "Let me make a call. Please wait a moment." A couple of minutes later she comes back. "The principal said it would be ok for Tanya to try Auto but the first sign of her failing, we'll take her out and then we will be back in this room again." I smiled at mom. Mom wanted to know if I wanted to go home with her and just have a half day. I said, "I'm fine mom." The coordinator told me that I'll start Auto the next day. I looked at her and said, "In the middle of the week?" in a shocked tone. She said, "Yes, the sooner you fill your empty schedule, the sooner you get back into a regular routine." I said, "Wow, that's quick." She handed me two slips, one with the name of the auto book

I must get at the book store at school and the other is a transfer slip to the auto class. I couldn't wait. I can't wait to prove to everyone that they are wrong about me.

One day I bumped into someone in the hallway. He actually said sorry to me. I just couldn't believe that. I smiled. At lunch I sat outside at the picnic table and the guy that pumped into me sat down at the same table. He looked at me and said, "Do you always sit by yourself?" I said, "Yep, pretty much." "Why?" I said, "Well, because everyone hates me? They grew up picking on me. I really don't have any friends except Lisa and she doesn't have this lunch so I sit by myself." He asked for my name and I told him. Then he told me his name "Adam Montano." I said, "It was nice to meet you. I wouldn't be upset if you left now. I'm use to it." He started laughing at me. "What?" He said, "You seem like a nice person to hang out with. Is that okay with you?" I said, "Sure." He stayed with me for the rest of lunch.

I finally made a friend on my own without Lisa to help me. I just had to keep him as a friend and pray to God that no one tries to take him away.

At the end of day I was saying good bye to Lisa and Adam showed up. He jumped right in front of me and shouted, "Hi!" I started laughing. Lisa just looked at me. I said, "Lisa this is Adam. I met him today." Adam said, "Pleased to meet you." Lisa just said, "Hi," like she was disgusted with him and started walking away. I yelled, "Lisa, I'll call you later okay?" She just waved her hand. I started walking to my bus stop and Adam followed. I started smiling and giggling. He said, "Whatchya laughing and smiling about?" I said, "Are you always so funny?" He said, "Pretty much, why?" "I was just wondering." He said, "You don't talk much do you?" I said, "Nope. I really don't have much to say." "Is it okay to walk with you for a while?" "My bus stop is right here." "Can I stay here with you until your bus comes?" "Sure." He was doing all kinds of stuff, just to make me laugh. He stepped on a block and tried to balance himself on it. He made me feel good. The bus came and I said bye. I watched him and he was watching me walk through the bus isles. I sat down, he waved and I waved while the bus was moving. I smiled all the way to my house.

I walked up to my house and I heard the phone rang. I hurried to open the door to answer the phone. I answered the phone, and it was Lisa. She asked, "Who was that guy that rudely interrupted us?" I giggled and said, "He was trying to be silly. He didn't mean to be rude. Like I said earlier his name is Adam. He seems nice, but I just met him today, so I'm not sure what type of person he is." Her voice seemed irritated at the fact I was meeting people without her.

I think she was upset at the fact that I was happy. Sometimes I just didn't understand her.

Jealousy was one of her pet peeves. She didn't like the fact that my attention wasn't on her, but when she didn't want anything to do with me and hung out with her other girl friends that don't like me, she expects me to brush it off when she comes back to me. I hated that. I didn't understand why she would break up our relationship just to hang out with the other girls. Isn't that playing a head game?

I'm not the type of person who'd take sides and cause all kinds of trouble. I like to take it easy and enjoy life. Take it as it comes. Why would I want to cause some thing to make it hard on someone? I just don't see the concept in that at all, but I liked her so every time she broke up our friendship, I just waited. She eventually came back. Her so called girl friends would say bad things to me in front of her and she wouldn't say anything. She let it happen. They would tell me I wasn't pretty and I was stupid, no wonder no one liked me. After awhile I just blocked them out. What they said to me would go in one ear and go out the other. I didn't care about what they said about me. I know they tried their hardest to get me to cry, but after awhile I became numb. It was best that I didn't have any friends. I don't understand why people have to cause problems. Why make up lies and stories just to see how hurt the other person gets? It just doesn't make since. I can't help but wonder what type of person others see in me some times, but I can help myself realize that people that like head games, lies, and back stabbing are the type of people I don't want in my life. After awhile I even stopped talking to Lisa, but that took a few years.

I looked forward to the next day of school. I was starting a class that I knew I had some knowledge of. I loved the fact that I was going to learn to work on engines and figure out how they tick.

Auto class was second period and every minute that went by I was getting more anxious. I wanted to start learning. I was thinking that if people saw me in auto class they would start treating me better, would respect me. I wanted to change my life even if it was just a little, but I also joined Auto to get my dads approval. Basically, I tried to do everything to get my dad's attention. I thought if I did things that he liked, he would come and visit more and do more stuff with me. I needed my father in my life. I was an emotional wreck, and cried about almost everything all through my life. I hoped that doing this would get me recognized and I would finally get the attention I deserve.

The first day was exciting when I walked in and everyone turned to see who was coming in. I walked to the teacher's desk and handed him the transfer paper. He said, "Welcome Tanya, pick any seat that you can find." I looked around and a boy pointed to a seat. When I sat down, he bent over and said, "Hi, my name is Chris." I said hi in a shy way. He said, "Whatchya in for?" I looked at him with a smile and said, "What?" "Oh nothing," he said, "just trying to make small talk." I just smiled and shook my head. The teacher said, "Tanya since you weren't here at the beginning of class, I need to go through the class agenda all over again." Everyone just looked at me. He continued. "The first three weeks, well the first week, we will be learning from the text book, but Tanya, you'll have to do three weeks worth of text book work to get caught up." I just rolled my eyes. "After we do the text work we will be able to work on real engines in the garage. Technically the school calls it a Lab." Every one laughed. Then he said, "Tanya, do you have any questions?" I said nope. "Then let's get to work. Mark, hand these work sheets out." It was a diagram of a transaxle. We had to recognize and find the names to all the parts and write them down on the sheet. I hated worksheets, but if I had to do them I will just to prove to everyone that I can. Chris showed me what chapter the transaxle was. I got the sheet done in a matter of minutes, so we talked for a few. The teacher saw that I was done and he came up to me to look at my work and I didn't have one wrong. He gave me another worksheet to do and it was the transmission. I looked at it and I looked at the teacher, I said, "Uhm, this looks like the transaxle." He smiled and said, "Uh huh, I got you there kid. Do your research and you'll see that they aren't the same." He chuckled and went back to his seat. Chris said, "This was yesterdays work." He showed me the chapter. I couldn't finish in all so I had to do it for homework. Chris said that the teacher was very easy. He hardly has homework, but since I wasn't there the first two weeks, I got tons homework. I love my Auto class even though it was the first day. Everyone was nice to me. I just had to keep it that way.

At lunch, I sat by myself again, and once again Adam came and plopped on the bench. "So how was your day so far?" "Not bad," I said, "I had an excellent day in Auto. He said, "Ohh, you like working on cars?" I said, "Yes I do." He said, "Very interesting. Can I ask a question?" I said, "You just did." He scratched his head and giggled. I said, "Go ahead." He said, "Who was that girl with you after school?" I said, "My best friend Lisa, Why?" "Well, she's kind of cute." I just shook my head. He said, "I know we just met but there's someone that I'm interested in that you know." I said, "Okay, it's Lisa, right?" She's prettier than I?" He said, "Uhm, well, yes." I said, "One of these days I'll let you meet her." He said, "Okay." "Just right now she's seeing my friend Warren." He seemed embarrassed so we just chatted about other things.

After school I was hopping Adam would come and bug me but he didn't. I think I scared him away. I tend to do that. I went to the bus stop without him.

I got home and mom was home. She said, "I got a call from your Dad. He needs to send Gayle back home to us. He can't handle her anymore and he thought I might since I have more experience in this matter. Your sister isn't listening to your Dad and she always goes out without his permission and all that." I looked at her and said, "What makes you think you can control her? You couldn't before." Mom said, "Well she has grown a little so maybe she'll change for us." I said, "When does she get here? Mom said, "Tomorrow afternoon or evening." "Great."

Mom's boyfriend came home and she told him. He just smiled. That night he made dinner. He made fried liver and onions, spinach and mashed potatoes. I hated liver. That was the most disgusting piece of meat I have ever had, but mom made me eat it because it was good for me. It was a good source of iron and I needed it.

Mom put some mayonnaise on my plate and told me it will help mask the taste of the liver. She was right, it did help a little. I can still smell the fragrance it made while it was cooking and it made my stomach turn. The smell lingered for a long time just like the smell of cooking fish. Yuck!!!

After dinner I did my homework and Mom noticed that I was very much interested in Auto. She came up to me and put her hand on my shoulder and looked at what I was doing. She said, "What is that?" I said a transmission. She said, "Oh, interesting. Do you like your class so far?" I said, "Yep," and continued to work on the sheet. Mom said, "Well okay, Jack and I are going to the Club. We'll be back later. You know where to call." I got my homework done then sat on the couch with Shallon and watched TV together. After awhile we went to bed.

The next morning came like every other day. Nothing but boredom greeted me. Shallon was already up and she was reading something. I didn't care. The phone rang and it was Dad. He told me that Gayle was on her way and she should be there in eleven hours. He told me which route the bus was taking, just in case something happens. I said, "So, she'll be home about seven pm." He said, "Yep, maybe a little bit early or a little bit later. Just tell your mom to call the station often to make sure where she is. Gayle is pretty much mad at me. I wouldn't be surprised if she hated me for the rest of her life." I said, "I love you Dad and I'll talk at you later." I hung up the phone, went to Shallon and told her the news. She was jumping up and down. Mom came out and noticed Shallon's excitement and asked, "Why is she so happy?" So, I told her everything. Mom smiled. Then she walked back into her room.

Mom went and picked up Gayle. I wanted to go with but she said it was best that we stayed home. Shallon and I kept on looking out the window hoping that they would get here soon. Time seemed to go by slow. Then mom drove up it was about ten pm. Someone got out of the passengers side. It didn't look like Gayle. We went outside to ask mom where she was, but it was Gayle. She just cut off her hair, wore make up, and wore different clothes. I gave her a big hug and Shallon hugged both of us. Gayle didn't seem too happy to see us. She grabbed her things from the car and brought them in. Mom showed her to her room. She went in and didn't come out. Mom said that she was just in a bad mood and that things will look up tomorrow."

My sister was home so it was bound to be interesting. I could only imagine what she was going to do next.

Mom had a friend help us with Gayle. She took her to places, hoping to get her interested in things. Sandy lost her husband to cancer and he left her with two children, so it was a God sent for Gayle to get involved with her and her children. Gayle always complained about going with her. One day Sandy took her to a car show. She met this guy named Pat. He had a 198 lemans, Pontiac. It was gorgeous. The car was light grey and Pat did the upholstery inside himself. He also rebuilt the engine. She started seeing him. I wished I knew him first to warn him about her, but she would always find a way anyways. Gayle was back to her old self again. She would leave with Pat without mom's permission and I was stuck at home with Shallon. There was nothing different about that.

Mom noticed how stressed out I've become, so she asked Sandy to Shallon for awhile. Shallon didn't like all, but after a while I guess she got use to it. I went to moms work often, just to hang out and help with things. She would pay me with a Super Big Gulp and a pack of cigarettes. There was this video game in the corner of the store and this guy would come in and play it just about every night. I guess to have something to do. Mom introduced us, probably thinking we would make a good couple seeing he was a day short of my birthday. His name was Warren. All I saw was a guy. I didn't feel any sparks with him. He liked working on cars with his dad. His dad rebuilt race car engines. We became good friends though. One night I asked Warren if he would like to meet my best friend. He would probably like her. He said sure. We went to her house and asked her Grandparents if she could go out with us. Since they loved me and knew me they said ok. Lisa was shocked. Warren and Lisa hit it off great. I didn't think that would happen. I was happy for them.

One night Gayle came home crying. Pat broke up with her. She just didn't care anymore, so she called a friend to come and pick her up. I asked who the person was and she said it was none of my business and not to worry about her. I said whatever.

While I was in the bathroom, she left. She didn't say bye or anything. I didn't even have a number just in case. That's the way she worked. I went to mom's work and told her what Gayle did.

Mom said, "Oh, don't worry, she can handle herself." I said, "I have a bad feeling about this. I don't think she should have gone out tonight." Mom said, "Stop worrying that's all you do is worry."

Warren just looked at me. I asked him, "Where's Lisa tonight?" He said, "Her Grandparents won't let her leave. They grounded her from seeing me right now." I said, "What did you do?" He said, "Nothing, just her Grandparents are really strict." I said, "Oh yeah, I forgot about that. I'm sorry." "Not a big deal, I'm here having fun." The store's phone rang and mom picked it up. It was my sister. Mom was acting worried and scared at the same time. Gayle was crying and very upset. Mom asked where she was, looked at Warren and asked him if he knew where the Giant Lumber Jack was. Warren said, "Yes, why? Mom said, "Will you do a big favor for me and go and pick up Gayle for me? She was left there from one of her friends." Warren said, "Sure, I'll go get her. I said, "I'm going too just in case." Warren said, "Well let's go, she's in a bad part of town." He sped through town and didn't get caught by the police. We got to the area but we couldn't find her even though we looked constantly. Then Warren saw a shadow at a payphone. He stopped the car and yelled Gayle. Gayle came running. I yelled to her to get in the car. Warren said, "Get in quick. We have got get out of here." She jumps in the front seat with us. I asked what happened but she couldn't talk. She was crying hysterically. She said, "Just take me to mom please." I was so scared for her and I believe for the first time in her life she was scared. Warren loved to drive fast and he knew how to get away with it too. I was so lucky to have him as a friend. All I know her friend was trying to sell her into prostitution and she escaped from him, but that's all.

She opened her eyes after that. She tried to change her ways by going to meetings to get help with her addictions. I noticed a lot of our friends went to the meetings too, but I think they went to just socialize with everyone. I went to get both. The meetings helped me stay in focus when things didn't go so well. I didn't know there were others that had problems like me or even worse, I also went to listen and to try to give as much support as I can. Sometimes I go to dwell over the things that did happen to me. Just to get it out because it still bothered me. Mom liked the fact that we went to meetings, probably because she knew where we were at. The place was a safe heaven. Everybody helped everybody. I loved it there.

Alano Clubs are the greatest support system in the world. If they are run properly that is. I miss the one in my home town. I miss the warmth and the friendships that I got out of it. I never felt anything like it again. One day I hope to go back. I know that it may feel strange to be at a place that

I haven't been in for years. But, just standing in a place that I grew up in and remembering the support and the good times will be all worth it. If you have someone in your family that has a drinking problem, you yourself can get help for them. Alanon is for family with alcoholics or people who have a drinking problem. There is also a support group for alcoholics called AA. I would love to put all the listings of the clubs in my book, but there are so many. Just go to google.com and look up Alano Clubs in your area. Once you find one, go right away, and they will treat you like family. You don't have to say anything or introduce yourself unless you are ready.

My First True Love:

Dick was dating my sister at the time I met him. Well, if that's what you called dating. I noticed him one night when he was over with Pat. I couldn't but help fall in love with Dick at that moment. He was tall, with black hair, brown eyes, and very skinny. There was something about him that caught my senses. I was sixteen at the time. Mom told all her friends and family that I was a late bloomer and to look out if I ever noticed guys in the near future. I guess girls at an early age are boy crazy for some reason.

One night Pat and Dick came over, I thought just to relax and to hang out. Pat sat there on the chair and Shallon was climbing all over him. But Pat didn't mind, I guess he liked children. I just sat there trying not to stare at Dick; I mostly watched the TV. Then all of a sudden Gayle and Dick got up off the couch and started moving towards the hallway where our rooms where. I said, "Wait a minute where are you two going?" Pat said, "Oh, just let them have their time alone. They need their privacy." I just started getting antsy. I was upset and angry and didn't know what to do. Pat said to just relax, not to worry, and come sit down. I did what he said. But it was too long. I said to him, "What if I go and knock on the door and say that mom was home? What would you think would happen? Pat said, "You wouldn't dare." I said, "I would and I'm going too." He's said, "No wait, they are probably almost done." I looked at him and said, "Done, what do you mean?" He looked at me and realized I had no idea why they where there in the first place. I said, "That's it, I've had it." I walked down the hallway banged on my door and yelled Mom's home and ran back to the couch. A few seconds later Dick hops into the living room adjusting himself and buttoning his pants. That just got me even madder. But I had to laugh. Pat just looked at me like I was dead or something. Gayle came out looked out the window and noticed mom wasn't home yet. She came towards me and started hitting me in front of Pat and Dick. Pat just laughed. Pat got up and Dick went to the door, Gayle said, "Wait she's not home lets go back," and finished. Pat looked at Dick and shook his head. Dick left and so did Pat. Gayle yelled

hold on let me come with and in a few minutes she was gone with them. I was very upset with her. She didn't have permission to leave the house and now I'm stuck watching Shallon all by myself. So I just sat there stewing in my anger and Shallon was watching TV or reading a book. Didn't pay much attention. I think I smoked at least a pack that night.

Shallon finally went to bed about 10pm. I just sat there either watching TV or listening to the radio. Sometimes I would hang on the front window looking out and day dream about what I might be missing out there. My sister came home at 11pm. She yelled at me and tried to beat me to death because I ruined her night with her "so-called" boyfriend. I just said you are lucky that mom wasn't at home because you would have gotten your ass beaten. I just laughed at her. For the longest time she didn't bring others to our house because she was afraid I would ruin her fun. They always picked her up and dropped her off.

One night there was a dance for all the Ala-teens and Pre-teens. Mom took us because she knew it was a safe place for us to have fun. But she didn't know that Gayle called all her friends and let them know where she'd be at. She said she would kill me if I told mom. But I didn't because I wanted to go. The music was loud and the atmosphere was filled with life and fun. I sat in the dark in the corner of the room smoking cigarettes and drinking Coca-cola and watching people going back and forth. Pat noticed where I was and came and sat down at the table. He had his girlfriend Jennifer with him. She never liked being called Jenny, so we had to call her Jennifer. A few seconds later Larry and Richard sat down at the table. Dick was out dancing with someone. He came over when he saw everyone sitting at my table. Thank God Jennifer was sitting next to me. I was very hyper, happy and scared at the same time. I finally bent over and told Jennifer that I had a crush on Dick for the longest time and I really don't know what to do since he's dating my sister. I told her not to tell him anything. Dick yelled,

"I'm going outside to cool off, anyone want to come with." Jennifer said, "I will just for a couple." I looked at her with a worried look and she just smiled. My heart was beating really fast. I didn't know what to

expect. A few minutes went and Jennifer came back, grabbed her boyfriend and the other guys to the dance floor. Then I saw Dick come towards me. I tried to hide in the corner hoping that he couldn't see me and move on to somewhere else in the dance room. But he didn't. He bent down and looked really close to see me and he spotted me. He sat down and asked if I would like to dance. I said no. He said that he couldn't hear me. I yelled, "NO!" He said, "Awww, come on I don't bite." I said, "you're seeing my sister and that's kinda wrong don't you think." He said, "Oh, um, there's something you have to know. Well, we aren't seeing each other anymore. There was a misunderstanding and she didn't like it to well. So we agreed to go our separate ways." I said, "Aren't you mad at me for interrupting your fun with her the other day." He said, "What that, no, I'm not mad at you. I thought it to be funny afterwards. You were gutsy. She could have killed you. Now, will you dance with me?" I said, "Um no, I can't. It doesn't feel right." He left and then Jennifer came back with her boyfriend and said, "Well, what happened?" I said, "What do you mean?" She said "You know." I said, "You told him, why?" She said, "I didn't tell him anything." I said, "He asked me to dance with him and I said no about three times now." She just looked at me and said "What's holding you back and why aren't you dancing with him." I yelled, "He dated my sister and I don't know how to dance." She just started laughing at me.

I thought I was safe because he asked me three times already and I thought that was the code. You know three strikes your out kind of thing. Well, I was sitting there smoking a cigarette and Jennifer nudged me and pointed. "Here comes Dick again." I felt my face become hot and my heart beating fast, it was like slow motion. He was taking his sweet time to me. Jennifer said, "This time don't say no, just go out and dance and have fun." I just thought to myself if only she knew how I was feeling right now. My palms started sweating, I was so nervous. How am I going to survive this feeling of embarrassment and uncertainty of what may come next. I wasn't taught any of this that I could remember. When he asked I said yes. He took my cigarette out of my hand, put it in the ash tray, took my hand and guided me to the dance floor. AC/DC was playing "Black is Back." Never heard of it before, but I tried my best to dance to it. We danced for a long time maybe about five songs. I started getting tired and hot so I let him know. He guided me outdoors to cool off and take a breather. All the while I was looking for Gayle. Dick said, "What's wrong?" I said, "I don't know where my sister is and I'm afraid she's mad at me for dancing with you." Dick said, "OH, well I saw Gayle take off with someone tonight on a motorcycle." I said, "Oh nice she better be back by the time mom comes and picks us up. I'm really sorry for interrupting you and my sister the other day. I didn't know what you two where up to until Pat told me. I believe in saving yourself for the right person. Making love is a secret and private experience between two people that truly love each other." I could feel my face turn red and I know he could see it. So I put my head down to cover the redness. He put his hand under my chin pulled up gently and said, "You shouldn't be embarrassed to talk about what's on your mind. That was beautiful." I said, "yeah right," and I put my head down again. He said, "I have a surprise for you and please don't get mad at me." I said, "Oh, ok." He said, "Close your eyes." So I closed my eyes and he gave me a kiss—my first kiss. I couldn't breathe, my legs felt like Jell-o and my heart was beating fast. I thought, "I couldn't believe this is happening". Someone I have had a crush on for awhile is kissing me. I felt like I was about to faint. I gently pushed him away to let him know how I was feeling. He looked at me and said, "Oh my, was this your first kiss." I kinda hit him and said yes. He said, "Well, hell of a deal!" That was his favorite quote; I have no idea where it came from. He stood next to me and said he was sorry, that he should have found out about that first before he gave me a kiss. I told him not to worry because I liked it, matter of fact I loved it. I started getting cold and asked if we can go back inside, he said ok, why not. So he helped me walk inside. I sat down and drank some of my coke. Pat and Jennifer were on the dance floor dancing along with Richard and Larry. "Stairway to Heaven" from Led Zeppelin came on and Dick pulled me to the dance floor, we slowed danced and kiss through the whole entire song. *I was so naïve, I didn't think anyone would ever hurt me. I didn't think that people were laughing or even smiling at us. I had no clue. I was on cloud nine and no one would be able to take that away from me. Well that's what I thought. I was finally in love with someone that I thought cared about me and*

understood me too. Have you ever just looked at someone and know from that moment on that you were meant to be? No one can ever take them away from you. That's what I felt. I thought he knew me and that's why he kissed me. Isn't that how it supposed to work anyways? God would have told me differently.

My sister came back right when the song ended and she noticed Dick and I dancing. She grabbed me and yelled, "What the hell are you doing?" I just looked at her in shock. She stood there for a second and then stormed out. I told Dick I had to leave and told him to call me when ever he felt like it. I ran out the door and Gayle was so pissed off at me. She yelled at me, "Why are you kissing and dancing with my boyfriend?" "He told me you two called it off and weren't seeing each other anymore." She said, "That's bullshit!" I said, "Gayle you know I had a thing for him for the longest time and you went after him just because you knew how I felt." *She really hated me at this point. I thought she was going to kill me. She shoved me a couple of times trying to get me to shove back but I wouldn't, not on church grounds.* God gave me a chance tonight with him and I enjoyed every minute together. "By the way where did you go?" She said, "I went with a friend to Village Inn for something to eat and a cup of coffee." I said, "Ok, I have every right to be pissed off at you for leaving me here all a lone tonight but our friends showed up and I have nothing to hold over on you."

"Dick said he didn't love you anyways." *I shouldn't have told her that. It made things worse.* Mom came driving up and we got in the car. Gayle was fuming mad and didn't say a word. I was just sitting there smiling and humming trying to keep my excitement in. Mom said, "What's wrong Gayle?" Gayle said, "nothing mom, I'll be fine." Mom said, "Tanya why are you so happy?" "I said I think I have a boyfriend." Mom gasped, "Wow, that was quick." "Well, I'm not sure yet. He said he'll call and we'll go from there." Mom said, "Good, take it slow. One of these days I want to meet him." I said, "Ok, mom you will."

Dick started calling me instantly, which was a shock. I didn't expect him too. The first call my sister answered the phone. She perked up thinking he was calling her. So she started a conversation with him. I just stood there waiting and listening to see if he was saying anything about me. Her voice changed and she said, "Yeah, hold on a second." She handed me the phone and gave me a dirty look. He said, "That was kinda awkward." I said, "Well at least you don't have to live with her." He said, "Yes, you got that right." We basically talked about how fun it was at the dance and he hopes he can see me again. He said I was an interesting girl. *These days if someone told me that I would just sigh and roll my eyes.* At the age of 16 his parents gave him his own apartment, just a studio but his own. I couldn't believe that. I told him he was so lucky. He said my parents are the manager of the apartments and I help landscape the property. At the moment I ride my bike every where except when Pat drives me. I said, "He's kinda awesome in that. I love his car. I would love to ride in it some day." Dick continued, "Well one of these days we'll go cruising with him." I said, "Really?" I was getting excited again. *Pat was an awesome guy and still is. I loved the fact that he was a down to earth type of person. He liked everyone. He was always smiling and joking around.* I've never been cruising before, matter fact I've never done anything without mom around. And we always did what she wanted. Dick said Hell of a Deal again. I just loved the way his voice sounded. So I didn't mind what he said. Mom tapped me on the shoulder and tapped her wrist stating in was time to get off. I said, "Dick give me your number so I call you back later. My mom needs to use the phone." He said, "Sure, but don't call so much it's my mom work phone and she can't use it for personal phone calls. Call it only if you don't hear from me." I thought to myself, this sounds weird. But I said ok. He gave me his number. I said good bye and hung up the phone. I just sat there for a few remembering the night before. Thinking to myself, what did I do to deserve this? Why am I being rewarded with a nice guy and new friends? *The voice in my head said because you worked hard for it. Plus its just apart of life. Yours will get better now just wait and see.* After mom got off the phone, I went on it again. She looked at me and I said no mom its not him, I'm calling Lisa is that alright with you. She left the room. I told Lisa what happened, she was so excited for me and wanted to know the details. So I told her everything. I heard her sigh. Then she asked if I wanted to come over and visit. I was shocked, she never asked me to come over before. I said, "Just a moment let me ask my mom." I yelled mom, "Lisa wants me to come over for a little while." Mom came in and said, "You're allowed to go but you have to find your way there. I'm not driving you everywhere." So I asked her for her address and told her I'll be there about noon. She said that was fine we'll have Egee's for lunch. I told her I can't eat there I don't have any money. She said, "don't worry we'll take care of that." I said, "great I'll see you soon than." I hung up the phone with her. This will be my first time going over to her house. The other time, I sat in the car and waited for her come out of her house. I don't know what to expect or anything. I showed mom the address and she said, "Oh, that's not too far. I'll take you there but you'll have to find your way back." I said, "Ok, at least I have the free city bus pass I can use." *Since I have a learning disability, I get free bus rides. I guess this is how the city likes to help or something. I didn't mind, well not yet that is.* Mom dropped me off and told me to be home by five and she gave me the bus information with the times. Lisa lived with her Grandparents in a beautiful part of Tucson, right behind Popeye's and a few feet away from Egee's. Her grandfather had a repair shop just walking distance from the house but had to close it because he was retiring and had to take care of his wife. They had a huge white house and at the end of the driveway there was a guest house. They even had a pool. I was getting excited just to be with Lisa at her home. I knocked on the door and she answered it, walked me through the kitchen and dinning area. Her grandmother was sitting at the small table. She introduced herself as Lisa's grandmother. I shook her hand. She said, "Aw nice, a polite one. You choose nicely Lisa."

I started to blush. Her grandmother gave Lisa the money to go to Egee's and gave her a list of what to buy. They asked me what I wanted and I said "I've never been there before. I don't know." Lisa said, "Try the Italian grinder. They are so good. You'll fall in love with it." I said sure I guess I can try that. So Lisa and I went to Egee's to get lunch on the way there I told her more about Dick and how he was dating my sister and all that. She just couldn't believe I was seeing someone that dated my sister. She said it was gross and she didn't trust him at this point. She said it didn't seem right to be dating your sister's ex. It made her feel funny. I didn't care because I was on cloud nine, happy as can be. I couldn't wait to go home and try to call him, But I also liked the idea of spending time with Lisa too. We were waiting in line at Egee's and I saw Pat's car drive by. I said, "Lisa, see that gray car? That's Pat's car." She didn't seem to care about cars and she seemed aggravated with me. So I stopped all together talking about the fun I had the night before. *All day I was thinking to myself my life is changing for the better. I'm happy and I hope this will never change.* Lisa gave the order to the person and she paid for it. We went to the end of the counter and waited for our food. The food smelled so good, my stomach started growling so loud, Lisa looked at me strangely. I said, "Hey, I'm hungry. Doesn't your stomach make noise?" She just shook her head. We walked back to her place. I opened the door and we walked in. I shut the door for her since she had her hands full. *Egee's is named for the drinks they make. It's like a slushy, but not. The flavors are all natural, no artificial flavoring. The color of the drinks are dyed I believe. Lisa ordered the Pina Colada slushy. It had chunks of pineapple and coconut—very delicious. I can drink that all day long if I wanted to. The sandwiches are out of this world. I've never had anything close to that again. I think it's the dressing they put on it. It's just like an Italian sub but a little bit different in taste.* We sat down at the table in the kitchen and Lisa served everyone. She got four cups and four spoons for the slushy. Her grandmother served the slushies to everyone. We had our sandwiches heated up. I was so in love with everything I had. I couldn't get enough of it. I made yummy noises and it just made her grandparents smile a lot. I guess they never saw a starving child before. After lunch, I helped clean up. Lisa took me to the living room where she played music. To me, she had everything. I was so amazed at all the music she had. All the records and cassettes and the stereo system she had. We just sat there listening to music and look at the albums and she told me why she liked RAT. She just couldn't get enough of them. They dressed like girls, with very tight spandex pants, long puffed out hair, and they wore make-up. She said that's why she liked them. They weren't afraid of wearing stuff like that. She also had the sound track of the movie called *Urban Cowboy*—one of my favorite movies in the whole world. We listened to that, too. We started talking about maybe living with each other when we graduated from high school. We were going to live in the guest house. We went in the guess house to check it out. It was pretty small. The living room turned into a bedroom and the kitchen was small the bathroom was even small. But I liked the idea. It would be fun living with her and not with my mom. We talked about what jobs we would get to pay the bills and we calculated how much it would probably cost to live there. I was having fun with Lisa that I almost forgot what time it was. I had to leave, I couldn't be late or mom was going to kill me. I asked her grandmother if I could use the phone to call mom to let her now I was leaving. Gayle answered and she said she wasn't home. I told Gayle I'll be home soon. I said thank you, my goodbyes to her grandparents, and told Lisa I'll see her at school tomorrow. I walked down the street to grab a bus to go home. I had to take two buses, but that didn't matter. I had a fabulous day with my friend. All the way home I was thinking about Dick and Lisa. I wished being happy wouldn't stop. I like the feeling. I got home five minutes after five and I was afraid mom would get mad at me for being late. But mom wasn't home yet. So I relaxed at bit. Gayle said that Dick called and he would be calling in a few. I said, "ok great, then I don't have to call him." About 7pm, he called and I told him how my day was. I told him how excited I was to even leave the house without my family. He seemed to like the idea of me being happy. We seemed to get along pretty well. So he said, "There's another dance next weekend and I was wondering if you were going?" I was shocked because I didn't know about the dance and I'm involved with the program. How did he know when he's not involved. He said that Pat, Jennifer, Larry and Richard talks to him about everything. I said, "I have to ask mom and she isn't home at the moment. I let you know when I find out." He said, "Great, tell her you have a ride both ways so she doesn't have to worry about you." I said, "Great, who's driving?" He said, "Who else but Pat." I looked forward to riding in his car. I felt it was privilege to be able to ride in his car. I couldn't believe that Pat would allow me to enter in his car. His car was so gorgeous from the inside out. I was afraid I would hurt it. I told Dick how excited I was and I couldn't wait for that night.

Awhile ago mom got me a diary, and I wrote in it constantly. Now I have some more to write about. So I did just that.

Mom called in to check on us and I told her about my date on Friday and my day with Lisa. She was happy that I was finally getting a life and she would have to talk to me later about it because she didn't have time to talk right now.

I was smiling ear to ear. I was, for once in my life, the happiest person in the whole world. I felt I won the lottery or something. For once in my life, something was going my way. Someone was interested in me for once. All week I thought about him. Morning and nights, that's all I did. I smile all day at school. I didn't let things get to me. I was trying to pay attention to my school work, but sometimes that was hard. I was excited—happy with life. I couldn't help but think about him. What school he went too or going to. When he was graduating or had he already graduated. What his dreams were and what he wanted when he grew up. I wanted to know everything about him. I couldn't wait to talk to him again.

During auto class, the guys noticed something strange about me. I was smiling and glowing. They asked questions—why was I in such a good mood? Why am I smiling? And how come I seemed spacey? So I told them the whole story, which I didn't think they wanted to know. Guys wanting to know what a girl said shocked me. Things were differently looking up.

Friday came slow. I counted down every minute to the day and time I got to see Dick again. Plus, I was very excited about riding in Pat's car. But

Dick didn't understand why I was fascinated about his car. I guess he never heard of a girl liking cars before. I just love beautiful vehicles. Pat pulled up to the house and Dick came walking up to get me. I opened the door and yelled in my house, "I'm leaving now!" Mom yelled, "Take your sweet time getting home but be home before 1." Dick smiled and said, "Hell of a deal." I'll never get tired of hearing that. It just makes me smile and giggle.

I got in the back seat of Pat's car. I was smiling ear to ear. Richard was on one side, I was in the middle, and Dick was on the other side. Richard didn't seem too happy about a full car or people. But he didn't say anything. Pat turned around and said hello and I said hi back. Than he said, "Hold on!" I was jumping out of my skin about that. I loved it. I love the noise the car made, how fast it could go, the person that was driving the car, and the music. I loved everything, even Jennifer in the front passenger seat. If only they knew how much I appreciate them. But I was so shy and afraid to tell them. I kept it to myself.

We went to the dance, and danced to our heart's content. I didn't have to worry about Gayle ruining my night she was busy doing something else. After the dance we all went outside the church and walked behind. The church roof was almost touching the ground, so it was easy to climb. Dick said, "Get down, you might break something." I said, "No, you come on up here. This roof is nice and strong." To prove it, I was jumping up and down. Dick couldn't believe I was doing that. I said, "Why would they build a roof so close to the ground if they didn't think it could stand the weight of any body. I play on roofs all the time this is nothing." He just stood there and asked me to come down—nicely. I said ok and jumped down.

Here's the fun part. We made out under the stadium. He was up against the building and I was up against him, kissing all over him. He slipped and my instinct was to put my knee up to catch him and he said, "Watch it! You don't want to harm my jewels." I said, "Oops, I forgot" and giggled a little. Pat and Jennifer came looking for us. It was time to go home. I really didn't want to but I didn't want mom to be mad at me either. We got there and Dick walked me to my door and asked if we can go out tomorrow night. I said, "I'll ask mom and you call me tomorrow. Mom's a sleep right now so I don't want to wake her." He asked what time he should call. I said about noon. He gave me a passionate kiss good night. Something I had always dreamed about and never experienced until now. I just about fainted. I closed and locked the door, went to the window, and watched Dick get into Pat's car and drive away. Then I went right to bed and just thought about the whole night. I was very, very happy. Nothing was going to take that away from me.

I woke up smiling. I couldn't wait to tell mom what kind of night I had. She wasn't a wake yet, so I watched TV until she did. I heard her alarm clock. I got up and went to the kitchen and made her coffee. I took it to her. She couldn't believe what I did. I was smiling and she said, "It looks like you had a nice time last night." I said, "Yep," sat down on her bed and told her just about everything. I even told her he asked me out again tonight. Mom said, "Two nights in a row? I don't know." I said, "Mom, you know I won't do anything that Gayle would do. I'm not that type of person." Mom said, "Well ok, but only if everyone that you're going to be with comes in for a few, so I know who is going to be with you." I said, "I'll ask Dick when he calls. I don't think there's a problem there."

Dick called just after I told mom everything. He's even on time. Wow, I can't believe it. Mom tried to listen to our conversation but I made sure she couldn't unless she picked up her phone in her room. She was really good at that, too. I asked Dick what Mom wanted and he said he would have to call me back, because he had to call Pat and ask him. I said, "Ok, I'll talk to you in a few." I waited patiently for him to call me back. After about a half an hour, he called. "Pat said that's fine, he likes it at your place anyways." I started giggling. He told me who else was coming over too. The whole group was coming to my house. I felt so special and popular at the same time. I couldn't stop smiling if I tried.

Everyone showed up at 8:30, right on time. I was so excited. Thank God Gayle wasn't around, she would probably cause problems. Everyone found a place to sit. Dick sat next to me, Jennifer sat on Pat (she's a small thing), Larry sat on the arm of the couch and Richard just stood against the wall. Mom came in and started asking questions right away. Pat, Jennifer, and Dick just started laughing. I was very scared to death on what would happen if they didn't answer mom, since Pat was driving. Most of the questions were for him. Mom asked, "Are you a safe driver?" That's why they started laughing. Pat said of course, adding, "I haven't gotten a speeding ticket or an accident yet." Then she said, "What are you guys going to do tonight?" Pat said, "just drive around, parking on Speedway and just hanging out. We might even go to a park or Golf 'N' Stuff. Don't worry we don't do anything that would cause any trouble. I like things simple." I was smiling. Pat knew exactly what to say to mom. I guess he had a lot experience in this.

Mom looked at Dick and I and said, "You guys aren't going to do anything stupid are you?" Dick looked at mom and said, "Not unless she wants to." I looked at him in shock and jabbed him in the side with my elbow. Mom just looked at him like she was going to kill him. Then he said, "I'm just kidding. I wouldn't do anything that may harm your daughter." Mom's face relaxed. I was able to breathe again. She finally said, "Ok, I'm satisfied, I trust you guys with my daughter. Everyone relax now. Bring Tanya back when ever you see fit Pat." She smiled and went to her room.

That interrogation only last thirty minutes, Pat said while we all walked to his car. Everyone laughed. Pat said, "But I like your mother, she has spunk." I said, "Ok if you think so. We got in his car and left. Pat was blasting his music—it was so loud I couldn't think. I guess it was supposed to keep us from talking all the time. I have no idea. But I was having fun, even if there were four of us in the back seat of the car. We did a couple of laps around Speedway and someone drove right up to Pat, challenging him to a race. Pat looked at Jennifer and then at me. "Go for it. I want to feel how fast your car can go." The other car was a rust color but I didn't pay attention to the make of the car. Pat blew him away. I was able to glance at the speedometer he was going over 120 miles per hour. I couldn't believe he could go that fast in this car, but I was having the time of my life. Then I heard Pat say, "Oh shit!" and all of a sudden he broke and made a hard right. We were going down a residential street. He turned down his radio and asked to keep an eye out on the cop car he noticed. I got scared. Richard took a look and said, "Nothing here yet." Then Richard said, "Oh, there he goes. He's after the other guy. You're safe." Pat said, "Good I was sweatin' my balls off." He made me laugh my ass off. Pat looked at me through his rear view mirror and smiled. He said, "That's enough fun for the night, so let's find a safe place to park and just hang out." He parked the car and kept the music going full blast. We got out one at a time. I sat on the curb by the car and so did Dick. Pat and Jennifer were in the car. You can guess what they were doing. Richard and Larry were just standing there talking to one in other. The guy who raced Pat finally showed up and told Pat he was an awesome driver. Pat said thanks, asking how he got out the sticky situation. The guy said I did what you did. But I parked and turned off the car and the lights. The officer went up and down the street but couldn't figure out where we were. Pat said, "Nice to know you didn't get caught." The guy asked if he wanted to race again? Pat said, "Not tonight. It's kinda hot out right now." The guy said, "You know you're right. Maybe next time." Pat said maybe. The guy said, "See you later than." Then he left.

I lit a cigarette and just watched all the cars drive by and thinking that nothing could get any better than this. Dick took my cigarette and took a couple of puffs and handed it back to me. I looked at him, but I couldn't say a word. I was so scared that I might say something that would chase him away. So, I just sat there and watched him. He finally said "What?" I said, "Nothing, I just like looking at you." He said, "Stop, you're creeping my out." I said, "What?" He said, "Just joking. Had to see what your reaction was." I slapped his arm in a joking matter. Then he grabbed me and gave me a kiss. Then wrapped his arm around me and held me for a while.

Pat said, "Ok, let's find something else to do. I'm bored now." So everyone got back in the car. I didn't mind; I enjoyed being in Pat's car. I felt safe in it. I think it was because it reminded me about Dad when he raced in his car. All I did was just smile the whole entire time. I think Pat was trying to show-off because he stepped on the accelerator, the tires chirped, and we were off, going down the speedway towards Golf 'N' Stuff. We went through the parking area. It was so packed that it took us a half an hour just to go through and back—so many cars and people. Saturday nights must be very busy here. We didn't stop we left and went to a park. We had to keep it down so Pat turned down the music. We got out, Pat went to the trunk of his car, and opened it. He grabbed a football and said let's play. I just looked at him. "It's dark out. How are we going to play football?" He said, "That's the whole idea. Playing football in the dark is fun." I said, "Ok, I'll try." I was on Dick and Larry's team. Jennifer didn't want to play. I think she was hoping I was with her. So we played against Pat and Richard. Pat threw the ball and I caught it. I tried to run through them to reach the other side and Pat tackled me down. The way he did it didn't hurt me that much. He grabbed me and held me close to him and he landed on his back and I was just lying there on top of him. At that moment I thought to myself that he really cares about us women. He didn't want to hurt me. Dick came up took my hand and asked if I was alright. I said I was fine and that was so much fun—I didn't know you could play tackle football like this. When I saw Pat coming towards me the first thing that came to my mind was, I'm going to be hurt. But that didn't happen. Richard helped Pat up. Pat patted me on the shoulders and said, "I'm shocked, you didn't scream or cry. I thought I might of scared you to death." I said, "I was scared but I was prepared to take what ever you where going to give me. I've always wanted to play football with someone and I'm doing it now. I love it." Pat smiled and we continued to play. A few minutes went by and Jennifer yelled that a cop was coming. We stopped playing and ran to the car. The cop stopped in front of Pat's car so he couldn't leave. Pat went to the officer's window and talked to him. I couldn't hear them. Pat came back and said, "Time to leave because the park is closed." So we got in and left. Pat took me home because it was late and he was pretty tired. Dick got out of the car before me. He gave me a couple of kisses and held me for a second. Pat yelled, "Come on, it's late." Dick walked me to the door and gave me another kiss goodnight. I said, "good night too." I yelled to Pat and gave them a goodnight wave. I opened my door and went in. I was watching Dick get into the car and they left. I was expecting Pat to step on the gas and make tons of noise with his car but he didn't. He was civilized. No wonder mom liked him.

I called Lisa the next morning to let her know what I did. She didn't seem too happy to hear from me. I asked what was wrong and she said, "I broke up with Warren and thought that's why you were calling me—to bitch at me for doing that." I said, "Why would I bitch at you. If you didn't like him it's really none of my business. Yes he's my friend but so are you. What happened that you broke up with him?" "Well, he wanted me to do things I didn't want to do and I got mad at him. I told him to take me home. On the way home he was driving crazy and it scared me." I told Lisa, "I'll be here for her and I'm sorry it didn't work out between the two of you. Is there anything I could do to help you? Are you all right?" She said, "Yes I'm fine. Just right now I'm shocked that you are fine with this." I said, "My friendship, like I said earlier, is important to me. I won't let anything get in the way of that. Besides you're my bestest friend in the whole world. I'm not mad at you." I think I cheered her up. Her voice changed. So, I told her everything that happened to me last night. I told her that I think I was in love with Dick. She said, "You were always in love with Dick. So, that's nothing new." I stuck out my tongue at her (like she could see that). There was silence on the phone. I said, "Are you ok?" She said, "I'm still kinda shaken up about last night. If my grandparents find out, I won't ever get to go out again." I said, "Well, then stop talking about it. We'll talk at school tomorrow about it. So, what are you doing today?" She said, "Nothing much, mostly watching TV and doing my chores." I said, "Same here, since I don't have any homework. Let me know if you need to talk, I'll be here for you. I need to get off. I'm waiting for a call from Dick." She said, "Fine, I'll talk to you later." We hung up.

Dick called at 11am. He said he couldn't wait to talk to me again. He got me at the phone ringing. He said, "I was wondering if you would like to come over to spend the day with me. We could go to the park near here and we can have lunch." I said, "Hold on. Let me see if I can wake up mom to ask." I put the phone down and went down the hallway to knock on mom's door. I knocked. Mom said what is it? I walked in, "Dick wants me to go to his place. Please can I go?" Mom asked where he lived. I said hold on let my check. I started to run to the phone. Mom said hold on, just pick up the phone here. Oh, duh. I picked up the phone, "Dick, mom wants to know where you live." "Tell her I live off of Ajo." So I told her. She said, "That's a little out of my way. I'm not driving you there. If you can find another way you can go." I told Dick that. He said, "The bus comes by here, so you can find out how to get here through the buses." So I told mom. She said ok, but told me I must be home no later than 6pm. I said, "That's fine because the buses stop running at 6." So, I got his address and told him I would see him soon. I looked up the schedule and the routes and discovered I only had to transfer buses 3 times. I made sure I could come home on time too. I had to leave Dick's at 4pm to make it home on time. And there was a bus at 4pm. Everything seemed to fall into place. But that only gave us a couple of hours together, which was the only downfall to riding the bus. I got dressed and kissed mom good bye and left. I was anxious—the bus rides where taking to long. I couldn't wait to see him, that's all I thought about on the way there. The amazing thing was Dick was waiting for me at the bus stop near his place. All I could do was smile and I thought that he must like me a lot to wait for me there. I jumped off the bus and ran right to him and just gave him a huge hug. I didn't want to let go. He said, "It is nice to see you too." I gave him a kiss and we started walking to his place. He said lunch is at my place and after that we'll go see my parents. I asked about the park, because we only had a couple of hours. He said, "We have time don't worry." We got to his place and he had sandwiches and chips with coke waiting for us. I sat down and started to eat. But I didn't eat much; I was too excited. I lost my appetite. All I could do was look at him. I wanted to pinch myself to make sure this was for real. I thought maybe I was having a dream and I'll wake up any moment and be disappointed. Dick said, "Tell me what you're thinking about?" I was shy and didn't know if I should. He said, "Tanya, you'll need to get use to talking to me. I can't read your mind you know." I told him what I was thinking. He pinched my arm and I said "Ouch!" He said, "See you're not dreaming—you are definitely awake." I smile and looked at him the whole time we sat there. He got done eating and asked if I was done. I said, "yep, not that hungry." So he picked up our dishes and emptied them in the trash and put the dishes in the sink. He said, "Ok, now lets go and meet my mom and Gary." I thought to myself, oh great, his parents. I was so afraid that they wouldn't like me. I was shaking and hoping that Dick didn't notice. He said, "Tanya don't worry, they'll like you. They like all my friends." His mom was on the phone and Gary wasn't anywhere to be found. His mom put a finger up to notify him to wait a minute. We just stood there waiting. I was taught when I was younger, don't listen into other peoples conversation. Just ignore it. So I stood there looking around and thinking about how lucky I was to have Dick. After a couple of minutes she got off the phone. Dick said, "Mom, this is Tanya, my new friend." She smiled at me and said nice to meet you and I said same here. We shook hands. His mother said, "So what are you two doing today?" Dick said, "Well, she has to leave at 4 so we'll go to the park for a little while and then she'll go home." His mom looked at him. He said, "Don't worry mom, we'll be fine." I smiled at her. She said, "Ok, well then have fun." Dick said, "Good bye Mom, see you in a few." We walked out the door. On the way to the park, he showed me the landscaping that he takes care of. I said, "It must be hard to keep all this up?" He said, "Naw, not really. You do a little bit everyday. You don't do everything at once." I said, "Wow, that's nice to know." We got to the park and we walked around, than we sat down on the grass. We didn't say much. We just watched others walk by and all of a sudden he started kissing me. We made out in the park in front of everyone. I was getting embarrassed at what we were doing. I put my hand on his shoulder and pushed gently. He stopped and said, "What?" I said, "Look, this is a public place in the middle of the day with a whole bunch of people walking about. Don't you think we should respect everyone?" He said, "I guess we can." I looked at him and asked, "Are you mad at me for stopping?" He said, "No I understand. Plus I know you want to take it slow and I understand that." I said, "You're my first and

I want to make sure we are ready. Making out is fun don't get me wrong, I just don't want you to think I'm a tease." He said, "Tanya you are never a tease. You're a wonderful person. And you're very sweet. I don't want to do anything you don't want to do. I'm very patient." I said, "That's nice to know. I'm still a virgin and I would like to keep that way until I know I have someone for the rest of my life. I hope that someday it would be you." I never thought I would get enough courage to tell him that. I was so afraid he wouldn't like me anymore. But he understood what I was saying. That made me fall in love with him even more. I looked at my clock and it was almost time for me to get on that bus. We started walking back. I took in the breeze, the sunshine, the clouds in the sky, the birds flying above us, people riding bikes, people running, and couples holding hands while they walked. Just like us. I didn't want this to end. So I tried to remember everything about this day. We got to the bus stop and we sat there until the bus came. He gave me a kiss and a big bear hug. The bus stopped and I didn't want to let go, but had too. I started walking up the stairs in the bus and waved to him. He waved back. I sat down and he watched me leave. I cried on the way home. I miss him already.

It was a few minute after 6 when I got home. Mom was a little mad at me. I said I can't help that the bus was running late. She said, "While you were gone a lot has happened. We have to move. The owner to this place is selling it and he wants it to be empty when he puts it up for sale." I said, "What? I love it here! Can't you buy it?" Mom laughed. I said, "How long do we have?" She said we have a month to pack up and find another place to live. I asked, "What about Gayle and Shallon?" "Sandy said she'll still have them and if you want you can live with her to until I can get settle down at our new place." I said that I would think about it. I asked, "Can I still go out with Dick and my other friends on the weekends like before?" For the first time in my life I have a whole bunch of friends. Mom said, "Yes you can still go out. I won't keep you from that. Maybe you can ask if they can help us move." I said, "I'll ask. Mom, can you please try to find a place near my school? I don't want to change schools again." She promised she would try.

I had to call Lisa and let her know. She said she was sorry to hear that I had to move. I also told her what I did all day. She didn't seem very interested in what I said. I think she was a little bit jealous that I had a boyfriend and friends besides her. Maybe she thought I didn't need her anymore. She just didn't seem to be interested in talking to me anymore. But that's ok, I was on cloud nine and very happy. I didn't care if the kids at school picked on me. I lost all interest in them. Maybe it was time to move on if she didn't want to talk to me anymore. I told her I had to go. I had a lot to do before we moved. "I'll see you tomorrow at school." We both said goodbye and hung up the phone.

I sat there watching TV, when my sisters came walking in the house. I was in shock to see them here. Gayle said, "Mom wants us here to help pack up the house." I said, "Great! We need all the help we can get." At least Gayle's and Shallon's beds were still here. I never went in their rooms. I had mine. I thought if Gayle is here and I won't be able to go out now. She always gets to go out. It's strange how she is only one year younger than me, but she acts like she's the oldest. It makes me wonder, though. Mom promised me that I could still go out. I just hope she'll keep her promise to me. Mom said, "Come here and give me a kiss and hug." So Gayle and Shallon went to her. Shallon usually goes to bed in a half an hour so she just sat down and read a book before bed. She didn't talk very much. She never did. Mom got up and got ready for work. She looked at Gayle and said, "You stay home tonight—don't go out." Gayle said ok, but she was pouting while she was saying that. Mom went in the shower and Gayle went right to the phone. She called someone I didn't know. She got off the phone and said, "Don't tell mom we are having company tonight. She'll kill us especially on a school night." I said I don't want anyone here. She said, "Oh stop being such a party pooper. Why do you have to try to ruin all the fun." I asked, "What about Shallon? Don't you care about her?" She said, "Of course I care about her but she'll be in bed when he comes over." "Oh great another guy," I said as I rolled my eyes, like I always do when she acts like this. "You just got home, why can't you just slow down a little and just relax?" Gayle said, "Are you kidding me? You aren't the boss of me! Now just leave me alone and if you tell mom, you'll know what I'll do with you." I hate it when she threatens me. I don't have the guts to stand up for myself. So I just let her get her own way. Mom came out of here room at 9pm and gave Shallon a kiss and hug goodnight and then sent her off to bed. Mom told us not to stay up to late and that she'd see us tomorrow. Then she left to go to work. Not even five minutes went by and there was a knock on the door. I opened it, looked up and said, "What did you stay out there until you saw mom leave?" He said yep and then walked in, which was rude because he didn't wait for me to ask him to come in.

I looked at Gayle. She just smiled. I didn't bother asking what the guy's name was because he wasn't going to stay long in her life anyways. He had a bag with him and he opened it up and it was a six pack of beer. I told my sister she was crazy. I told her to keep it quiet, I was going to bed. I just told her that because I didn't want to be here in the same room with that rude and ignorant stupid asshole. I just pretended to go to bed. Something told me to listen in time to time. I just lied there and thought about Dick and how I was going to see him again if she is back. I missed him already and it has only been just a few hours since I've seen him. Time went by quickly, I heard a lot of commotion coming from the living room. I got up and went to investigate. The guy was teasing Shallon with her teddy bear and Gayle was laughing at the situation. She didn't see anything wrong. I had to do something. Shallon seemed upset and was about to cry. I asked the guy to give Shallon her teddy bear back so she can go back to bed. He wouldn't . Gayle said that Shallon was having fun. I said, "Look at your sister! She isn't having fun! She's terrified, can't you see that?" I asked the guy one more time to give my sister her teddy bear or I'll have to get it for her. He said, "I'd like to see you try." I said, "Get out, if you know what's good for you. I'll call my mom and she'll be so mad at the both of you." He said, "No, I won't go unless Gayle wants me to." I went up to him and grabbed the teddy bear but he had a good hold on it. So I did the only thing I could think of—I punched him in the face. He got violent with me. He growled, pushed me, and tackled me into the couch. I heard my back crack and I felt pain. My sister Gayle grabbed him, started pushing him towards the door, and told him that it was time for him to go. I got up went to Shallon and gave her teddy bear back and told her to go back to bed. Gayle said, "You had no right to hit him." I said, "I had every right, because he wouldn't give back Shallon's teddy bear." She said, "We were just playing with her." I said, "No you weren't, you were teasing her. I suggest you go to bed now and pray to God Shallon doesn't tell on you." Gayle said she wouldn't because Shallon loved her unlike someone else she knew. I told her to grow up and went to bed. Mom came home and made sure I was up along with Shallon. I was waiting for Shallon to say something but she never did. Shallon smiled at me for the first time in a long time. Matter of fact I don't remember her ever smiling at me before. I smiled back.

I talked to Dick just about everyday on the phone. Didn't have time to talk to Lisa except at school. I told Dick what Gayle did and he asked if I was alright. I said nothing I can't handle. He was so concerned about me.

It was a strange new experience for me. I liked the fact that someone else was concerned over me. I liked the fact that someone was paying attention to me. But in the back of my head I was putting myself down—I'm no good, so why is he paying so much attention to me? What does he see in me? I'm no one special. I'm ugly and stupid. I hope he'll never leave me because of that.

Friday came, so I had to make sure Pat picked me up early before Gayle would try to sneak out. I need to spend time with my friends. Pat didn't mind picking me up first. He came and picked me up at 8pm. One hour before mom woke up. Mom knew what I was doing and said it was ok. See, Gayle would sneak out after mom left for work. This time I was smart. Gayle was furious with me. I left before she did. Before I left, I told Shallon what she needed to do if she did. I gave her mom's work number. If she felt unsafe at any point of the night and I wasn't home yet give her a call. Back then we didn't have cell phones, we had pay phones. It was only fifteen cents a call, but I didn't have that to call in from time to time.

Mom hardly ever gave us money. We just lived without it.

After Pat picked me up, we went to pick Dick up. It was only the four of us tonight. We went to Village Inn for something to eat and sit around for a little while, just getting to know each better. I never saw someone so much in love as when I saw Pat and Jennifer together. To me, they where the perfect couple. They never really argued and they always had that spark in their eyes. I loved watching them, because they knew exactly what love was. It was so amazing. I thought Dick and I were like that too. I had so much love to give him and I showed as much as I could. My shyness sometimes got in the way. But something told me Dick knew exactly how I felt about him. He didn't do anything in a negative way towards me. That's how I knew he was right for me. At dinner, I told Pat about us moving. He said he'll see what he could do. I said great mom would be happy to hear that. So I said what are we doing tonight? Pat said just hanging around and stuff, nothing special. I said, "Every night I'm with my friends is something special. You guys are like family to me and I love it." Pat and Jennifer smiled. Dick gave me squeeze and a kiss. After awhile Pat said lets go, so we got up and left. We drove for a while and then Jennifer said, "Lets go to the park and hang out there." Pat said, "Any objections?" I shook my head no, and Dick said that was fine. It was a chilly night. Pat had everything you can think of in his trunk. He took out blankets from it. I looked at him with amazement once again. Then I whispered into Jennifer's ear; he sure does come prepared. Jennifer said, "Yes he does, that's why I love him." I just smiled. Pat and Jennifer disappeared in the dark somewhere at the park. Dick and I went to the play ground. I sat on the swing and started swinging. Dick pushed me a couple of times. Then he joined me on the swing next to me. We had a contest on which one could swing the highest. Each time I went up in the air, I got a tickle in my stomach and I giggled. Dick said, "What are you laughing at?" I said, "I love swinging it tickles my stomach sometimes." He agreed. I looked at the direction of Pat's car to make sure it was still there. It was so quiet at the park. I wanted to make sure Pat didn't leave us there. Dick said, "Don't worry Pat won't leave us here." I looked at him and said, "How did you know I was thinking that." Dick said, "Well that's a mystery." He always says little things like that to make me melt and fall deeply in love with him. I started getting cold and we decided to wrap ourselves up in the blanket that Pat lent us. We went under a play ground gym set. The sky was clear and the stars were really bright. We were making out in the park in the middle of the night—under the stars. I thought to myself, nothing can get any better than this. I didn't want it to end. I was staring at the stars and a vision came to me—well popped into my head. It was so strange. I blurted out, "Dick, one of these days, I'm going to have your child and we will be married." He just looked at me. I said, "I hope I didn't say anything wrong?" Dick said, "Nothing you say is wrong." He continued to kiss me all over. Some how my shirt was off, but I didn't mind. He was keeping me warm. Pat and Jennifer ran up to us and said it was time to go. I looked up and said, "Already?" My top wasn't covered and Jennifer noticed and just walked away. Pat said, "Hum, Tanya cover up." I looked and noticed and immediately put the blanket over myself. I was blushing so hard at that time; I couldn't stop giggling. I asked what time it was and he said past 1am. I said, "Wow, time went by quickly." Pat left towards Jennifer. I put my top back on and got up. I ran to them and apologized to Jennifer. She said, "Oh don't worry about it. It happens to the best of us" and I smiled. We left. We stopped at mom's work since the park wasn't that far from her. I asked if there were any problems after I left. She said only Gayle complaining that you get to go out and not her. I said, "So she's home now?" Mom said she better be, if she knows what's good for her. Mom looked at Pat and said, "Nice to see you again Pat." He said, "Likewise, I'm sure." They smiled. Mom said, "Ok, what's on the agenda now?" Pat said, "I was thinking about dropping your daughter off at home, taking Dick home and taking my girlfriend home and you know take myself home." She said, "This early? I would think you guys would be out all night long." Pat said, "No, I'm tired." We left and said goodnight.

I got home and Gayle wasn't up. It didn't dawn on me to check on her. I just went to bed. Once again I was having trouble falling asleep. I kept on playing the events of the night in my head. I thought to myself that I'm the luckiest girl on this planet. I noticed that I say that a lot.

The next morning came quickly. I just laid there in bed and day dreamed. I didn't want to get up. Shallon popped her head in to see if I was awake, then she jumped on me. I said get off you little turd. She just smiled at me and asked me to watch cartoons. I said, "You usually get Gayle to do that." She said, "She's not here." I got up and looked. She wasn't home. I looked at the time and it was 6:55am. I didn't sleep that much and Shallon's up early. I said, "You did the right thing to come and see if I was home. Where you up when she left last night?" She said, "Nope, I was in bed." I said, "I should have stayed home. What if something happened and you where here by yourself? I wouldn't forgive myself." We heard the front door open and I got up to see who it was. It was Gayle. I said, "You left Shallon here, alone? Why did you do that?" Gayle said, "She's fine. I'm going to bed for a little while. Don't wake me." I told her that mom will wake you when she gets home. "I'm going to tell her what you pulled," I threatened. She looked at me like she was going to kill me and proceeded to go to her room. Mom called about 9am to let us know she was coming home, because she stopped at the Alano Club to relax. I told her what happened. She wasn't happy at all. She made me go and wake her up so she can talk to her. Here we go. I can just hear Gayle now. I woke Gayle up, she went to Mom's room since it was closer and she picked up the phone. I heard yelling, a whole bunch of yelling. I didn't dare to listen in. I waited for signs that mom was done yelling and Gayle going back to her room before I picked up the phone. Mom told me that Gayle was grounded and she's not aloud to leave. I said, "How am I going to keep her home? She'll just beat me up anyways." Mom said, "I'll be home soon." I said ok and hung up the phone.

Shallon paid some kind of attention to me. She sat next to me on the couch and we watched TV. I guess Gayle is starting to bug her a bit. I know she felt neglected and I didn't want her to go through that. In my own way,

I felt bad for ever leaving in the first place. I didn't trust Gayle anymore. It was hard for me to deal with it. In the long run I blocked out most of what Gayle did. I didn't want to feel guilty; matter of fact, I didn't want to feel anything towards Gayle ever again. I was really made at her. I didn't want Shallon to experience what we went through. I don't know what will happen when mom comes home and I really don't want to know. Mom could be down right mean and scary at the same time. Shallon and I had breakfast together. It was actually nice spending time with her. But I was still thinking of Dick and wondering when I would see him again. The phone rang, it was Dick. I said, "What are you calling me for this early in the morning?" He admitted he couldn't sleep. I said same here. I told him what happened. He said not good at all. I said, "I know, right?" He said, "Ask your mother if we could go out again tonight?" I said, "Really, I didn't think I was going to hear from you again after what I said to you." He said, "Oh, about that, it didn't bother me." My mood perked up, and I felt excited for what I heard. I'm thought to myself, he must love me then. I didn't scare him away. I was smiling ear to ear. I'll ask mom, she should be home shortly. Besides I believe she's off tonight and I don't think she'll say no because of Pat. She loves Pat. He said, "Hell of a deal" again. I just wanted to melt. Look it, there are a few things in my life that I didn't want to end and one of them was Dick. I loved him with all my heart and soul. I would do just about anything for him if God permitted me. I looked up to God all my entire life. I looked for signs and I listened to everything around me—the birds, wind, other animals, and really, any noise that caught my ear. I didn't want to miss a thing of what God had to say. That's how I felt with Dick. I didn't want to miss a word that he said. I wanted to be able to be with him every minute of the day. I knew God loved me because we had a relationship like no other. I talked to him all the time and sometimes he would answer me back either by voice or a sign that I saw. I knew God wouldn't throw stuff at me if I couldn't handle it. I hoped that one day Dick and I would be that close. I prayed for it every day. I prayed about him period.

Pat picked me up at 8:30 and Mom followed me to the car. "Pat I was wondering if you could help us move in a couple weeks. You look pretty strong, and if you know of anyone else that would love to help—you know, the more the merrier." Pat said, "Sure, I don't mind helping and I'll see if I can find anyone else." Mom said, "Great, I'll talk at you later," while I sat there just rolling my eyes. We drove off. Pat didn't turn the music on, instead he started talking to me. "So, you're moving—why?" I said, "The landlord is selling the place." "When where you going to tell us?" "Well, I was supposed to tell you last week, but you know, you would rather do fun stuff instead." He was acting like my father or something. He said, "Tanya this is important. You always find time to help you family." I looked at Pat and said, "I wouldn't want to help my family especially the way I was raised. Anyways, I didn't think you would consider it." Pat said, "I love helping friends out. Friends are family. You are apart of my family now." I felt the rush of warmth go through me. I was satisfied at the thought that I had added more people to my family. I said, "I've always considered you to be my big bother and always will Pat." I wanted to give him a hug but he was driving.

He stopped at a store and told everyone he'll be right back. I couldn't get enough of Dick, even though we sat right next to each other. We held hands and kissed a couple of times. Richard said, "Can't you two love birds just keep it down for once?" That made me blush. Jennifer was looking in the back through the mirror on the visor. I looked and said sorry. Jennifer smiled and said, "Aw, don't worry about it. I know exactly how you feel." Pat opened the trunk and put two paper bags in it. We stopped at Larry's. Pat said, "Sit tight, I'll be right back." After just five minutes, Pat came running out and got in the car and said, "We are off!" I looked at Dick and asked where are we going this time? He said, "Just wait, I think you're going to like it."

While Pat was driving down the road, I was trying to figure out where we were going too. We were getting closer to another part it the city. I said, "We are going to a party?" Pat said, "Not exactly, but close." We drove past the part a little ways and then he turned off. It was deserted behind the park. Pat said, "No one goes back here. Well, we do, but no one else. We can sit here and watch everything in the park and no one will ever notice we are back here."

Pat popped the trunk and grabbed the bags. I had no idea what was in them—maybe food or something like that. He grabbed a bottle out of the bag and it was some kind of alcohol. He opened it and started drinking it. Then passed it to the next person, and so on. When it got to Dick, I was wondering if I should try it. I never drank that before. All I'd ever had was a sip of Dad's Gin and Tonic. Dick took a drink and he said, "You don't have to have a sip. This stuff is really strong. I don't think you'll like it." But, I took a little sip and he was right it was strong, but it didn't taste too bad. I've had worse. I read the bottle and it said Jack Daniels. Of all the things to try out—hard core whiskey. Then Pat took out these giant cans. They were blue and gold trimming. He threw one at Dick and passed the rest out to everyone that showed up. There were Larry and Mark with the 442 Olds. *I never rode in Marks car. But that's ok. I got to ride in Pat's car. His car beats everyone else's.* Dick opened his can and took a sip. He handed me the can and I took a sip. It was a strong taste of beer called Fosters. I didn't care for the taste. I looked at Jennifer and she was drinking orange juice. I said, "Jennifer why aren't you drinking." She looked at me and said, "I am drinking. I'm drinking a screw driver." I started to feel strange and then hyper and happy. I was hopping and dancing all over the place. It was so relaxing to be around friends outside in the middle of nowhere—figure of speech—no one telling us what to do. We were ourselves. Pat brought out a small radio and turned it on. I just looked at him. He has everything. We sat there listening to music drinking and having a good old time. I caught myself looking at the stars. But I didn't think anybody cared. Arizona stars are so amazing that I didn't want this night to end. Dick told me that he wasn't in high school anymore because he dropped out, but that was ok because he had a job with his mother. Then he told me he played the guitar. I said which one and he looked at me. "Electric or acoustic?" He said both. "Awesome, someday I would like to hear." I touched my face and realized it was numb. I asked, "Is it normal to lose some feeling in your face from drinking?" Everyone in the group started laughing. I said "What?" Pat said, "Nothing—you're so cute." I said, "Thanks! Pat you know you're like my big brother right? I'm mean, you the brother I never had." Pat said, "Yes Tanya, I know. You're drunk." I said really, "I don't feel any different. He said, "Yep, no more for you." Then he tried to hand me a coke, but I thought he was playing with me because I couldn't grab it. But then he moved his hand a little to keep me from grabbing and I got it. Everyone was laughing. I sat down next to Dick and started drinking my coke, but he was still drinking his beer. Pat said, "Ok guys, it's late—time to go." I didn't bother asking what time it was. I was so lucky I had friends like this. Pat looked at Mark and asked if he could drive Richard home because he wanted to spend a little time with Jennifer by himself before she went home. Mark said no problem. Pat said, "Great, see you guys later." We left the park. I got home and there were lights on in the house. I thought mom's up. She's never seen me drunk before. How am I going to explain this? Pat said, "We'll all come with you and explain." I said, "WHAT? You're going to take the fall for this? Are you crazy?" Pat said, "This is what friends do Tanya. Anyways I already told your mom what we were doing tonight. She's the one who bought the booze." I'm exclaimed, "What! When did you talk to mom?" He said, "Earlier today when I bumped into her at the Club." I was in shock, "You talked about alcohol at the Club. Did anyone here you?" He said, "Just her friends." They were laughing about it. Matter of fact, they pitched in too. WOW, my own mother! I just couldn't believe it. Wow! So everyone got out of the car and walked me to the door. I opened the screen door and then mom opened the house door. She was smiling at me. Then she looked at Pat and said, "did she have fun?" Pat said loads. I tried to stand up straight and talk but the words didn't come out that well. Dick gave me a kiss good night. Pat said, "Thanks Sally, you're the best." Then he left. Mom looked at me and said, "How was your night?" I said, "Pretty fun, why?" Mom said, "Just checking. Isn't it your first time drinking?" I said, "Yes, but I didn't think you would be ok with it. I was afraid you'd get mad at me. I didn't know you helped until Pat told me a few minutes ago. Sometimes I don't even know who you are!" I said, "So, how was your night? Did Gayle pull any guilt trips?" Mom said, "Nothing I couldn't handle. Go to bed, because tomorrow's another day." I said good night and stumbled into my room. I didn't change my clothes, I slept with my them all on.

The next morning I was rudely woken to noise in the kitchen. It sounded like pots and pans being thrown everywhere. I got up and it was Mom, she was making breakfast. I walked in and mom asked how did I feel today. I said, "I have a headache and still pretty much tired. Will you please keep it down so I can get more sleep." Mom giggled a little, "Oh no sweetie, you'll have to learn to cope with the symptoms you have afterward if you want to drink." I knew it was to good to be true. Mom did that on purpose to teach me a mean lesson. I said, "You didn't do this to Gayle? Mom said, "It's because I was never home when she went out." I went to the living room and Shallon was smiling at me and reading a book. "What mom told you what she was going to do and you didn't come and warn me?" Shallon just stared at me. Gayle came walking out her room and gave me an evil glare. Like she couldn't wait for us to be alone glare—she was going to do some damage to me. Mom banged the plates on the table and yelled, "BREAKFAST IS READY!" Shallon jumped up and ran to the table. I got up and walked to the table slowly. Mom slammed a bottle of Tylenol on the table and said, "Eat something first before you take these. It will help." I looked at her like I was going to kill her if she didn't stop making so much noise. She sat down with us and just smiled. Gayle pouted; Shallon was busy eating.

Mom started eating, too. She looked up and said, "We have to talk. At the moment I can't find a place to live. There's an apartment complex that has a studio apartment and in three months a one bedroom apartment will be available. I've talked to Sandy to see if she can board you until I find a bigger place to live and she said she wouldn't mind. You guys can visit anytime. So what to you think? We'll have to store some of our things in a storage unit until then because there isn't enough room in the studio." I said I don't mind living with Sandy for awhile. It would be cool. Mom said, "She has rules to be followed and she's home all the time, that way she can take better care of you." Gayle didn't like that to well. Mom said, "Just give it a try and we'll go from there. The landlord gave me an extra week to pack and move, so we don't have to rush." Gayle jumped in and said, "I don't want to live with Sandy. Couldn't you and I share that apartment for now?" Mom said she would think about it.

I called Lisa to let her know I'll be moving in with my mom's friend, who I basically grew up with. And then, once again, told her everything about my night with Dick. She didn't seem to care that much. I told her I'll call later, I have to make another call, just had to tell you. "Oh, one more thing, I'll still be going to the same school." She said that was great. I'll talk to you later. I hung up the phone. And I just sat there. Shallon said, "Are you calling anybody else?" I said no, I just didn't want to be on the phone that long with Lisa. She hasn't been herself lately. Shallon just looked at me strangely. I said, one of these days, you'll understand.

The following week was pretty busy. I didn't have much time to think about Dick, let alone to talk to him on the phone. Mom would call us every hour on the hour to make sure we did what she told us too. For four hours we had to pack. The first hour we had to pack the kitchen. We had to start from one cabinet to the next. Making sure there wasn't anything left except four plates and 4 bowls—those we will be using in the mean time. We had to pack the spice cabinet, except the main seasonings that we use everyday, and we packed up just about all the pots and pans and cups and mugs. Then we emptied under the sink. We got all that done in less than an hour. We got to breath for 10 minutes. Then mom called again to pack Shallon's room. I hated to pack other people's rooms. Shallon didn't have much, just a lot of toys and books and stuffed animals. We told her, she would have to live with one stuffed animal for a while. She picked the stuffed teddy bear that I recovered for her that night—I smiled. We got her room done. This time we had 15 minutes to spare. I think mom knew how long each room took to pack. It didn't take that long. Mom called again, this one is going to be a challenge, pack and clean Gayle's room and then yours. Don't forget to pack the things that will go into storage because you won't need it at Sandy's. I won't call for a couple of hours. This will take awhile. Seven thirty came and we didn't have dinner yet. I was starving. The door bell rang, I opened it and it was Domino's. The guy said, "Pizza delivery." I looked at him and said, "Are you sure you got the right place?" The guy chuckled and read the address and the name. "Ok, that's us, but I don't have any money, who ordered it." He said, "Sally did, and you don't pay it's already taken care of." Wow, mom didn't call us about the pizza, but I grabbed it and said thank you. We devoured the pizza like it was the end of the world. There wasn't any more left by the time we were through. Mom called a eight. "How was your pizza?" I told her it hit the spot thanks. She said, "You didn't make anything to eat before that, did you?" "No mom we were trying finish our packing done." "Ok, good, I'm glad you guys liked it. Did you get the packing done for the night?" she asked. I said everything is done. The weird thing is I didn't get a call from Dick tonight and it strange. We usually talk everyday. Pat would have called my if anything happened.

Thursday was just like everyday. At school, classes where the same, I enjoyed Auto—the class I looked forward to everyday. The next semester was starting and I took two Auto classes this time. I couldn't wait to tell mom. At lunch, I sat inside because it was chilly outside. Adam found me and sat right down. He said, "You look happy today." I said, "I just found out I have two Auto classes and it will be like that for the rest of the year." He smiled and gave congrats. I said thank you. "Where have you been?" He said, "Family problems, my mother died." I said, "Oh my, are you ok?" He said, "I'm fine now, but it was really hard for me to deal with and that's why I wasn't in school for the past four weeks." I gave him a great big hug. "I didn't know her that well, because I lived with my grandparents for the past four years." "My friend Lisa lives with her grandparents too. But I haven't talked to her in a while." He said, "The one that was so nice to me that day?" he said, sarcastically. I said, "Yep, that's her." I told Adam about my boyfriend and how much I loved him. Adam was still the supportive person he always was. Then we had to go back to class.

At the end of the day, it was the same routine as before. But this time, I couldn't wait to go home to tell mom what classes I was taking next semester. Adam jumped at me like he did before. "Where is your friend?" I said, "I have no idea, she could have went home already. We're not talking that much lately. She does this all the time. I'm use to it." We were walking to my bus stop. "So how are you doing?" He said fine. "I'm sort of glad to be back in school. It helps keep my mind busy." "Yeah, I would think so. It's hard to do anything if you are constently thinking of your mother." "I couldn't even imagine what you are going through." "Hey, she's in a better place." He said, "Tomorrow after school do you want to come to my house? It's just down the street from here." I said let me talk to mom first. I'll let you know tomorrow. *I couldn't give out my number until mom knew about him. She was strange that way.*

I walked in the house and all of a sudden, Mom told me Dick called. "He'll call you back later." I was excited to hear he called. I said, "What did he say?" Mom said, "The usual—is Tanya there and so an so." "Ok so what time will he call?" Mom said, "I don't know, he just said later." "Oh ok." So I told mom about my good news. She was happy to hear I had a good day for once. She told me how proud she was with us in getting the house ready to move. Saturday is when most of our things go into storage. The house will be just about emptied Saturday. All that will be left is the daily stuff we will be using. I asked mom if I could go out tomorrow night with everyone. She said, "No, you'll have to stay here and watch you sister. Gayle is going to a meeting." "Ok, well can I go out after she comes back?" Mom said, "You know your sister won't come right home. She'll take off to somewhere. Why don't you ask your friends to visit you here. I don't think they'll mind." "Oh ok," I said. "I'll see what they want to do."

Dick called and I answered the phone. I said, "Where have you been? You haven't called in a while." He said, "I called today and you weren't home yet." I said, "I'm talking about all week." He said, "Oh, I had to do all the landscaping for mom. The big bosses came today. I had to make sure everything looked nice for them. I couldn't talk to anyone if I wanted to." "Oh," I said, "I missed talking to you." He said same here. "What are we doing tomorrow night?" I told him I'd have to stay home. "Gayle has a meeting to go to tomorrow night and don't know when she'll be home and besides Saturday we have to move most of our stuff. I was wondering if you and everyone can come over here?"

"I'll find out. What time do want us over tomorrow?" I said, "How about 9pm? That's when Shallon goes to bed." He said, "Ok, but I'm not making any promises." I said ok. He said, "I'm getting a car soon. I've saved up almost enough money to buy a car." I said, "That's great and I'm very glad to hear that. What kind of car? He said, "It's a 1967 blue Chevy Impala. A very big car. Pat is going to help me restore it so I can drive it around." I said, "That's great I can't wait to see it." I was very excited for him and I couldn't wait to see him again. He said, "I'll call you back later." I said ok, goodbye and we hung up the phone.

I never got a call back from Dick. I started feeling abandoned, like he didn't want to be around me anymore. I couldn't believe what I was feeling—is he just going to forget all about me and pretend that I never existed? Does this mean that I won't hear from Pat and Jennifer too? All these thoughts were going through my head. I couldn't but help wonder if everyone was just going to forget all about me. I started crying and looking out the window. I didn't want to lose all of them. I was afraid to call Pat or Jennifer. Somehow I knew they wouldn't be home anyways. I was very nervous. I knew something was up—I had that feeling. Shallon told me not to worry so much. Pat didn't even call me. Maybe I was boring and they didn't like me anymore. I just don't know. At 9pm Friday night, I told Shallon to go to bed. After she went to bed I started crying my eyes out. I put the radio on, hoping that would help me. I was putting myself down. If had did done something to Dick that he wanted maybe you'll still have him. I told myself I was saving myself for later and it was alright to do that. I was going crazy. Nine thirty came and I heard Pat's car coming down the street. I jumped up went to the bathroom and washed my face dried it really quick and ran out the door. He just parked the car. Everyone got out of the car, Larry, Richard, Dick, Jennifer and Pat. A great relief fell over me. I jumped on Dick and said, "You never called me. I though something happened to you or Pat and Jennifer didn't want to come over." He said, "I'm here now." Pat said, "Tanya we like you. Stop worrying." Pat brought another brown bag. Oh my God, I really do need a drink right now. We went inside and Shallon came out of her room to see what the commotion was. I said Shallon it's only us now go back to bed. She stuck out her tongue at me and left.

Pat laughed at that. He said she is such a cute kid. I rolled my eyes. I was just happy I had my friends with me. Pat said we aren't staying that long but Dick said he'll stay with you for a while and about 1am I'll come and pick him up. I looked a Pat and mouthed a thank you. He said, "No problem." He handed Dick a couple of beers and said we'll be back later. I gave Pat and Jennifer a hug goodbye.

Dick and I sat there on the couch with one light on. He opened a beer and started drinking it. I had a couple of sips as well. I said, "I was worried I wouldn't see you again." He "asked why would you think that"? I said, "Well, you didn't call me back and I had a strange feeling." We sat on the couch quietly. Then he said, "I would never leave you hanging and I'm sorry I didn't call you back. It was hard to get an answer from Pat." He looked into my eyes and said, "I do very much care about you, so don't think I don't." Then he gave me an passionate kiss. My heart melted and I just didn't want that moment to end. I loved him and it would just kill myself if I never saw him again. He said, "Why don't you turn off the light and let the moon light, light the room." I said sure. I sat back down and we held each other. But I still had that strong feeling that I was going to lose him. We started making out on mom's couch. Time went by so quickly. He looked into my eyes and said, "Look into my eyes, what do you see?" I said you. He said, "Don't you see the darkness in my eyes." I said, "What?" He said look again. "Now do you see? I'm not who you think I am. I have a dark side and I don't want to hurt you because of it. Someone told me I wouldn't succeed in my music because of my dark side." I said, "Stop you're scaring me. You don't have a dark side. You need guidance and I can help you with that." He said, "I'm going to have to let you go for now. I don't think I can handle myself right now." I said, "No don't go, don't leave me—I love you and that's all that matters." He said, "I need my own space and maybe one day we'll be back together again." He told me a little saying that I knew about all my life. It was March 22, 1985 and he whispered:

If you love something,

Set it free,

If it comes back to you,

It is yours,

If it does not,

It was never meant to be.

I said, "I go by that every day." He said, "Well then you would understand what I'm about to say. I'm going to leave you for a while to figure out my feelings. But don't worry I'll come back to stay." I just couldn't believe what I was hearing. Why would he say that now? I knew it, just knew it. I didn't want him to go. I didn't want him to break up with me. He hurt me. I was so much in love with him. I started to cry. I told him I knew he was going to do this to me. I wasn't stupid. He grabbed me and held me for a long time. He tried to say sorry; he didn't mean to hurt me. At one, I heard Pat's car, I started crying even more. I didn't want to let him go. I told him please just stay with me. Don't break up with me. He said that he have no choice. "I don't know who I am right now and it isn't fair to put you through this." How can someone just turn on and off feelings like this. I got up off the couch with him and walked him to the door, I didn't want to let go of him and then he left. I didn't even feel like walking with him to the car to say hi and bye to everyone. I was devastated and didn't want to see anyone right now. I cried so loud, I wanted God to hear me. I felt my heart breaking. My chest hurt so bad. I though I had a true friend and a boyfriend wrapped up in one. I thought I found my soul-mate. How could he have done this to me? I called mom and let her now. She was shocked to hear that too. Warren was at her store and she told him right there on the spot. He said he was sorry to hear that. Does she want anybody right now? I told mom to tell him no, I want to be alone right now.

The next day, I just wanted to mope around and feel sorry for myself. But I had to help move our things. I did that. I was a zombie in a way. I was so devastated I couldn't think straight. I just wanted to sleep all day. No one called to check on me to see how I was doing. To this day, I still wonder how I survived the emotions of a break up. Sometimes God plays dirty tricks on you to see how you handle certain situations. But this was down right mean.

On Sunday, we went to Sandy's to start our so-called "new" life with her. Mom told Sandy what happened to me and to be supportive. Sandy understood. On Monday, I went to school as usual. I was moping even in school. I didn't feel like doing anything at all. My Auto teacher noticed. He came up to me and asked what was wrong. I told him everything. He patted me on the back and told me, "Everything happens for a reason and one day you'll find out what that is—now let's have some fun in the shop. There's someone I would like you to meet and maybe you'll cheer up a bit. I don't like seeing any of my students upset and depressed. It just isn't right." I followed him into the shop. All the guys were looking at me with concerns on their faces. I can't believe they were all concerned about me. They don't really know me. I walked all the way to the other side of the shop, where the engine crane was. There were three guys standing there and smoking cigarettes (my Auto teacher let us smoke in that area). He let us know when someone with authority is coming by buzzing his bell. He said, "Guys, this is Tanya and she's not having a good time in her life right now. See if you can do something to cheer her up." There was Carl, who was tall skinny and handsome; his brother John, who was not as handsome; and Billy, who was my height a little over-weight but handsome. All the guys smiled at me. I smiled back. Carl offered a cigarette and I excepted. They asked what was wrong. I said, "Do you really want to know. I mean, I'm a girl, don't you have anything else interesting to do beside listen to a girl?" The guys said, "We love to hear girl's sob stories. It helps us understand them better." I just rolled my eyes and told them anyways. Carl couldn't believe I was still a virgin and a matter-of-fact, none of them believed me. I asked, "Could that have been the problem with me? I wouldn't put out like you guys want it in the first place." Carl said most likely because he put you up on a pedestal. "When he said he'll come back when he finds himself, all he's doing is going to another woman to satisfy his needs. If he gets bored he'll most likely come back to you. I suggest you not to trust him. He's a snake." I looked at Carl, "You're just saying that to get me interested in you." He said, "No, I'm telling you like it is. Some of us men, don't like to be tied down. We look for easy women to have fun and then run. They don't even know what hit them until it's too late." I said we've been going out since December 29th of last year and now it is almost the end of March—that's four months. The guys looked at each other and all most at once they said. "Yep, that's how long a guy will date someone of interest and if he doesn't get any thing he moves on." I looked at them, knowing he wouldn't do that to me. I thought he was my friend too. I started to cry again. Carl came up to me and gave me a hug. My heart was fluttering and breaking some more. How could I be so blind? Why didn't I know stuff like this in the first place? No one told me the rules or explain things to me. Well, now they did. I wish I knew it back than. Billy said, "After school today, can I drive you home? I don't think you should be by yourself." Carl nudged him and laughed a little. I smiled a little, "Only if you keep to yourself and not pull anything." Billy promised. "Meet me here, well out in front of the shop, and I'll take you home." I said, "Ok, but I don't live with mom anymore. I live with her friend, so I don't know how she'll react to seeing you." "Oh, I'm not getting out of my car, so I'm just dropping you off." It sounded ok.

At lunch time, I didn't feel like eating. I lost my appetite. So I was just sitting there day dreaming, trying to find the answers to my sorrow. Adam plopped right down and said "Hi!" I looked at him in an empty glare. He asked, "What's wrong? Your eyes are red and puffy." So I told him everything. He started eating my lunch and tried to put some in my mouth. But I didn't eat. Before the bell rang, I told Adam that I had a ride home so I'm not taking a bus. I also told him I was living with my mom's friend until mom finds a place for all of us. He said, "Wow, you are having a difficult time aren't you. I said, "As if." I started to cry again and he came to me and hugged me very tightly. "See this is all you need. In no time, you'll feel better." I said to him, "I hope you're right because I don't know how much more of this pain I can take."

I walked to the shop to see if Billy was there. I just hope I didn't get stood up, because that will only prove one thing. Guys like to do, or say, something to get a women's attention and if they are not satisfied with the outcome, then they forget all about you. I was looking all around, seeing if I could see him anywhere. I didn't. I saw cars parked in front of the shop. I saw a hand above one car. It was a small Honda, I believe. It had stickers all over it and it was yellow. I laughed to myself. It actually made me smile. He opened the door from the inside and I got in. I had to put the seat belt on just to be safe. I never was in such a small car before. He said, "This little thing is great on gas mileage and it works only when it wants too." That made me laugh. I told him how to get to where I lived. He tried to talk to me but I couldn't think or listen, I mainly thought of Dick. I told Billy that I was sorry, I'm not in a talkative mood. He said, "Oh, don't worry, it takes time to get over something like that. I understand." Then I smiled. He stopped right in front of Sandy's house and asked for the phone number. I said, "I have to go ask Sandy because it's her phone—hold on a moment." I got out and went to the door. I knocked out of habit. I still don't feel it to be my home. One of her kids answered the door. Sandy said, "Tanya you don't need to knock, just come on in." I said, "Oh, ok, I have a question?" She said, "Shoot." I asked if I could give my friends your phone number? I forgot to ask you yesterday. She said, "Of course you can." "Um, can I have it please? I don't know it." She gave it to me. I said, "I'll be right back—a friend of mine drove me home today and he's waiting for the number." She said sure. I walked out and went to the driver side and gave Billy the number. He said, "Thanks, when can I call you?" I said, "I don't know. I don't know Sandy's rules yet. I've got to go. I'll see you tomorrow?" He said, "Yep, I'll be there." Sandy's front door had an iron screen door, so I couldn't tell if she was stand there or not. I walked right up to the door, she startled me, she was standing in the door watching me. I opened the door and she started to move away. I admitted that he was wondering when he's allowed to call. What should I tell him tomorrow? She explained that he could call anytime as long it is reasonable. "I don't like late calls. They startle me." I said great I'll let him know. "Who dropped you off?" "Just a friend, he was being helpful, telling me I shouldn't be alone right now." She looked at me and said, "You are taking this really hard aren't you." I said yep. "I don't understand why he left me like that. I know it's only been a couple of days, but the pain won't go away. It's like someone ripped my heart out." She said, "It's like someone you love died on you. You are grieving right now. In time your pain will get easier to deal with. It won't completely go away, but you will learn to live with it." "I don't want to learn to live with it. I want him back." She handed me a notebook. "I said what is this for?" She said, "Write what you feel in this book, it'll help deal with your pain." I told her I have a diary. "I write in that all the time." She said, "Good, maybe use the notebook to write a story then. Do something with it to keep your mind occupied." "Ok, I'll think of something. Thanks." She just smiled. "Now come in here and sit down. We are going to watch a movie." I asked how? She said, "We have a VCR. It cost a lot of money but I figure in a long run it will pay for itself." I was stunned about the whole thing. "We don't have one of those and mom never took us to the movies." We watched whatever is on the TV. My first home movie I ever saw was

Cat People. Talk about a messed up movie. When you try something new, I've noticed it tends to stick with you. We watch loads of movies at Sandy's house. I loved it. But Sandy did get mad once in awhile. Her house was always a mess. I had to clean just about all the time. I didn't have a chance to do my homework. I ended up doing it in Auto class.

None of the guys where at class the following day but that was alright—I think I could handle being by myself for a little while. All of a sudden out of no where I started crying again. Chris saw me and sort of came to my rescue. He said, "Oh, Tanya cheer up, I don't like seeing you like this." I told him I'll be fine. "I just wish this pain would go away already." *I hope after what I went through the guys learned a lesson not to treat women in a bad manor. I hope so indeed.* Chris said, "I know what will make you feel better." "What?" He said, "You can help me work on my Camaro." I exclaimed, "What?!?! Are you sure you want me to touch your car?" He said, "Yeah, why not. I don't think you'll hurt it or anything. After school you can test it out if you want." I said, "What do you want Chris?" He said, "Nothing, I just want to watch you work on my car." I said, "You're a pervert Chris. Is that all you think about—girls and how they look on or in your car?" He scratched his head and said, "Would you get mad at me if I answered yes?" I laughed and shook my head. I said, "Whatever floats your boat Chris. But don't touch the merchandise you hear." I was still laughing. He said, "You can work on my car tomorrow. That way you can wear something more comfortable." I looked at him. "Chris, stop it. I'm not here for you to drool over. I'm here to help you with your car. Do you what me to help or what?" He nodded an ok. "Then let's get started. What do you need done." He said an oil change and spark plus. I said, "What about spark plug wires?" He said he already changed them. "Great, let's get started." I rolled under his car with a pan and wrench and started draining the oil. Rolled out, got up, and worked on getting the spark plugs out. He just stood there watching in amazement. I just smiled at him. I gapped the plugs to the specifications that was recommended for his car and put them back in. I asked him for the oil filter for his car and he got it out of his trunk. I grabbed a filter wrench and went back under the car. I change the filter and put the bolt back in the oil pan on the car, rolled back out, and told him he could put the oil in his car, which he did. His car was done in forty minutes. He just looked at me and said "WOW!" I don't joke around with cars. "Now go start it up." It wouldn't start. He got out of his car and said I broke his car. I said no I didn't, let me look. I found the problem, someone loosened the distributor cap. I looked at him. I said, "Did you do this hoping to get me into trouble or to see if I can find the problem without help." He said, "No trouble, just to see." I said, "Now start that car." By then everyone was watching me. Chris started his car and everyone clapped—even my teacher. I loved working on cars for some reason. Maybe its because I love the attention it got me. I don't know. My Auto class always kept my mind busy. I guess it was because it was something I loved to do. I felt it got me closer to my dad and the people around me. Auto class was a whole different world. Everyone helped everyone, no one picked on anyone, and it felt safe to be there. I wasn't judged or picked on in there. If I could get away with it, I'd probably would have Auto as all my classes but the school wouldn't have it. So, I had to deal with only two classes.

At lunch time, I went across the street to smoke a cigarette because I really needed it. I hung out with a group of kids on the corner and I started talking to them about what happened to me. I was having a hard time coping with the loss of someone I really loved. One of them, whose name I will not reveal, came up to me and said I have something that might help you feel better. I said, "Ok, what is it?" She said a joint—pot. I said I never tried it before and I don't do drugs. She said lets go somewhere and you can try it, it might help make you feel better. I said, "Ok, what do I have to lose?" I followed her and someone else behind an apartment complex and she took it out from her purse and lit it. Then she handed it to me. I took a drag and started coughing and gagging. She said that was normal and the next time try to hold the smoke in for a few seconds. I did that. Pretty soon I started feeling funny, dizzy and happy. It made me feel good inside and I was happy. I looked at the time and realize the bell was going to ring soon. I started to panic—how I was going to go to school in this state. She said, the feeling will go away in a little bit. Just try to enjoy it in class and stuff. No one will notice.

I walked into my next class—thank God I sat in the back. It was math anyways, he just tells us what to do and sits down and reads the newspaper. So I was safe in this class, but I felt very tired. I wanted to go to sleep. I put my head down on the desk. The teacher didn't say anything. Next thing I know it the bell rang and the class was over. I got up and went to my next class. I just sat there too. I didn't realize this stuff last a long time, but I didn't care. For the next two weeks that's all I did at lunch time. I didn't see Adam or anything. The last time I smoked the stuff, she told me it was laced with acid and I only had a few minutes to live. She said, "So what are you going to do for those few minutes." Without saying a word, I turned around and ran out into the street in front of oncoming car. She pulled me out of the way just in time. She grabbed me, "Tanya, I was joking, it wasn't laced with acid. I wanted to see what you would do. I didn't think you would do that." I just looked at her and said, "I'm tired." She said it was time to go back to school. I said, "Um no, I can't I need to sleep a little." She said ok, "We'll go back in the bushes and you can take a little nap. I lay down on some rocks and closed my eyes." A few minutes later, I felt a part of my arm getting really hot. I moved my arm to brush what ever it was away and opened my eyes and said, what was that? She said it was a bee. She got it away from me. I didn't believe her. I think she was trying to burn me. I tried to get up to go back to school and she said, "If you go back now they'll catch you and then you'll get into trouble. I suggest we just sit here for a few and wait." I waited a little bit and just decided to go home. I hoped that no one would recognize me while I was walking to the bus stop. I got home, my arm was hurting, so I looked at it and there was a blister. That was it, I don't trust her and I'm going to stop smoking pot.

Sandy wanted me to clean out her office so she can be able to work in there again. I told her was so tired from today and that I didn't think I have enough energy to do it. She said, "You are living in my house and I'm doing this as a favor for your mother. She is not paying anything for you to stay here. At least you can help me out by cleaning." I said, "Can't I do it tomorrow? I'm just too tired." She said, "Whatever!" I went to my bedroom and fell asleep for a couple of hours. Shallon came in and woke me up. Sandy said to wake up, someone is here to see you. I asked, "Who is it?" Shallon said, "I don't know." I got up and went to the door. It was Billy. He said hi and I said hi back. I went out by the brick fence and sat on it. He followed. I asked, "What's up?" "Oh nothing, I haven't seen you for a while and thought I would check in and say hi. Plus I wanted to know if you would like to go out sometime?" I said, "Billy you know I can't see anyone. I'm so tied up with Dick that I can't see straight. I wouldn't be good company. I'm sorry I can't." He said, "Can I just give you a kiss to see if there is anything?" I said just one, "but I'm telling you there isn't anything there between us." He gave me a kiss and like I said I didn't feel anything. I looked at him and said, "See I only see you as a friend." He seemed a little upset with himself and said, "Well, I have to get going. By

167

the way, I'm moving to Colorado, so you won't see me anymore." I said, "Oh nice for you to tell me after I said no to dating you. What would have done if I said yes?" He said, "I would have waited on moving and then hopefully, if things worked out I could have moved you with me." I said, "Billy we just met what about a month ago? This is basically the third time I've seen you. It would have taken a lot of time to get to that stage." He said, "Yeah I know, but I would have waited." I didn't see the logic in what he was saying. I said, "I'm sorry Billy, you're just a friend." He said, "Ok then, I'll say my goodbyes." He walked to his little "put-put" car, got in and left. I walked inside shaking my head and with a confused expression on my face. Sandy said, "What's so confusing?" So I told her. "Some boys just don't know how to talk to us. They get mixed up in their words and sometimes they think ahead hoping the girl sees it the same way. Most of the time the guy is the one who ends up confused more than the girl especially if they don't know how to talk to a girl." I just shook me head.

Shallon and I tried to wash the dishes and clear off the kitchen table for dinner. There was so much. I thought to myself where does she store all this. I don't think there is enough cabnets to store it all. I got tired fast. We didn't do that much. But I did enough to make mac and cheese and hotdogs for dinner. I know it's not a healthy meal, but that's all she had. There wasn't one veggie in the house. I don't think she ever gave her kids veggies. But I was a kid and had to keep my mouth shut. During dinner Sandy said, "You'll finish the dishes after dinner right?" I said, "No, I have homework to do." She said what? Then grabbed my arm, pulled me off my chair, and started yelling in my face. When this happens I shut myself down. I don't let anything get to me and will try not to get to me. I just vegged out. All I was thinking, if you lay one hand on me…..I didn't even hear what she was saying, just her yelling at me. Shallon got involved and tried to push Sandy away. But Sandy was too big for her to budge. Eventually she stopped, without me thinking, I went to my room grabbed my book bag and some clothes. Shut the door and left. Sandy tried to run out the door, she wobbled out the door yelling at me. You better get back here if you know what's good for you. I just kept walking. I went to the old house to see if there was any sign of mom being there. There wasn't— everything was gone. I started to cry. I didn't know what to do. I sat in front of the house for a few. I felt something, but no one was around, then I heard something or someone tell me go to your mother's work. I got up and walked to the bus stop I always used. The Alano Club was on the way, so I stopped there to see if she was there. No one saw her today. One of her friends noticed I was stressed out. He showed some concern over me. I just told him, I'll be fine when I see mom. I'll just go to her work and wait for her there. I said my goodbyes to everyone. At that place, when you come in to the door, yell "hello everyone," and continue to do what ever you want. And when you leave you're suppose to yell "goodbye everyone" and wait a few seconds before leaving just in case someone says something in return. I love the place. It is a great big family. Everyone cares about everyone. So, I yelled "goodbye everyone." And just about the whole room yelled, "Goodbye Tanya, we hope you feel better." I left and walked the rest of the way to mom's work. I got there at 10pm and Anne, mom's boss, was there along with Warren. He loves it there because of the video games. I went to him, he was busy playing and didn't pay any attention who was coming in or out of the store. I poked his ribs and he jumped so high that I thought he was going to do something to me. He said, "Oh, hey Tanya, why do you always do that? You know I don't like it." I smiled at him and said, "Oh bullshit, you don't." He gave me a hug and asked what's up. I said, "I need mom—the person I'm suppose to live with is a total bitch. I can't take her anymore." Anne heard me and said, "She should be here soon. She always is an half hour early." I said thanks Anne. Warren bought me a supper big gulp. I stood there watching him play that game. We were just shooting the breeze and getting caught up with stuff. He asked, "How was Lisa doing?" I admitted that she doesn't really talk to me anymore. I told him what Dick did. He said, do you want me to rough him up or something? I giggled, I said no because I still very much love him. I just wish I knew why he left me though. Warren said, "He must be after another girl or something. Some guys are like that you know." I said, "I just want him back." Mom came walking into the store. I said hi, but she looked at me and said, "There you are! I was worried sick about you." I said, "Really, why?" She said Sandy called me. I said, "Oh, how nice, she had your number and I didn't." I started getting made at her. Mom said, "Now hold on young lady. A week ago I gave her my number and made her promise me that she would give it to you. She said she would." I looked at mom and said she didn't in an angry tone. Warren turned to me and looked. I said to him, "What!" He said, "I never heard you raise your voice before–it's a shock. And by the way, don't talk to your own mother like that." I rolled my eyes. Mom said, "Ok, well that's over and done with." She said she would like to work thing out with you. I said, "Hell no, I'm not going back there. I don't want to see her face again." Mom said, "Then what are we going to do?" "Mom, just let me come home. I'll sleep on the couch, on the floor, in the tub. Anything I just want to come home." "Well, let me think it over. Since you're here, you want to help me tonight." I said, "I don't mind if your boss doesn't mind." Anne said, "I don't care." I helped her stock the store. Warren stocked the alcohol. Mom took care of the customers. Mom called the place to talk to Gayle but she didn't answer. She left a message on the machine. A couple of hours later Gayle called her back. Mom said, "I found Tanya, I was wondering if it's alright with you if she comes home. I know there isn't any room but she's not going back to Sandy's." Gayle said it didn't matter. Ok, well don't stay out to late and try to say out of trouble. She hung up the phone with her. I said thanks mom. Mom said now I have to call Sandy to let her know you're here. She threatened to call the police. She left and went to the office to call her. She probably thought I would yell at her while she was on the phone. "Just keep an eye on the store and let me know if anyone is here." I waited patiently for her to come back and let me know what she said. Mom came out looked around and said, "She wanted to know what to do with your stuff." I said I didn't know? I don't even know how to get it all. Mom said hold on. She came back out. Ok we can go pick up your stuff in two weeks. She'll have it all waiting for you out side. I'll go and help you retrieve it. Mom sighed, "I don't know what to do with you kids. One minute everything is fine and the next you guys are causing problems." I just ignored her and thought to myself that if she were a responsible mother, we wouldn't be in this mess in the first place. I looked at Warren. He said keep me out of this. I said, "You're such a great friend." He smiled at me.

I was getting tired. I did all the work that mom needed done before she left her shift. Warren was still there. Mom asked Warren if he could take me home and she would give him gas money. He said no problem. It was about 2am when we left. I said to him, "Do you always spend all your time at that store?" He said only my spare time. I asked him if he ever went to sleep? He said, "When I'm tired, I go to sleep." How often is that I asked? Not that often he said. "I can stay up for days if I wanted too." I just looked at him. I said, "I'm the opposite of you. I have to have a lot of sleep." He just smiled again.

I got to mom's apartment and Gayle wasn't there. So I made myself at home found some sheets and pillow and made a bed on the couch. I know that when Gayle came home, I'd probably have to move to the floor because I won't sleep in Mom's bed—I just can't. I fell asleep. The next thing I knew, it was morning and mom was walking in the door. I opened my eyes to the glare of the sun light coming in to the apartment through the door. I covered my eyes with my arm. Mom closed the door. I told her Gayle, didn't come home last night. Mom said, "She called me and told me she was spending the night at a friend's house." I thought to myself, I wonder what friend—a boy or girl. Mom said, "I'll be right back, I'm going to the landlord to see if we can move into a one bedroom apartment for right now. I can't figure how we can live here without interrupting my sleeping patterns." I said ok and went back to sleep. Mom came in and said, "We can move into one today." I was startled and jumped up. I said what? She repeated it. I said ok, "When then?" She said, "How about now. We don't have very much to move and I call Gayle to get her ass home and then we'll be set." My sister got home at 10am and by 1pm we were at the other apartment. Mom said, "I'm going to bed now. Please try to be quiet." Gayle and I just sat there watching TV, then she said, "We can go swimming?" I looked at her and said, "It's not warm enough yet." She said, "Well, I'm bored and I need to do something." I was fine just watching TV. She said, "I'm calling a friend and I'm taking off." I said, "Are you allowed too?" She said, "Mom doesn't care as long as I don't get into trouble." I said whatever.

So everything was doing just fine. I was thinking in the back of my head that something was about to happen because of how relaxed I was in life right now. Don't get me wrong, I do very must still miss Dick, that will never change. I still don't know how I'm going to live without him. When you thought you have a bond with someone, it's kind of hard to get over him or her. I learned that. You feel alone, no one to turn to, and you feel your life is falling apart. Mom didn't help, all she said, you'll get over it. No emotional support from her. My sister was still pretty much mad at me over the whole Dick thing, so I couldn't get help from her. Lisa would just listen on the phone and try to help; but, I needed more help. The emptiness I felt inside wasn't going away. Everything I tried to do, wasn't working. The pot thing was only a tempary fix. It made feel good for a little while but then the world came crashing around me again. After awhile it didn't work anymore. I didn't see why I was smoking it in the first place—I didn't like the side affects. So I decided to quite smoking the stuff and try to get my life back in order. I had nothing to lose.

Monday came fast. I got to school and had a cigarette before going to Auto class. I was walking towards the class and all the guys just stared at me while I walked bye them. I thought to myself, now what? I know, the teacher found out I was smoking "the stuff." I walked into class and the whole room emptied. They didn't say hi or anything. The teacher came up to me. He said, "Tanya we need to talk." His voice seemed concerned. I said ok, shoot. He said sit down. So I did. He scooted a piece of paper with my name on it and the classes I'm taking with the grades on it. He looked at this. So I did. All my classes had F's except his classes, they were A's. He continued, "I've been watching you closely after your boyfriend broke up with you because I knew how sensitive you are. I even told you if you needed any help to come right to me and I help you. My little birdies have told me you go and smoke weed at lunch time and don't do your work in school. I'm glad you love my class, the grades prove you do. But if you don't get these grades up, I'm going to have to drop you." I was in shock, my heart dropped, and I started crying. He said, "I'll give you two weeks to get these grades up. During the two weeks you can't have cigarette breaks in my class and I don't want to hear that you left the school grounds at all. You have to stop smoking the stuff or I will report you to the principal. You have two weeks, Tanya, and believe me I'll be watching you even closer now. Carl is here with his brother, I told him what happened. If you need to talk to him go ahead and go." I said, "Just to let you know I stopped smoking weed Friday. The so called friend was doing mean things to me and I just didn't like it. I rather just stay on school property anyways. This weekend I told myself to straighten up and take control. But it's so hard to deal with a loss of someone you love. No on told me this was going to happen. No one explained to me that love hurts. I just don't know what to do." He said, "Take one day at a time!!!!" I know that slogan. He started saying something about school. "Since you failed all these classes, you're going to have to make them up. They have an after school program you can go to, to put your grades up. It's 6 weeks of night school, but you can't miss one night. Pay attention this time. If you do this and pass all the classes there, I won't tell the principal about the weed." I said good because I can't tell him who the girl is because I don't like to make enemies. I said, "I promise I will go to these night classes and pass. Just wait and you'll see." He said great and "I look forward to getting good reports from your other classes and I look forward to seeing how well you do with the night classes." He smiled at me and told me to join the rest of the class. I smiled back. On the way to the shop, I was thinking, my teacher really cares about me.

No other teacher would have taken the time to sit down and talk to me. I was diffently the luckiest girl in this world. I got the support I needed, the firmness of a father, and caring from a friend—from a teacher no less.

I walked into the shop and everyone stopped what they were doing and just looked at me. The teacher scolded them to get back to work, everything is alright now. I looked around and just couldn't believe all these guys, worried about me. I didn't think it would be in them. The bond got even stronger now because everyone in my class showed some kind of caring in their own way. I never had that before. It was hard to hold back the tears, but I managed to do so. Carl was outside and he motioned me to come out, since he can't come in during school hours. He's not a student anymore. I looked at the teacher and he said go on. So I went. Immediately Carl hit my arm, and said, "That was stupid of you. Why didn't come to me or anyone her for help?" I said, "I didn't think anyone cared. So, you know, I just did what I thought would help." He said, So did he give you a lecture about the grade thing." I said yep, "I told him I would do anything to keep this class. He's enrolling my in night school at a different high school. I'll be going to school 12 hours a day for 6 weeks. How fun!" Carl said well that's important. I know. Carl lit up a cigarette and he asked if I was going to have one. I said, "I can't for two weeks. He grounded me." Carl started to laugh, "I don't think he'll mind now. Here you can take a couple of drags off of mine." The teacher came out went to the welding shop and got the teacher from there. They lit up a cigarette and started talking. The teacher called for me and I went over. The welding teacher told me I was doing the right thing and not to worry everything will be all right. Then he said, "Not all the teachers are like this one. I hope you know that?" I said I do and smiled. They told me to go back to class.

The two weeks of the grounding was hell, but I worked my butt off. If I had problems with certain work I was allowed to take to Auto and someone there would help me. Everyone helped me in their own way—the support I got was amazing. I loved everyone in my class. The last day of my two weeks the teacher called me in from another class. I had to go from one end of the school to the next. I ran—I didn't walk, I ran. It was my Auto teacher and I didn't want him to wait to long. I got there and he was sitting at his desk with a worried facial expression. I sat down next to him and asked what's wrong? He looked at me and said, "I got your estimated quarterly grades here." I said, "Oh, um how do they look?" He said, "Why don't you look for yourself." He handed me the piece of paper. I saw B's and C' in my other classes. He congratulated me on staying in his class and I started to cry. He patted my on my back and said, "See how weed can really screw up your life?" Now I know; I won't ever touch the stuff again. He said, "Ok, you are no longer grounded in my class. Just keep up with the good work and finish the night classes. I'll see you later. Now go back to class." I thanked him so much for his help and ran back to class. I had a big smile on my face for the rest of the day. Every one from Auto class would pat me on the back if they saw me walking past them. The word went through the school like wild fire, but this time I didn't mind—I felt appreciated.

The rest of the four weeks were the hardest I've ever dealt with. I got sick in the middle of it, but managed to go to school. One time, I missed the bus to my night school and I didn't know what to do. I called home and Gayle answered the phone. She said mom was asleep. I said, "I missed the bus to night school. I need her to come and pick me up and take me to school." She said she'd do it. I said "You? You don't have a license." She said, "But I know how to drive. Besides if I get pulled over, I'll tell them I don't have my license with me and tell them it's a Denver Colorado license. I'll be fine." "Ok whatever—I just need to get to class." She was her in ten minutes and we were off. If we managed to get there, I'll only be late ten minutes and I can explain myself. My sister got confused and so did I on which street to turn off at. There was a cop in the middle of the road not going anywhere and we didn't know what to do. So she just turned down the street. The cop followed and pulled us over. I started freaking out. Gayle told me to just calm down, she'd handle everything. The officer came to the window and asked for driver license and registration. She handed him the registration paper and said she lost her license. Her license was in Denver Colorado. He said, "Did you know what you did wrong?" Gayle replied no. "I was confused and didn't know about the way things are here yet. I'm still learning." He explained that she cut in front of him. She said, "But officer you stopped in the middle of the rode. I thought you were letting me go first. I didn't know." He said, "I have to give you a ticket for reckless driving." She signed for it the ticket and by the time everything was done, I was too shaken up to go to school so we just went home. Mom wasn't up yet. I was still scared to death of what will happen when she found out. Mom was a little bit mad, mostly at me for being irresponsible like that. I said, "I didn't want to miss a day of night school. How am I going to explain to them what happened? Oh, my mom couldn't take me because she was sleeping for work that night. They wouldn't except that, mom. You know it!" Mom asked why I missed the bus. I said, "I had to go to the bathroom. I couldn't wait." "Well from now on wake me up if you miss the bus. I don't want anything else to happen. Now we have to get your sister her license and pray to God we can get her off these charges."

I had to make up the classes I missed on Saturday, so I couldn't go out or anything until Saturday night. But that was ok because, I didn't have anything to look forward to. I missed hanging out with Pat and everyone. They never came looking for me to see if I wanted to hang out, probably because Dick was with them. But I did see them time to time at the Club. I guess that's all I needed. They never talked to me about Dick. That was a sore subject. They tried to keep it as simple as possible. They knew I was still having a hard time with it all.

After the six weeks of class, I had to wait to see what my grades would be before I could celebrate. I waited anxiously all week to find out. Thursday, I walked into Auto class, thinking to myself that today is the day and I can't wait—it has to be here. The teacher looked at me and shook his head. He told me to relax, it takes time. I dropped my books on the table and went to the shop. We were tearing apart a automatic transmission today, so I was looking forward to that. The teacher came out and started giving us a lecture on how the transmission worked and how to tear it apart. It was interesting on how something so complex can make a car move. The automatic transmission had all kinds of bands on it. There were different sizes and everything. I didn't pay much attention to it because all I was thinking was my grades. I think he noticed. He told us to get to work in naming all the parts to the transmission and write them down on the work sheet. Then he went back to the room. I stood there and copied off of everyone, because I didn't feel like doing the work myself. I don't think they minded either. The end of first period class was soon. The teacher walked out into the shop and yelled, "Can I get everyone's attention please." Everyone stop what they were doing and waited for him to say something. He said I have a piece of paper here (he waved it up in the air). It has Tanya's grades on it. My eyes widened, my heart was beating fast, and I felt like I was going to collapse. He looked at me and asked, "Can I tell everyone what they are or do you want me to tell you in private?" I took a deep breath and said, "Everyone helped me here, it should only be right that everyone found out the same time I do." He nodded. "Well everyone," he paused for a second, "I don't know how to say this, so I'll just say it. She passed all her classes." Oh my God, I started crying, I couldn't believe it. Everyone cheered all at once and came rushing towards me. If they could I know they would have lifted me up and carried me for awhile, but they couldn't. I got a lot of hugs and pats on my back and someone slapped my ass. I can only guess who did that—Chris. I was so proud of myself (I know it was against school rules but I had to do it) that I ran to the teacher and gave him a great big hug. He patted me on the shoulders and said, "Great Job Tanya, I knew you could do it." *My auto teacher was the closest thing to a father. He was the only teacher who believed in me when all else failed. I will never forget what he has done for me. He encouraged me to succeed. Matter of fact he was the only one in my life that did that at that moment in time.* I was happy. I loved life. The next class period came. Everyone sat down while the teacher was just sitting there with a straight look on his face. The class was silent. There were just a few of us from the class before. He said, "There are a few that already heard what I'm about to say. So I'm just going to say it again. Tanya passed all her classes. The whole room roared into hurray's, congrats, and pats on the back. I looked out into the shop and I saw Carl outside. I had to wait for the teacher to release us into the shop before I could tell him. The teacher said, "Our lesson for today is the transmission, now go and study—here are the worksheets." I didn't need one because I already did it. I looked at the teacher and looked outside. He noticed too and said, "Ok Tanya you've earned it. You can smoke a pack if you want to." We just laughed at that. I went to Carl and I told him. He picked me up and gave me a big hug and swirled me around. I enjoyed that. He put me down and said we have to celebrate. "Let's go out tomorrow night with my friends and go to the drive in movies." I said sure. I gave him my number so later he can call me. I couldn't wait for school to end. I wanted to go home and tell mom. At lunch, Adam came to me. He said, "Hello stranger, where have you been?" I told him the whole story, which practically took the whole lunch period. He wanted to know why I didn't come to him for help, but I explained I had to do it the way the teacher wanted. I didn't think you would want to. Besides it would have been boring. He said nothings boring when it comes to you. I said, "Awwh, your sweet." I told him I had a date with a friend tomorrow night and everything. He said, watch out, I wouldn't trust boys if I were you. They are pretty tricky. I said, "I'll be fine besides my teacher would just kill him if he harmed me." He said that's good you have a teacher on your side. He smiled at me. The bell rang and we went our separate ways.

The school ended, I walked across the street to catch the bus and Lisa came to sit with me before she walked home. She said, "I'm sorry, I haven't been the bestest friend to you for the past few months. I just didn't know what or how to handle you being friends with Warren and how that would make me feel. I am glad, however, that you let me have my space. A lot of friends won't do that." I told her, "I don't hold grudges and I knew you needed your space so I let you have it—bestest friends for the rest of our lives. And, it's ok, because Warren understands too. He doesn't talk to me about you or anything. It's like a totally different life." I gave her mom's new number so she can call me anytime she wanted. She asked about how I was holding up of the loss of Dick. I said, "I rather have him back than to deal with this pain I have inside. It hasn't gone away yet. But I'm managing I guess. I got a letter from him the other day. Do you want to read it? His spelling sucks and his grammar is awful. But at least he's writing to me." She said sure. She smelled the letter and looked at me are you serious. And he said he just wants to be friends. I don't think so. The letter went like this:

Dear Tanya,

Hows it going? Good I hope. Well last week I wrecked me bosses. 1985 Chevy 4 weel drive What a mess. Oh well hell of a deal ha ha.

I don't know what the reason why everbody is asking if you heard about me...... Mabie its becaus I havent written any body for awile. Boy Angie still has got me all screud up. I don't know why. I cant stand her. she had the nerve to call me on my birthday. I just siad what the hell do you want. She siad I love you and she wished me a happie birthday. I siad I dident want to hear from her agen. and hung up. she hurt me so bad and it still herts. to think about it. How culd she do something like to me. I treated her like a Queen. Oh well lifes a bitch. So how are you doing. good I hope. Im coming back to Tucson next weekend to buy a car. then im coming back up here. after I get the car paid off. Im coming back to stay. then mabie me and you can go crusing. or something. and get to be friends agen.

If your not mad at me. I though you were. because you diden't want me to know your address. at first. Why.??? I still love you a lot and always will. Im just trying to find my self agen. I don't know who I am any more. she screued me up so bad its not even funny. well I wanted to wish you a happie valentines day. well its getting late see you later ___love you___your friend always Dick

"I just love how he writes his letters," Lisa said. So many mistakes.

"I know can you believe he wants to keep in contact with me?" Lisa just shook her head. The bus was coming and she gave me a hug. "I'll call you later, ok."

I got home, but mom wasn't awake yet. So, I tippy-toed into her room and jumped on her. She woke startled and then she started yelling at me. "What are you doing waking me up this way?" I said I have some good news. I told her. She said that she was so proud of me, but asked, "Now can I go back to sleep?" I said, "I guess so, but, first, can I ask if I can go out tomorrow night with some friends to celebrate?" She was ok with it, so thanked her, left her room and shut the door. At five the phone rang, I quickly picked it up so it wouldn't wake mom—it was Carl. I told him that I was able to go out with him tomorrow and he said, "Great, I'll pick you up around eight, so we'll get a great parking spot." I said great and gave him the address.

School was taking too long to end. I was very excited about going out. I couldn't wait. I told Lisa in class what I was doing and she said, "You're going out with a cowboy?" I said, "So, I like cowboys. They are so cute and all." Lisa's so-called other friends were looking at us—like they wanted to kill me. They hated me with a passion and I had no idea why. Dino, one of the other in the class, nudged me and said congrats on my big news. I thanked him. Mr. T, our English teacher, was very proud of me too. He told the whole class, "See what happens when you put your heart and soul into something." For a couple of days I made an impression on the school, even people I didn't know came up to me and congratulated me. *But that didn't last long. By the next week everyone had already forgotten and everything was back to normal. That was ok though.*

When I got home, I was in a good mood. My heart was fluttering with excitement. My sister was sitting the couch watching TV. I said I need help trying to find something to wear tonight. Gayle just sat there and I rolled my eyes. I decided to wear jeans and a cowboy shirt that I love so much. It reminded me what my dad wears and my cowboy boots that my mom got me on my sixteenth birthday. I hardly wore them because I didn't want to ruin them. I didn't wear make up because I didn't believe in it.

Gayle made dinner—chicken and rice with veggies. I sat there eating it, fidgeting all the while. Time seemed to go slow. She tried to pick a fight with me, asking what is so special about this date because it's not really a date if there are others with you. I just told her, "You're right it's not a date, I'm going out with a bunch of friends to a drive-in movie. Nothing special in your eyes, but it's a big deal in mine. Since I don't go out that often with friends like you do. I can't help but get excited about going out. It's fun compared to staying here all night and doing nothing."

Mom woke up just in time for Carl to pick me up. I made her coffee, so she wouldn't have to start yelling or anything like that. I wanted her happy so she wouldn't change her mind about me going out. At least I asked her and didn't sneak around like my sister. Mom was sitting on the couch when he knocked on the door. She got up to answer it. It was Carl. Mom said, "Come on in and your name is?" He said his name like a gentleman, "Ma'am, my name is Carl. I'm here to pick up Tanya." Mom smiled, "You don't have to call ma'am—call me Sally." "Yes, ma'am…I mean Sally." She was curious about the movie we were going to see and he told her, "Jaws!" Mom looked at me and said, "I thought you didn't like horror movies?" I said, "I don't mind when I'm around others I know." "Carl, Tanya is allowed to be late as long as she wants. The only thing I want from you is to make sure she doesn't get hurt or lost," said Mom. I rolled my eyes but he agreed with a smile. I told her goodnight and pulled Carl out the door.

There was a gentle breeze outside. I ran down the stairs because I didn't want to be here anymore. Carl's friends were waiting in a pickup truck—a 1970's Chevy truck, I believe, white with blue stripes on it. It fit four people with no problem. We got to the drive-in at 8:45 and it was dark already. Carl was complaining because it was dark already and we might miss the beginning of the movie, but his brother told him to calm down because they don't start until 9. He was right. We parked and got out and sat on the tailgate and in the bed of the truck. They had a cooler full of beer and wine coolers. I looked at them and they said, "We are just friends here. It's ok, we won't tell, so just enjoy yourself." I had a couple of wine cooler and a couple of beers, but they didn't seem to drink that much. They told me they never saw anyone drink so much. I just said, "Well, I only drink to have fun and four drinks is about it for me." I even told them that I drank Jack before as well. I really didn't pay much attention to the movie because we just sat drank, smoked, and talked. After the movie Carl asked, "Do you want to come over to my friend's house and after that I can drive you home." I said sure, I'm in.

We got to his friend's house and it seemed that everyone disappeared. His friend told us that he was going to bed, because he had to get up in the morning for work. His wife followed. He looked at Carl, smiled, and said just keep it down. Carl nodded. He put on some country music and asked me to dance with him. I said sure but I didn't know how to dance. That was no problem because he would teach me. I didn't know what to expect next. I was pretty much buzzed and I was feeling great and relaxed. He was teaching me how to two step. He spun me around and I laughed so hard, he said, "Shhh, you'll get my friend mad at me." I covered my mouth and smiled. He asked if it was ok for him to kiss me and I didn't object. He kissed my mouth and then started kissing my neck. Then he put his hands on my breast. I pushed his hands away, but he guided me to the couch and laid me down. He told me that everything will be fine and just relax and in no time it will be over with. I said, "What? I'm not ready for this." He said don't worry you'll be fine. Next thing I knew, one pant leg was off, then the other, and then my underwear. He whispered in my ear, "It's ok to squeak and make little noises but please don't scream or cry out. That will wake my friends up." I couldn't get him off me—he was too strong. I told him no, I can't. But he didn't listen to me. He did what he wanted. It hurt a little and then I didn't feel that much after. I did cry a little, during, because I was saving myself for someone who really did love me. I only thought of Dick during the whole thing and I was praying to God to help me. In a matter of minutes he was done. He said, "Ok, you can get up. Please, go upstairs and clean yourself up in the bathroom." He gave me a kiss, but I just didn't know exactly what just happened. I did what he asked. I came downstairs and sat on the couch in a daze. He asked if I wanted a beer or something. I just said a cup of water please, but he said, "It's getting late we should take you home." I was ok with that. On the way home he asked if I was all right and I answered, "I guess." He said the first time is usually hard for a woman. I said, "I think I can handle it." He gave me a kiss and held me all the way home. I said you'll still come and see me right and maybe call me. He said sure, "I wouldn't just drop from the face of the earth after tonight." That was good. We got to my house and he gave me another kiss and said goodnight. I walked up the stairs to my apartment and went to bed. I woke up the next morning excited about what we did the night before and waited all day for him to call me. He never did. I waited the next day, again he never did. Then I was thinking well, he'll be at the school Monday, I'll see him then. He didn't show. Matter of fact he never came to the school again. I started talking to the friends we both knew, maybe they can give him a message for me or something. They turned on me. Next thing I knew, Carl's brother came up to me and said my brother says Happy Mother's Day in a very rude way. I didn't have those friends anymore. I started thinking maybe I was raped. Someone took something from me and then tore me apart mentally. I told mom what happened. Because Carl was 19 and I was 17, Mom thought she could get him for statutory rape. But according to the information she found, I was too old for that. I couldn't accuse him of rape because, in a way, I consented. I had to deal with this on my own. I wrote to Dick and told him what happened, hoping I could get a response from him. I never heard from him. The feeling of being alone came back. I was depressed once again. I didn't know what to do next. I had no one. Then one day I got a letter from him and I was in shock. I opened it quickly:

Dear tayna

Hi how are you?

sorry for not writing sooner but Ive been so bussy. And I got alot to get out of the way with the trobel im in. what ever you do dont tell my mother that im in trobbel. so how are you In doing ok I gess. I hope your not mad at me. I relly like your letters. pleas dont stop writting me. I miss everbody back there so much. O well today I made 10 sets of golf seats and im tired tomorrow im going to the air port to make a plain cover. I know big deal well I just though ide wright to say hi and dont stop writting tell your friend Lisa to wright to. I miss everbody. I gotta go see you latter

Love,

Dick

I was hoping he was writing to let me know he got my last letter and he was sorry to read what happened, but he didn't. He seemed distant from me in this letter. I'll just keep on writing him. Maybe someday he'll wake up.

One night I went to hang out on Speedway. I like sitting at Jack 'N' Box. I walked there because I didn't have anyone to drive me. I just sat there watching the cars drive by hoping maybe I would see someone I knew. No one showed. The Jack 'N Box was closing, so I left and walked home. When I opened the door, all the lights where on and I heard yelling in Mom's room. I saw Mom hitting Gayle with the phone cord and Gayle was on top of my baby brother—who I didn't know we had. I yelled at mom, "What are you doing?" She turned around and saw me and then slammed the door. I managed to open it and pull on mom. "Stop!!!!" Gayle managed to get off of our brother and run out of the room. Mom came out after us, I told Gayle to leave and get help. Mom went out after her, yelling, "That's right, you little bitch, go and run away like you always do!" When I heard that I went out the front door and headed to my favorite neighbor's for help, but they didn't want to help. They said they couldn't get involved. I hid on the top floor at the bake, hoping if I hid long enough, maybe Gayle could get help and I wouldn't get beaten up like she did. I fell asleep outside. It was quiet when I woke up and it was still dark. I thought to myself I wonder if everything is alright. How was my baby brother? I hope he didn't get hurt. I started getting worried, so I went back to mom's apartment. Biggest mistake I ever made. When I got to the apartment, the window screen was off and behind the screen was a bottle of Peppermint Schnapps. I thought to myself, mom's drinking? I opened the door and mom was sitting on the couch. She said in a very, very mean voice, "Where have you been?" I shut the door behind me—another big mistake. She got up off the couch and asked the same question. I said, "I fell asleep outside behind the apartments." She came towards me and started hitting me. She cornered me up against the door and the wall and just hit me and punched wildly. I didn't know what to do. I pleaded for her to stop, but she didn't. I hit back, even though I didn't want to. I had no choice; I had to protect myself. I hit her really hard on the side of her head and she lost her balance. I escaped from her, ran out the back door under the fence, and headed toward the 7-11 for help. I asked the clerk for help, but he couldn't. He said there's a pay phone outside if I needed to call for help. I hurried out, went to the pay phone, and dialed 9-1-1—I didn't know what else to do. I was in shock, and I didn't know anyone I could trust or where my sister was. The emergency operator picked up, "9-1-1, what is your emergency?" I said, "My mom just beat us up. My sister and I escaped, but my baby brother is still there. I'm afraid for him—please help!" The lady asked where I was and I replied that I was at the 7-11 at 5ᵗʰ and Pima. "We'll send someone there to help you. Now stay on the phone just in case something else happens." I was shaking, breathing hard, crying, and I couldn't think straight. The clerk came out with something to drink and he asked if I needed anything. I said, "Thank you, do you have a cigarette? I left mine at my apartment." He said hold on. He came back out with one. Then I heard sirens. I told the operator what I heard and she said, "Let me know when they get there." I told her I couldn't hold on the phone much longer. I'm very tired and just want to sleep, but she pleaded with me to just hold on a few more seconds until the ambulance and the police showed up. When the officers arrived, the operator needed to verify it, so I handed one the phone. I sat down on the curb and just started crying. The EMT's came to me and started checking me to make sure I wasn't bleeding or suffered any broken bones. They asked me if I needed to go to the hospital? I didn't think so. A female officer started asking me questions. "Where do you live?" I told her, "Not far from here and gave her the address." "Where's your mom?" "She's at the apartment with my brother. She's the one that beat my sister and I." "Where's your sister?" "I don't know. You need to go to the apartment to check on my brother." I gave them the number to his father, so he can come and pick him up. The officer asked if there was anyone they could call for me? I said, "I don't know of anyone," so they helped me to one of the patrol cars. The other police car left—to go to the apartment I guessed. Then a few minutes later, they took me there. I heard mom yelling and crying. Then I heard my baby brother crying. I stayed outside sitting on the curb. I saw Mark drive up. He got out the car saw me sitting there, went to the door, and he told the officer who he was, so they let him in the apartment. He took my brother outside, looked at me and said, "Tanya you did the right thing. Are you alright?" I was fine, I told him. He said, "Do you need anything?" I shook my head no, "Just take care of my brother." He left and an officer came to me and said I want you to go behind me because your mother is coming out now and I don't know how she'll react to seeing you. So I hid behind him. I watched them take mom away—her hands where hand cuffed behind her back. She was struggling. It looked like she was trying to escape from them, but they had a good hold on her. The put her in the car, shutting the door as she looked out and saw me. She started hitting the window with her shoulder and head. An officer opened the front passenger door and said, "I suggest you calm down before you hurt yourself." I heard mom call out, "That's my daughter there. I need to talk to her." But the officer shut the door. The officer that I was behind took me to a car. He told me that they would have to find a safe house for me to go to since I didn't have a place to stay. I was crying and I didn't know what to do. I ended up at some house with iron bars all over it. The yard didn't look like it was taken care of and the whole house was dark. How did they know someone was there? We walked to the door and they knocked. The door opened and a light came on. *I tried very hard to forget this part. I hated it here.* They were nice to me around the officers, helping me to a room with lots of beds with other kids. A woman gave me pajamas that actually fit and helped me to bed. They told me in the morning, which wasn't long, we will tell you the rules. I got there at 4:15am and they woke everyone up at 7am—talk about being tired. We sat at a table for breakfast and before we ate, we prayed. We ate oatmeal—I hated oatmeal, but they made me eat it, saying we don't waste food here. You must eat it. Then they told me the rules: no smoking at anytime; no TV; no radio; and, no phone calls unless you asked permission first. You can read, but only the bible because you must have done thing wrong for you to be here. The bible will help you to be forgiven. I said, "I didn't do anything wrong to be here—my mom did. I didn't have anywhere else to go. So they sent me here. I need to call my dad in Colorado to let him know what happened." They said, "We can't let you use the phone until we hear from your case worker to see if it's ok. That may take a week." I started crying. I can't even call my friends to tell them I'm alright? "No, I'm sorry." "What about school? Can I go there?" "No, not until we here from someone," they continued, "Everyone has chores to do. If the chores aren't done no one will eat. So make sure the chores are done." I think I shut myself down because I don't remember being there that long. I remember calling my dad and telling him where I was, finding out he couldn't help me this time. He promised when he heard from my sister, he'd tell her where I was, so I gave him the number. At that point, I felt abandoned by my own father. Three days later, I think it was my sister came to the house with her boyfriend. She started crying. I said, "Why are you crying? I'm the one that should be. Your free to do what ever you want. I'm be punished for something I thought I did right. I got mom arrested, I saved you and our brother and what do I get? I'm in a prison, too. I can't go to school, smoke, or watch TV. And dad won't help." The lady that was taking care of me gave my sister my caseworker's phone number and told her she had to leave now. I told her to find a way to get me out of here. Then, the lady shut the door and I shut myself down. I don't want to remember about that place because it was pure hell. I felt sorry for all the kids there. My case worker called and said they found a close friend of the family to take care of me. They told me that her name was me Delene, but I don't know a Delene. My case worker said, "You're mother pick her to take care of you. She said to tell you the Alano Club, whatever that means." I said, "Oh ok—it's ok then." I was more relaxed now. But when did I leave? She said, "I'll come and pick you up at 4pm and take you to her." I couldn't wait. As soon as I got off the phone, I told the creeps about the call. They tried to get me to clean some more before I left, but I wouldn't comply. Rather, I just sat on their couch with my arms folded on my chest and ignored them, watching the time the whole time, waiting for 4pm to come. Finally, 4pm—nothing, which made me worry and wonder if she forgot about me? Then someone knocked at the front door and I jumped up. The lady opened the door and I wanted to leave right there and then, but the lady had to sign papers to let me go. It didn't take me that long to get to Delene's house. It was across the street from school and not to far away from my old bus stop. I was shocked. Why didn't I know her?

Delene took me in. She had a pack of cigarettes with a lighter waiting for me—it was my brand. I sat down and lit a cigarette. I said, "How did you know what brand I smoked and If I smoked at all." She said your mother told me. I said, "Great, but I don't ever want to talk to her or see her again!" I was shaking because I was afraid she was going to make me. She said, "I'm here to help *you*, not your mother. I will try my hardest to protect you. I'm here for you Tanya. I've already called your school to let them know that I'm watching and caring for you. You can go back tomorrow or the next day. Either way you have to start this week. You already missed three weeks of school." I didn't believe it—three weeks? Where did it go? She shrugged her shoulders and said, "I don't know." The cigarette made me cough and got me dizzy. But it was so nice to have one. Delene said your mother dropped off your things. "I didn't go through it, so I don't know what's all in it. Let me show you where you're going to sleep." She took me to a small room that had a couch a table and a chair in it. I thought this will work. I'll sleep on the couch. She was the nicest caring person I had ever met. I fell in love with her immediately. She woke me up in the mornings, helped me make breakfast. She sat there with her son and I while we ate our breakfast and she talked to us. She gave me lunch money. I was able to enjoy school lunch. My Auto teacher knew what happened and gave me a signal that he was hear for me. None of the students knew what happened and that's the way I liked it. To this day Carl never showed his face. I didn't care, because things were looking up for me. I tried out for tennis—made it. Delene took me to tournaments, and even though I didn't win, it was nice that I could try. We went to her son's, Brandon, baseball games. I gladly helped with household chores. She even had a swimming pool. I was safe for two months. One day Delene showed me some papers I had to sign. It was to drop charges against mom. I said, "I don't want to sign these. She deserves what she gets." Delene said, "Tanya she paid for what she did to you and your siblings. She'll never forget what she did to you. It's only right to sign these papers. I promise she will never hurt you again." I asked if I could still live here and Delene said absolutely. I signed the papers. A few days later mom showed up and I was very upset. I said Delene, "You told me I wouldn't see mom anymore, now she's here?" "Tanya she learned her lesson. Did you know she gave me money to take care of you? She supplied everything you ever needed." I said, "I'm not going to be able to go to tennis now. She won't take me. She won't do anything with me." "Tanya, your mom moved to another apartment. It's bigger and everyone will be able to live under the same roof. I promise you she has changed. She's been sober for three months now. She's been going to meetings to get help. It's time for you to go home." I begrudgingly said ok, but I didn't like it. "If your mom acts up again you can come back, I promise." I said ok, adding, "I'm still mad at her." She said, "You have every right to be still mad at her." Delene went to the door and signaled mom to come in. Mom wanted to hug me, but I wouldn't let her. She said, "Tanya I'm sorry you had to go through this, but I promise I won't harm you or your siblings again." I didn't say anything. I stayed quiet. Delene helped me pack my things and helped carry them out to the car. I gave her a hug and started crying. She gave me a kiss on the head and said good bye. Mom and I went home.

The apartment is behind Kost tires, off of speedway. I thought to myself ok, this looks great. Mom helped me carry the stuff up to the third floor. It has an elevator and a security door. That same night that I came home there was commotion behind our apartment and we saw ambulance with a couple cop cars. Mom turned on the news. The landlord's children found a little girls body in an abandoned car. The girl went missing the night before. It was horrible. It turned out that her step dad killed her and dumped her body there to hide the fact that he did it. I felt sorry for both families—the landlord's and the victim's. I was able to go out every weekend since speedway was right there. I was looking forward to a better life. I had to take the city bus to school again but I didn't mind.

I ran into a lot of friends at Wiener Schnitzel's, a hot dog fast food place. I even made some. I met "Lurch," a very tall and skinny boy with white hair. He was very nice. I met Lonny, who was a doll—easily the nicest person I could ever meet. He had a gentle soul. Everyone that hung out there knew me. I would yell from the balcony to everyone before I came down. One night, Pat and Jennifer parked there. They didn't know I moved here. Instead of yelling from the balcony, I just showed up and tapped Pat's shoulder. He turned around and was very shocked to see me. He said, "Tanya, where have you been? We haven't seen you around." I told him somewhere safe. "I just moved here" and I pointed to the apartments. Well, that's nice. I said, "How are things going?" Jennifer and Pat said at the same time, "Really good—no complaints here." I said good. "How's Dick?" "Oh well, he's with my ex Angie—they've been an item forever now." I said it doesn't bother you? Pat explained that she's crazy, "It's better him not me. She's living with him in Phoenix now." My heart just broke and I started to cry. Pat asked what was wrong and I cried, "I needed Dick and you guys, but you weren't around. Gayle said she tried to find you to let you know where I was and what happened but she couldn't." I told him everything. He gave me a big hug and said, "We won't dessert you anymore Tanya—I'm sorry. You want to come over this weekend to Jennifer's. I'm working on her new car and thought you would like to help." I perked up and said, "Absolutely, I would love to!" My big brother was back. He said I should meet him at Jennifer's at 1pm tomorrow and we'll get to work. I couldn't wait.

Someone in the back ground called me name. I turned and it was Lonny coming towards me. I said, "I'll talk at you guys later and I left them." Lonny just wanted to hang out and talk so we basically did that. About an hour went by, I saw someone show up and park next to Pat and Jennifer. I didn't recognize the car at first. Then I saw Dick get out of the car. He got a new car—a 1972 Cutless Olds Mobile with two doors, a white top, and it was bright green—a gorgeous green. I don't like green, but this color I could handle. Before I could go over to him, Dick left. I think Pat told him that I was here, so my attention went back to Lonny. Lonny's been a good friend, but I had the strong feeling he wanted to be more than a friend. I just didn't feel anything more than that and it seemed, he didn't mind. Lurch came running in and yelled, Lonny let's go. I waved to Lurch and he waved back. Lonny said I'll see you later and I gave him a smile. Nothing else was going on so I decided to leave for home. I started walking outside and noticed Pat and Jennifer were still there along with Richard, Larry and some other guy. I didn't dare to go over there because I was invited, so I just waved to them and continue to walk towards home. Pat yelled, "Tanya, over here?" I didn't know what to expect, but I went over nonetheless. Pat said, "Tanya this is Chris, you haven't met him yet." Chris said hello and returned it with a smile. Pat asked where I was going. I admitted home because I was bored and was surprised, "Tanya is never bored. What's wrong?" I said, "You know what's wrong? I saw him and with a new car." "Oh, Tanya, you haven't gotten over him yet?" I shook my head, "I don't think I'll get over him. Where did he get that car?" Pat said, "I helped him find it. Isn't she beautiful?" "Gorgeous!" He explained that's why he wanted me to come over to Jennifer's tomorrow, "I got her a beautiful Pontiac from the same place and I wanted to you to see it." He asked if I would you like to hang out with them tonight. I said, "Sure, I have nothing better to do...Where did Dick go anyways?" He said to go and get Angie. I said sarcastically, "Who's Angie?" Pat laughed but Jennifer was being quiet. Chris left to get something from Wienerschnitzel's and came back with a drink. He seemed like an good person. A few minutes later Dick came back, hesitating to drive closer when he realized I was here. Pat signaled him to come over. He pulled up Pat whispered into my ear, "Just play it cool and don't show any emotions or he might just leave. Don't you want to see him again? Just try to act normal and don't show that you're still thinking of him. Angie can get pretty jealous—if you know what I mean. I don't think Dick told her about you yet." I had to hind my feelings for the greater good of our group. I stayed away for a very long time and none of them knew what happened to me. I just don't know what to do at this point. So I just leaned against Pat's car and lit a cigarette. I saw Lurch and Lonny drive back up. I yelled to the group, I'll be right back and I started walking towards Lonny. I got to him and whispered to his ear, which I think he liked very much, "My ex is here, so could you act like my boyfriend just for tonight?" He said sure and I replied, "Thanks, you're a true friend." Lurch started picking on us and I said, Lurch I would have asked you but you are way too tall from me. I laughed a little. And he said,

"Well I wouldn't have accepted because you are way too short for me." I laughed at that. Lonny gave me a hug and a kiss on the cheek and started holding my hand. We started walking around the parking lot to talk to others and the Angie came to me and said, "Look what Dick gave me." She held out her hand and there was a ring on it. "He said it's his grandmothers, we are engaged." I felt my heart drop. Lonny somehow knew how I was feeling and helped hold me up. He was a true friend always there for me, making sure nothing happened and always available to listen to me. I hid my feelings and congratulated her, all the while Lonny holding on to me for support. Dick came running up to Angie and said, "Hi Tanya! It's been awhile—how are things?" I looked at him and noticed that Lonny was very much supporting me. I said things couldn't have been better. "You should know I wrote to you once." "Oh yeah, I got that letter." Angie was getting impatient with this situation because the attention was not focused at her. I said, "I'm surviving with help of my dear close friend here." I gave a little kiss on Lonny's lips and he liked it. I looked into Lonny's eyes, which were screaming yes, she kissed me. I smiled and so did he. Dick said I guess Angie told you. I said, "I bet I was the very first one she told?" He said that Pat and Jennifer found out before me. Dick said, "You can continue to write me if you want. I will read the letters." I said I would think about it. Lonny nudged me and motioned for me to go inside. "Congrats guys, I hope you'll have a happy life." Lonny held onto me until we sat down at a table. He went and got me something to drink and a couple of napkins because he knew what was going to happen next. He held me and watched out for those two so they didn't see me cry. Matter of fact, Lurch noticed through the window that I was crying. He walked up to the building and stood in front of us and motioned for all his friends to come over where he was. I was able to cry sort of in peace, with the help of all my new found friends. There was a tap at the window. Lonny said, "Someone's coming in." I wiped my eyes and asked if you can tell I was crying. He said yes. "I'll be right back, I'm going to the bathroom." He was right. I looked horrible. I splashed some water on my face like Mom taught me, dried it off with paper towels, and straightened myself up, and thought that I looked almost good as new. I walked out, looked at Lonny and saw his eyes looking over into the line where you place your order. I knew what he was looking at and I didn't look, for fear of them noticing that I knew they were there. I walked up to Lonny bent down and gave him a little kiss on the lips and sat right back down next to him. Now it was safe to look. Dick, Angie, Pat, and Jennifer were in line. I whispered into Lonny's ear, "Thank you so much for being a good friend." He gave me a hug. Pat and Jennifer came up to me after getting their food. Pat said, "I guess you won't be hanging out with us tonight?" I gave him an emphatic "Nope!" He said will I still see you tomorrow? I said of course Pat because I loved working on cars and I love you guys. "I'll see you tomorrow...I promise. Pat and Jennifer smiled at me and I smiled back. They left and I pretended not to pay attention to Dick even though I saw him look at me. Lonny just held me. After it was all clear, I broke down crying again. Lonny just held and rocked me. Lurch was still at the window looking out. My heart was breaking even more. How could that be, it's been a year since we broke up. I didn't think I could hurt so much after a year. Lonny said, "Maybe you should go home. I'll walk with you so you won't be alone." I would like that very much because I should go home. We walked outside and I yelled to Lurch, "Thank you—I'll see you tomorrow night." Lurch smiled and waved to me. Lonny and I held hands and walked very close. Everyone was still parked there. I had no choice but to walk past them. I waved to them. Everyone waved back and I heard Pat yell, "Goodnight Tanya, I'll see you tomorrow." I just waved again.

I got to my apartment, went right to the balcony with Lonny we sat down on the floor and watched. Lonny said, "Why do you want to put yourself through this? He'll never want you back. He has someone now. Let me be your boyfriend." I said Lonny, "You're just a friend. I don't see you as anything else. I haven't seen anyone else that I think is attractive. No one will ever catch my eye again. I just need you to be my friend. Can you please do that for me?" He said, "Yes Tanya, I can" and he held me.

About a half an hour later, my group left the parking lot. It was still early and I wanted to go back out there, so we went back out to Wienerschnitzel's. Lurch came to me and asked if I was all right. I said I'll be fine. He asked, "How did you know they left?" I pointed to the building and said, "Third floor, 4th balcony over." "Now I know why you like it here." I said, "Yep I can see everything." I smiled a little. He gave me a hug and said, "I'm glad I could help tonight." I said thanks.

A blue gorgeous Pontiac came driving in. I loved that car. Lonny said, "You just got done crying over your ex and now you're creaming over another guy's car. I just don't know you." We both laughed. I want to get to know the person in that car. I watched it turn into the next building. He parked at Kost tires. I said I'll talk to you later. I'm going to check this out. Lonny asked if I wanted him to come with me, but I nodded nope, "I'll be right back." I walked along the sidewalk on Speedway towards Kost tires, trying to look as if I wasn't on a secret mission. He was sitting on his car with one of his buddy's. I just played cool sort of speak. As I was passing the car, I said "Hi." The guys said "hi" back. I stopped and started a conversation, "I'm sorry, but I couldn't help notice your car. What year is it and model?" One of the guys said, "It's a 1972 Lemans Pontiac, but I'm trying to convert it into a GTO." "Nice! My name is Tanya. I live in this area and just had to let you know that no one is allowed to park here. The company frowns upon it." He said, "Don't worry about it. I have permission to park here." He smiled, "My name is David but everyone just calls me Dave." I said it was nice to meet him. I told him that I hang out at the Wienerschnitzel's almost every weekend. "I'll be there tomorrow night if you're interested in hanging out. I know just about everyone there." He said thanks, he'd think about it and he winked. I said, "I have to get going. I hope to see you soon." I continued to walk towards my home. I went upstairs and went to the balcony and just sat there. I could see Dave's car just fine where I was at, so I had two places to watch. I saw Lonny walking towards my place. I guess he noticed that I was on my balcony. I went to the side door of the building and opened it. I saw Lonny walking up the stairs. I let him in. We went back to my place and out to the balcony. We sat there. He asked me what I found out about the mystery car. I told him and added, "We will see if he shows up tomorrow and I'll go from there." Lonny said, "I just don't understand why you just don't go out with me. I treat you better than anyone else." I said, "Like I told you earlier—you're just a really close friend. And I love you for that. I need that kind of relationship from you now."

Before I left for Jennifer's, I looked out my balcony and looked at Kost tires parking lot. I saw a blue car there that looked exactly like Dave's. I was curious, so I went down with my bike and rode over to Kost. Inside I saw Dave putting tires on a vehicle. I thought to myself, oh so that's how he got permission. But I didn't notice the car there before. Made me more curious, something to ask him about when I see him tonight. Then I started going to Jennifer's.

Pat asked me who the person was that I was with last night. I couldn't lie to him, so I told him. He said, "Tanya, don't be playing with people's heads like that. Do you want to become like Angie or even your sister?" I said no and I'm not going to be. "Lonny is just a very close friend. That's all he is, I swear, besides there is someone else that caught my eye. I met him last night." Pat asked who because maybe he knew him. I said Dave. Then I told him everything I knew about him. He didn't know him. I proceeded to tell him what happened to me during the past year and he felt sorry for everything I went through. He asked me why I didn't call him for help and I told him that I didn't think he would help me. He stopped what he was doing and looked in my eyes. "Tanya I think of you as my sister. I will always be here for you, no matter what." I said now I know. I certainly wish I knew that before because that place I stayed at was unbearable. Pat said, "Well at least your out of it now and you're alright." "You think so? I'm still hung up on Dick." Pat said I noticed despite doing my very best to hide it. Pat got the head off of Jennifer's engine. He handed me 16 valve lifters and a can of oil. He said, "Please pump these until they fill with oil." "That sounds fun." He said not as fun as you think. I said I never did this before and I've been working on cars for a few years now. He said, "Well, you don't have to put oil in these. I like to do it because it helps the engine start faster. I like to oil all the parts that need it before I start the engine. So it's not a hard start." That's sound logical I thought to myself. He was right it wasn't that much fun. But at least I got them done just in time for him to use them. He showed me the old ones. They didn't look to good. He said this is what happens when the engine is over heated and burning oil, It gets caked on like this and the engine does poorly. One of the symptoms is it will stall. Plus you burn oil. "I was able to get this car really cheap because the owner couldn't afford to fix it. So he sold it." I asked how much would this car really cost to get it fixed. He said with the hours into tearing it apart and putting it back together and the parts involved, around $1100.00 dollars. "It's worth ever penny because once it's done and you take good care of the car you won't need to do it again. The guy neglected his car. I'm surprised he didn't blow his engine." I helped Pat as much as possible. Then I had to go home and get ready for tonight. He said before I left, "Don't do anything I wouldn't do?" I said and what might that be when you do everything anyways. We laughed.

I got home around 6:30pm. Mom was hardly ever home. I never got to see her that much. In a way it was a good thing. I was still pretty much pissed off at her. The less I saw of her the better. What was so great about my apartment was that I could watch outside and wait for everyone to show before I went out there. I didn't have to guess and try to get there just in time or end up waiting there for a long time before anyone came. Everyone seemed to show up about 9pm, so I went down there when I saw Lonny arrive. Lonny smiled at me and gave me a hug. The blue car came in and I casually walked over to it. Dave got out and smiled. I said, "You made it?" He said, "I couldn't resist." I asked him how long he had been working at Kost because I never noticed until today. "Well, I've been working there for a couple of months now. But how did you know I worked there, we only briefly met last night?" "I told you I live around here, so I keep my eye on things!" He smiled.

We hung out together the whole night. He took me for a ride in his car up and down Speedway. I noticed Pat's car going towards the hangout. So, I smiled. Dave asked what I was smiling about. I said, "My big brother is going to be at the hang out." Dave said, "You have a brother?" I explained he wasn't my actual brother just a close friend of the family, but I call him my brother. We went back to the hang out and I introduced Pat and Jennifer to Dave. Pat shook hands with him and said "I'm her big brother." I just chuckled a little and Pat winked at me and smiled. I smiled back.

After that night Dave and I saw more and more of each other. He took me to meet his family. I found out his dad had polio and coincidently, he's the substitute teacher for my school. His sister has a mental disorder and I couldn't remember what was wrong with his mom. I felt kind of weird being there, but I tried not to show it. I was trying to be polite. I hope I was.

After meeting them he took my little brother and I to Saguaro National Park—we drove through it. He asked me if I wanted to drive his car but I told him I couldn't, I didn't have a license. My brother said, "oh come on, you can drive." But I wasn't ready.

One night, we were making out in the back of his car at Lookout Mountain. We were passionately into each other. Dick kept on popping into my mind. I told Dave we should stop. But he wouldn't, saying "Oh come on, you know you want too." I said I can't I'm not ready. Some how I got hit in the face, I think it was his elbow. It hurt my jaw. The next think I knew, we were doing it. Talk about pain—I never felt this much pain before. I started screaming and crying, wishing for it to stop until he finally did.

He just lied there on top of me for awhile. I finally cried, "Please get off me I can't breathe." He got up, put his pants back on, and I did the same. I said, "Why did you do that?" He said, "I thought you wanted it." "I told you to stop." "I didn't hear you," he blurted. "How could you not hear me?" He scooted next to me and wrapped his arms around me and apologized to me because he didn't mean to hurt me. He gave me a gentle kiss. He said, "You were my first, so I really didn't know what to do or how to do it. I'm so sorry. Next time, when you're ready, you'll have to guide me." I didn't know what to do at this point and I asked him to take me home. I was sick to my stomach at what just happened. He wasn't the one for me. He walked me to my apartment. Mom was home. She said, "Hello Dave. How are you two doing?" Dave said he was great. Somehow the subject of him moving in came up, but it all went so fast. He was moving in. He said, "This is great. All I get to do is walk to work. It'll save on gas and mileage on my car." I couldn't believe what I was hearing. I couldn't say anything, because I was afraid of what mom would say—not to mention Dave. So I just let it go. He moved in Sunday. He had his own bed and I had my own. Mom told us we sleep in separate beds and no sex. I just rolled my eyes (if only you knew mom). I started to hate him. I didn't know what to do. I was so trapped and confused.

Jennifer called me and invited me to her birthday party. It was on Halloween and it sounded like fun. Dave and I wore black clothes and painted our faces black and white. It was alright. I was with my friends. Then Dick showed up with Angie. My heart was beating fast. Angie noticed I was there and she started in on Dick but I couldn't hear the argument. I didn't like seeing it. I thought to myself, he doesn't need that—that's not a relationship because I don't see love there. Dave held me and kissed me and was being gentle to me. We didn't argue—of course I felt I didn't have my own life anymore so there wasn't anything to argue about. Pat noticed how distant I looked. He always notices stuff about me. I don't know how but he's amazing. We had to leave early because Dave had work the next morning. Pat said, "Tanya I'll take you home if you don't want to go home." But I told him it was fine, I needed my rest anyways. I said good night to everyone and we left. On the way home Dave asked if I was ok, I said, "I'm fine just tired that's all." We got home and I went right to our room hurried and got my pajamas on and jumped into bed. He came in and realized I was in bed already. He shut the door and came to my bed. He started kissing me, but I wasn't in mood and besides I was still recovering from the last time. He said that was over two weeks ago. I said, "I'm still sore." He sat there and then he asked, "Why did I move here than? I thought you wanted me to move here." I said, "No my mom wanted you to move in. I didn't know what I wanted so I listened to mom." He suggested trying one more time and if it hurt he would stop, but I told him I couldn't. He forced himself on me and ripped my underwear off. He was so strong. I couldn't get him off me. Why on earth do I have to get involved with forceful people? I don't know how I manage to go through this again. I couldn't figure that out. Maybe I just shut myself off. After he was done, he said, "See, that wasn't so bad was it? " I got up and went to the bathroom, puked and then took a shower. When I got out, he was in his own bed so I went to mine and there was blood on the sheet. I said great to myself. I got a small towel and put in on my bed. The next morning, he was already gone for work. He didn't wake me. I looked at the time. Mom should be home. But she wasn't.

I called her at the club, where she was playing Pinnacle. She told the person who answered the phone that she would call me back. She never did. So I had to take things into my own hands. Dave came home at 2pm. I told him I needed to talk to him, so we sat at the table. I said bluntly, "Dave, it's time for you to move out. I don't love you. I can't handle what you've been doing to me. Please give me you house keys, get your stuff and leave immediately." He said, "Tanya I love you. I promise not to hurt you again." I said, "I can't love you—that's been destroyed. I've tried to forgive you but I can't. I don't want to call the police over this, so please leave." He said, "What about my bed?" "Call me later when you have someone to help and I'll let you in. Just please leave now." He grabbed all his things that he could carry and left. I was able to breathe again.

My sister came home from whatever she was doing and I told her what just happened. She said I liked him. I told her how he forced himself on me twice now and that I just couldn't deal with it anymore. She was stunned and sorry. I said, "Look he's coming back to get his bed. Please be here to let him in. I don't want to be here." I left and rode my bike to the club. Mom was still there playing cards. I said, "Mom I need to talk to you. She said ok hold on a moment." I sat there and watched them finish their hand. After the hand everyone left the room to take a break, Mom finally asked me what was wrong. "I broke up with Dave and I kicked him out. I'm afraid at what he might do." "What happened?" I simply said that he would not

195

take no for an answer. She said, "Oh, anything happen?" "No I stopped it." Mom said, "That's a shame—I really liked him." "That's what I've heard." I told her that Gayle would let him in to get the bed and she assured me everything would be fine. I didn't want to go home until she did, which worked for her. I noticed in the next room they were playing Canasta. I went over there to see if they needed a player. They did—everyone was playing the dummy and they needed a player. They asked me if I wanted to play, so I killed some time until Mom was ready to leave.

The phone rang. I heard a call for Sally, "Mom yelled I'm busy, I'll call back." "It's emergency please take." I saw mom walking out of the room with her cards so no one will cheat. A few seconds later she came into my room and said Dave is at the apartment to get the bed and was hoping you were there to talk to. He was hoping you would change your mind. "Tell her to tell him no." *I liked that Dave didn't know anything about the club. Gayle knew he didn't know about it. She knew it was our safe haven if needed be. I'm glad she didn't tell him. Mom would have killed her.* After awhile the phone rang again and someone announced a call for Tanya. The girls said go ahead and take it—they'd wait. It was Gayle letting know he was gone. I said thanks and told Mom he had come to take his bed.

I wrote to Dick every chance I could get. I told him what happened with my life. I let him know that I still thought of him and that I wrote poems about him. I did just about anything to get him to start talking to me to me again. Here's a poem I wrote. Don't laugh, when you're young. Sometimes you don't make sense.

I'm lost in the world of Pain

I had him for a while,
Then I lost him.
He was the one for me.
He understood me in every way.
Now he's gone, Oh he's gone.
I'm lost in the world of pain.

Everyone told me I'll get over him,
But I haven't.
He hurt me so, I can't live
Without him.
I'm lost in the world of pain.

No one can help me,
He's the one who can.
I need his love.
Oh, why did he set me free?
Does he still love me?
He hurt me so.

I'm lost in the world of pain.

He's the one who put me this way.
I'm alone, no one to love.
I love him.
I need him so.
I'm lost in the world of pain.

Doesn't he care for me?
Doesn't he love me?
Why did he do this to me?
I'm lost in the world of pain.
April 2, 1986

I made several. But this one was the best of them all, after reading them again after all these years.

I still went to school everyday. One day I realized that I was late for my cycle (period)—I like to say cycle because it doesn't sound so sick. This was in December. I asked my sister if she can help me find out. She said she knows of a place that gave free pregnancy tests. But don't really talk to them because they are crazy. I said "And you want me to go there?" I asked her not to tell anyone, especially *him*. I don't ever want to see *him* again. I went to the place. While I was waiting for the test results, they put on a video of a woman having an abortion. She was screaming and shaking. I just shut myself off like I learned to do. After the video was over, the lady came I, sat down, and said that I was pregnant. I was in shock. They she proceeded to ask me questions. I looked at Gayle and said, "I thought you told me they don't ask questions. She shrugged, "Mine never came out positive. So I didn't know." I shoved the lady out of my way and ran out the door. I started crying, I couldn't believe this is happening to me. My mind was racing—I thought what the hell am I going to do now. I found a pay phone and called mom at work. She was working dayshift today because someone called off. I said mom, "I have something to tell you." I

198

sounded upset. She said it better not be about the car. I told Gayle to be careful with it. I said no, nothing to do with the car. I told her. She was flipping out, yelling at me. "Why are you telling me this over the phone? I'm working! Don't call me again!" and she hung up. I started balling my eyes out. Gayle said, "What's wrong?" I said, "Mom doesn't want anything to do with me, she hates me. Of all her kids, she thought I had the head on my shoulders. She doesn't want me to call her again." Gayle said, "Well then we will go to her." I couldn't because she was so mad at me. I don't want to see her now. I don't know what to do. Gayle said we can tell Dave. I said, "Hell no—hate him! He can never know you hear me." She tried calming me, "Ok, ok." Gayle helped me into the car and she started driving. She suggested going to mom's work and talking to her. But I said no, "Let's just go home and I'll call Pat for his guidance. He might tell me what to do." I noticed we were going to mom's work. I told her "No, go home!" She wouldn't listen. I said I'm saying in here, I'm not getting out of the car. She said fine, I'll go and talk to her. To top it off, Warren was in there playing that game. Doesn't he ever work? I watched mom through the window. She was yelling at Gayle and she was pointing her to leave. Warren came out of the store and walked to me. He said, "Are you alright?" "No, I'm not and never will be for the rest of my life. He said, "Tanya you'll be fine. You'll work this out. I know you can. You always have and always will be." He put his head and arms through the window and gave me an uncomfortable hug. That did it. His hug made me cry so hard, I couldn't stop. Gayle came out of the store and said you're right. Mom doesn't want to see you right now. I suppose to take you home now. And you're supposed to wait there. I said, "Where do you think I'm going to go?" I don't have anywhere else to go. I cried some more. Warren said, "Don't worry Tanya you'll be fine." Gayle took me home. I wrote Dick another letter telling him what I found out and how mom was reacting to it and how I was reacting to it. I told him I was totally lost.

About 3pm mom came home. I never saw her come straight home like that. She wanted to know who the farther was. I told her. Her face was getting red. Then I said, "That's why I broke up with him and kicked him out. He forced me. I hated him for it. I didn't know this was going to happen." "Does he know?" she asked. I said, "I'm not telling him, he doesn't need to know." She agreed that we should keep him in the dark. Gayle stepped in, "Mom don't you think he should know, I mean it is his baby? Mom started yelling at Gayle, "I wouldn't talk if I were you!!! Now keep you mouth shut!!!!"

Mom said, "We have a couple of options, but the one that I think is best should be the only option—you're going to terminate the pregnancy immediately. You have your whole life ahead of you. You're too young to have a child now. God will understand. I'll make the appointment." I heard Gayle sigh. Mom called and made an appointment tomorrow to find out how many weeks I was along and to see if abortion was possible. "I hope it's not to late," she sighed. Mom looked at Gayle and said, "You better not tell Dave if you know what's good for you." Gayle promised not to. The next day Mom and I went to the doctors office, where they asked me a couple of questions. When was my last menstrual cycle? I answered. Are you sure? I said yes. The doctor came in and said we were safe and made the appointment for the procedure. It was on Mom's birthday of all days. The day before the procedure, I received a letter from Dick. It said:

Dear tayna,

Hi!

Thank you for wrighting me. it picks up my speruts to when ever I hear from you. and when I see you in person it relly gives me a good felling inside to know that you're my friend I relly love the pitcher you sent me. you are so butiful not just on the outside but on the inside to you understand and listen when no one else will you are a loving person and that is verry special. Please dont change. you have something verry few people have and you give it freely and ask nothing in return. I felt relly special and good About my self when we were dancing. I miss being Able to go dancing Alot I rember when we usto dance it ws great. And Im looking forward to dancing with you Agen if you will. next time I come into town I gess in alot of ways im still in love with you. I Always will be. What I like the best right now is our friendship it will never die in my sole its burns like a fire that will never go out. As far as what your doing. it is your desition and up to you. Please dont think im mad im not it is proply for the best. I want you to know that I well be here for you to talk to. when you need to talk to someone. That's where me and you are o much Alike. we cair for people so much and verry few people see it. Or take time to see whats inside.

All they do is look at whats on the outside and thats it. one day somebody well see it but intell they do all I can do is keep riding on. wright me a letter and talk to me. Ill listen and try to understand. After all that's what friend are fore well its getting late and I have work tomorrow hope to hear from you soon. Or see you. I wont be coming down for awile because im going to Michigan on the 27 of jan I just gotta get away for ahile. I think Im going crazy. I well wright when I get back. hope to hear from you befor I leave?

Love your friend

Dick

I wish he would learn how to spell and use proper grammar.

I won't go into great detail, but I went through with it. Yes, I was awake the whole entire time. I prayed all the way through, asking for God's forgiveness.

I had to take it easy for two weeks, so no school. The first week I needed to just rest and the second week I could do stuff, but no lifting.

Mom went to the drug store to get my medication for pain and an antibiotic, which I have to take to ward off infection.

I was lying on the couch just resting and watching TV. There was a knock on the door. I thought to myself that's strange they are suppose to buzz us first. Gayle answered the door. It was Dave, he shoved her away came towards me, grabbed my arms and pulled me up to his face and started yelling at me. I couldn't do anything. He was screaming, "How could you? I would have taken care of you?" "How did you find out?" He said your sister told me. He was shaking me. Mom walked in and saw us. She started yelling, "What the hell are you doing here?" Gayle played dumb. I yelled for me mom to help me. She came and shoved Dave away and I collapsed on the couch. Mom said, "Leave now and never come back!!!" He left. Mom said "How did he get in here? And most importantly how in the hell did he find out?" I said Gayle told him. Mom was furious at Gayle this time, she almost smacked her. Instead she said, "Why the hell did you have to tell him?" She claimed he should know because it was his child too. Mom said, "You told him after the fact not before. You just wanted to cause problems. You don't care at all about your family. You only think of yourself—just leave. I don't want to see you right now." Mom came over to me to see how I was doing. I told her I'm having a lot of cramping right now. He was shaking me pretty hard. Mom just gave my sister an evil look. "You just don't know what you did to jeopardize your sisters health, do you?!?!"

Mom told me I had to pay her back once I could get up and move around better. But I didn't have a job, so she suggested The Village Inn. But now, I should just sit there, relax and take my medication. I fell asleep. *My sister put me into danger that day. Dave could have killed me. I will never trust her again. I saved her a couple of times. I just didn't understand why she didn't do the same for me. What I did I know in my heart it was the only thing I could do. But I know that I will be paying for what I have done for the rest of my life. I don't want anyone to go through what I went through. It's very difficult to even think about. Please do what ever you can possible not to get yourself in this situation. Like don't have sex until you are married (laughing)—if you can help it.*

I wrote Dick another letter telling him what I did. I told him how hard it was for me to go through it. I told him what Gayle pulled. I told him everything, I thought to myself, like he's going to answer me.

Well, I did get a couple of letters from Dick. I didn't expect them and I was so thrilled to have gotten them. They came 9 days apart.

He actually wrote back. Here's what they said:

Jan 13,1987

Dear Tanya,

Hi how are you?

I hope your doing good.

I dont know if you got my last letter or not? Please wright and let me know? well im going to michigan on the 27 of januwary and comming back on feb 1ˢᵗ. im flying out of tucson and returning to tucson on the 1ˢᵗ and I will drive back to phoenix on the 2ⁿᵈ. I will be comming to tucson on the 24. saterday of januwary to see all you people. And I want to see you, especialy. I want to sit and talk like us usto do. I rember when I culd sit and talk to you for houres at a time and I want to do that mabie go on a picknick me, you, Pat, Jennnifer well I hope your doing well. Ive been berry worried about you latty.

I haven't had tine to wright. becaus things at work are kinda upset. but that's all behime me now.

I sincerly hop your not upset at me for my last letter??! I ment every word I siad in it. listen if I dident men it I would not have siad it. it came from my heart + soul. It seams funny I havent siad Anything from my heart and soul for a long time. (Thank you.) well im doing ok. I might be in a band agen soon. we are called Phoenix Fire Birds. well it getting late hope to see you soon.

Love,

Dick

Here's the next on, I'm so sorry about the way these letters are. Can you imagine typing all this and making sure not to change any words that the computer corrects automatically? I hope you enjoy trying to figure out what he is saying. I took me a few times myself.

January 22, 1987

Dear Tanya,

yes I recived your last letter the Day I maled your letter to you. well I relly liked your lost letter Alot. The little nots brought back alot of good memories and sad to. but I have never forgot them and never will. so how are you doing? I relly do worry about you alot. I can under stand what your going through. and I know its not easy. but please listen to me. every day that gose by it will hurt a little less and you well fell a lettel better. here is a pome wroght by

(Sherokee Isle)

Tomorrow will come.

The pain will ease.

But you will never forget.

It takes time and love.

For the healing to take place.

Remember along the way.

To accept but not forget.

I know what its like. And it hurts so bad that you cant stand it. but that's when people like you and me are set aside from all the rest. we learn to accept but never forget and we go on with our lives. I like to see hapie. When your happie and when your sad im sad. The band audition went ok but it looks like. (IM IN) (YEA)

To answer some of your questions now. yes _I still love you. I always have and always will._ you're a _special_ person and _I want to see you happie._ The reason I never talk about my self is my letters much is becaus I dont know if im redy to. im not sure where I need to talk is person to person. To regaine what I tought you to let it out. Talk about it. not hold it in. well it seems I lost the ability to do that. but I gotta get it out soon that's why I want to sit and talk to you like we ust to do. I learnd alot from you that what the Thank you is for. Well the consert was great. I took the guy Andie who is the leader of the band. And the anwer to (wll I ever forgive you for trying to get me back for the past 2 year) no problem. I was never up set for you trying. And the past about forgiving you for not at first becaus at frist I saw a replay of my daughter christina marie but look at it this way the babie is in gods arms now and I loved more than we *culd ever emagen. Well I gotta go hop to see you saterday the 24th in Tucson. I want to go daacing how about it? tell me when I get there*

Love,

Dick

I had to put this little drawing he did in the letter—isn't it cute?

I was able to get a job at Village Inn as a bus person, clearing off tables and washing dishes. How fun! But I had no choice. After working for only a few hours I needed at break. I asked my supervisor if I can go and have a cigarette. She said that will be ok.

I went through the back, sat down on the curb and lit a cigarette. There was this guys standing up against a grey truck. I didn't think anything of it. I didn't care. So I just smoked my cigarette. He came up to me and with the sun was in my eyes, I couldn't see him very well. Then he said, "Hi there, stranger." I stood up because I recognized Dick's voice. He said I got your last letter and I had to come right away. He had a bouquet of flowers with him and he gave them to me hoping they would make me feel better. The first thing I did was gave him a huge hug and then I started crying. I couldn't let him go. I was holding him for so long that I forgot about work and I blurted, "I have to go back to work or I'll get fired for not being there. Come back at 6, when I get off. I would love to spend more time with you." He told me he couldn't because we had plans right now. "I'm here to pick you up. I asked your supervisor if you can have the rest of the day off, because we haven't seen each other for a long time. And, she said yes." I said really, "I didn't see you any where." "I did it an hour before you came to work." I hit his shoulder with my fist and said, "You little Devil."

Then I smiled. He started laughing and said, "How many times did I tell you not to call me that?" I spent the rest of the night with him. We talked for hours catching up on things. He told me that Angie was pregnant and then lost the baby due to drugs. The baby died in his arms at the hospital. He broke up with her because he found out she had been lying to him from the start. After all the talking, it didn't take long for all the old feeling to come back. We got back together on January 24, 1987.

After Dick came back from his trip to Michigan we started seeing each other again. You couldn't tear us apart if you tried—and believe me his ex tried. True love overcomes everything. Just keep that in mind when things don't look too good, God always finds a way to help you through the difficulties in your life. I'm definitely a witness to that.

Every other weekend he would send me money to take a bus to go see him in Phoenix. And every other weekend that I didn't go, he would come down here to see me. He showed the effort that he really cared and loved me. Mom didn't think it was a good idea because he hurt me so bad before and she was afraid it might happen again. I told her I can handle it this time and that things will be better. She said, we will see.

Whenever I went to Phoenix, I stayed at his mother's place. We didn't do anything to jeopardize our relationship. Instead, we went to concerts, parks, lakes, movies, friend's homes, and parties. The parties where mostly at Char and Linda's and since they were Dick's friends—we mostly stayed there when I came up. Char was funny in his own way, while Linda was a very energetic, loving person. She always had to do something and couldn't stop until it was done. I understand where she was coming from. Running a big house like that with her kids, can be a challenge in and of itself. She was more relaxed when she had a drink or two. We would have barbeques, cook outs, and Linda would make her famous seafood spaghetti—which to this day, I've tried to get the recipe for. She had lovely kids—Desiree, Amber, Kendra, and Amanda. I had another family that I loved. I looked forward to seeing them whenever we can. I thought maybe we should all live together since I loved everyone. But, then again, I would probably overstay my welcome because moving in with friends can actually ruin friendships. So I didn't bring that up. I just enjoyed their company.

One night, while we were doing vodka shots, we played a game where you have to bounce the quarter in the shot glass. If we didn't make it, we had to drink. Well, I wasn't that good at it. They teased me about it. I had to take a break from drinking all the alcohol. Desiree said let my play with your hair. I said sure but don't cut any of it off. She said I won't. I was sitting there enjoying my buzz and Desiree was doing something to my hair. I felt tugging and brushing and pulling. She wouldn't let me see it until she was done. Her sisters would come in and look then giggle and take off. I think I saw Linda come in at one point. Everyone was having fun. She was finally done. She let me look at it. I started laughing so hard. She made all my hair in the front stand straight up. It was hilarious. Desiree did her hair like that all the time because it was the style in the late 80's. I wish I had a picture of it. I would be great to show it off. That's just one of the times we had together.

Besides going to Phoenix every other weekend, we would write love letters to each other. Dick even went as far a recording his voice on cassette tapes. We would spend hours talking on the phone with each other. Sometimes we just sat there with the phone to our ears just to listen to each other breathe and we'd watch TV together. It was awesome. Something was different about our relationship this time. I felt very secure and happy. Maybe it was because I never gave up on him. I knew we were meant to be. God told me and I felt it. I just had to wait for Dick to open up his heart and soul and search for the true meaning of love. The true meaning of love is God. It doesn't matter what religion you are, God is what brings everything together.

Dick and I started talking about living with each other when I graduated from high school. The closer I got to graduation, the harder it was for me to see Dick. Mom didn't think it was a good idea to keep going to Phoenix every other weekend. Instead, she thought I should be studying and getting ready for the finals. I said, "Mom, don't worry I'll pass—I always do. I have a great support system in my Auto classes and my English class. I know what I'm doing so please don't worry." That didn't please her.

My Auto class teacher gave me information for a great technical school in Phoenix that would give me a degree in mechanics and would be a great place for me. I showed Mom the information and she made an appointment for them to come and explain everything.

The schooling would take two years. It'll give me my degree and ASE certification. Then, they will help me find a job in that field. All they asked was for a $250 deposit, so a spot could be reserved for me. Mom looked at me and asked, "Are you serious about being an mechanic?" I nodded emphatically. "That's what I want to be." She said ok and she wrote out a check for the amount and handed it to the guy. She had to sign some documents and then everything was done. I was so happy. I gave Mom a hug.

Finally, after all the talks about my moving after graduation, we did it. My mom's reaction was not expected—yelling and telling me I was going to be making the biggest mistake of my life. She reminded me about what he did to me in the past. I wished that she could see that we've grown up and he changed. "Why don't you want me to be happy?" She said, "I want you to be happy, but this isn't how you can get it." " I can't believe you, you don't support my decisions, you just want to control me and to keep me from experiencing life. I'm leaving here mom—just accept it," I stated frankly. She said, "Why don't you just get your own apartment and go to school that way? He'll try to control you if you move in with him." I said, "Why can't you just support me in my decision mom?" She never answered my question. She grabbed her purse and slammed the door as she left the apartment.

I called Dick to let him know what mom said. "I hate her. She can't support me in my decisions. I wish I had that." He said, "Tanya be patient because it's only a few weeks now. You don't want to do anything stupid. I said, "I know, I just wish I could graduate now and leave because I can't take her anymore. I wish she understood me. I wish she could be happy for me." Dick calmed me down and reassured me, "I'm here for you. Soon we will be together for the rest of our lives. Think about what we can do together. Think about the freedom you will have when you leave you her. It's right there for you. Just try to patient for a few more weeks." I said, "I miss you, I need to see you, and I need to hold you. I can't believe she can keep me from seeing you. I'm 18 now. I just want to live my own life." He said, "I want to see you too. I'll see if I can come down soon to spend time with you and our friends." We both said "I love you" at the same time.

The last few weeks were pure hell. Mom found just about anything to argue with me about. I had to start sneaking out without her permission just to get away from arguing.

The closer graduation (and freedom) got, the more excited I became. I called Granddad to see if he could come to my graduation. He said he would love too, depending on his work. "I'll check my schedule to see and I'll get back to you." I hoped he could make it. He told me that he was so proud of me. I was jumping up and down with excitement that he might be at my graduation. My sister came in and asked why I was so happy. I told her Granddad might be able to come see me graduate. The face expression I got from her wasn't what I expected. I asked, "What's wrong?" She snarled, "Nothing" and walked away. I also called my dad to let him know about my graduation. He was happy for me, but he couldn't come. He had to work, which upset me and I started to cry. He said, "Let me see what I can do. I don't like to hear my little girl cry." Then I explained to him what mom was doing. He said, "She's just afraid you'll get hurt again. I don't blame her." I said, "But I want to live my own life right now. I just don't understand." He said, "One day when you have your own children, you'll understand." I vowed to never treat my own children like she treated us. Dad chuckled a little and promised to do everything he could to attend "my big day." I said, "I love you," and "I love you, too." We hung up. I called Pat and let him know about my big event and he said he'll call everyone else.

Dick called me again, which was strange because I just got off the phone with him a few minutes ago. He said, "I'm sorry Tanya, but I can't come down for your graduation. My boss just called me and told me we have a big account to do and he's not sure how long it will take to get it done. I can't leave Phoenix until it's done." I started crying, "Oh come on please, you'll get to meet my family—my Granddad and my Dad. You can't do this to me! I've looked forward to this my whole life. Please find a way." He said, "I'll try but it doesn't look good. But I will be there this weekend to pick you and your things up to move up here." I sighed in relief, but was still upset that he wouldn't be here for my important day. I told him I loved him and he said the same. We hung up. These up and down emotions are going to drive me crazy. Why can't anything be easy?

When the big day finally arrived, I got up at the same time I did when I was going to school because I couldn't sleep in. I rolled out of bed, went to the bathroom, and took a long shower. I got dressed in what I would wear to my graduation. I tried to figure out what to do with my hair but nothing seemed to work. I just gave up on it. I went to the living room and just sat there looking out the balcony window, trying to keep myself calm—inside I was going completely crazy. My mom and sisters woke up about 10. They where shocked to see me ready and dressed. Mom said, "After I get my coffee let's go to the club and get breakfast." My sisters ran in there room and got dressed and we left. Mom was smiling the whole entire day. I thought it was because she was very proud of me—I didn't know she was up to something. After breakfast we played a couple of card games and everyone there congratulated me. I was so happy. Mom asked what I wanted for dinner and I told her I would love steak or lamb. She said, "We'll see what we can do. Let's go to the store." I didn't pay much attention to how much food she was buying. We got home and there were messages on the machine. Mom went to check them. The first call was my favorite Uncle in the whole world who said congratulated me and then he added, "Sally you know where I'm at give me a call." The second call was from my dad, which perked me up immediately. He said he would be here at 4:30—it was already 3. I screamed and was shaking with excitement and Mom smiled and told me to be calm. "I forgot something at the store and I'll be right back. Just relax until I get back," she said. I was very happy that I didn't ask questions. I went out to the balcony and had a cigarette to calm my nerves. But it didn't help. 3:30 came quickly and the door buzzer went off. My sister answered it. It was Dick disguising his voice, "I have a flower delivery here for Tanya." My sister buzzed him in. When I opened the door and looked toward the elevator, there was a tall man with a hat that Dick liked to wear all the time. I knew it was Dick immediately! I ran down the hallway and jumped on him—we almost fell. Pat and Jennifer were there too. I was crying—I couldn't believe he tricked me this way. Pat and Jennifer were smiling and I wanted to jump on them too but I refrained from doing that. They came into the apartment and I was shaking so hard it was hard for me to breathe. Mom came home soon and when she opened the door, peeked her head inside, and opened it completely to reveal Uncle Will was with her. I just about fainted. I ran to him and gave him a great big hug. I looked outside to see if Granddad was there, but he wasn't. Uncle Will said that Granddad wasn't feeling well. He showed me the plane tickets and he was right, Granddads name was on it. But duh, his name was the same too. I just started to laugh. I felt my world was finally coming into focus. Mom was in the kitchen with Gayle making dinner. Uncle Will was sitting at the table just watching me with my friends and my boyfriend. I truly loved it—one big happy family. The buzzer rang and I looked at the time. I went to the buzzer and said one moment please door is broken. I knew who it was, so I told everyone I'd be right back. I ran to the elevator and waited to take me down. I got to the door and there was my Dad. I was so happy, I opened the door and ran out to give him a great big hug. We went up and it was a great big party. I had a time of my life. Time went by so fast that it was time to go. Dick wrapped his arm around mine and he escorted me to the car. He opened my car door and let me go in. Then he shut it for me. My dad sat next to me and my sisters sat next to him with Will in the front seat. Dick jumped into Pat's car and we left for the graduation ceremony. When we got there, Pat's car had already arrived. Dick ran to mom's car and opened my door. He motioned for me to take my hand and I got out of the car. Everyone gathered at the car and gave me hugs. Dick walked my to the auditorium where everyone is suppose to meet before we walk on the field. Dick came in with me to show everyone who I came with. Dick gave me a kiss and hug, smiled, said I'll see you later. He left me by myself. I just sat there waiting. One of the kids came up to me and asked who just came and dropped me off because I didn't recognize him. I smiled and said, "That's my boyfriend that I told everyone about. We broke up with me a couple of years ago, but I got him back!" I think I was glowing that night. When it was time to walk onto the field, I was so nervous. The girl next to me said, "I'm sorry I didn't get to know you in school, I just want to say congratulations, you deserve it." I smiled and congratulated her. We were in the field getting ready to sit down in the seats, when all of a sudden I heard my friends and family yell out in unison, "We love you Tanya!" I shook my head because they weren't supposed to do that. The principal got on the microphone, asked for everyone's attention, and requested that everyone's applause be held until all graduates were called. The guy that was walking along side of me said, "Wow, you must have a lot of friends and family that love you!" I said yep, and thought that I didn't even know until now. How ironic is that?

The ceremony started and it took awhile for them to announce my name but I was patient. Finally, the principal got to our row and I saw my dad on the field. He took my picture and smiled. One step at a time, one name at a time—I was getting closer to the stadium. They called my name and I walked up the stairs smiling all the way, shook the principal's hand, grabbed my diploma with my other hand, and said thank you. The principal said, "Congratulations! Tanya, I knew you could do it." I wanted to hug him but you're not supposed to. I had to sit back down and wait for everyone else before I could join my friends and family. I was so happy that words could never explain exactly how I felt. The last name was called and the principal said, "Class of 1987, congratulations on completing your high school years at Rincon High!" Everyone cheered and threw their hats in the air except me because I couldn't bare the thought of losing it. My family was already on the field—everyone took turns taking pictures with me. Dad pulled me aside and he was crying. He said, "I'm so proud of you. I'm sorry I wasn't there more often and I hope we can change that." I gave Dad a hug and said I hope so too. We both smiled. Mom finally announced, "Who's hungry?" Lots of hands went up around me. She said, "The last one to the apartment is an rotten egg." Everyone made a dash to the cars. Dick gave me a kiss, opened the door, and shut in when I got in. Dad commented, "He's a perfect gentleman, isn't he?" Mom just stared through the rearview mirror. I just smiled.

We got to the apartment and my friends were already there—like I knew they would be. Mom laughed that it wasn't fair because Pat drives too fast. My friends laughed. After dinner, Uncle Will took me to the balcony and we talked. "I know you are moving to Phoenix with Dick this weekend," he said, "And I wish you the best of luck. I hope everything turns out for the best. Your mother doesn't like it, but I know you want this. Here is your graduation gift from Granddad and I. He's very proud of you too." I cried my eyes out. I held him for a few minutes. I loved my Uncle with all my heart and he just made my life a hell of a lot easier. Not because of the gift, but because he showed up to my graduation. Uncle Will said, "It's too bad I can't stay for the next couple of days to celebrate with you but I have to go back to work. I'm taking a late flight out tonight. I said, "Uncle Will, I'm so glad you came in the first place! If it weren't for the support I received today from all my friends and family, I wouldn't have gotten the reaction I did at school tonight. I thank you for coming on your busy schedule." I gave him another hug and realized that everyone was watching us. I just blushed and we both walked back in. I saw Uncle Will go to my mom and gave her a warm hug and kiss that only a brother and sister could have cherished together. Mom's eyes were swelling up with tears. Then my Uncle went to my dad and shook his hand and said it was nice to see him after all these years. Dad said like wise and both of them smiled. Uncle turned to everyone else and said, "It was fun and a pleasure to meet you all." Dick came up and shook his hand. Mom followed Will outside where he got a cab. Few minutes later she was in the apartment again with a wet face from crying.

My dad was stuck here for the whole weekend, but I didn't mind one bit. It'll give mom some company. Dick asked my mom and dad if it was ok to take me out with my friends to celebrate. Mom and Dad said, "Go ahead but don't drink" at the same time. Everyone was shocked to hear that. Pat asked if he could use the phone. Mom said sure. I gave Dad a hug since I hardly got any from him and said good night to everyone.

Dick took me to his truck and Pat and Jennifer went to his car. We met up at the fast food joint on the Speedway stripe. Pat said it's a quiet place where no one would bother us. I didn't mind I was high on life. I didn't care where we were at as long as I had my friends. Everyone else—Larry, Richard, and Chris—showed up a few minutes later. Chris jokingly asked us if we wanted 'shrooms. Dick turned on his radio, blared it, and we danced in the back of his pick up. Cars were driving by, honking there horn, and yelling out of their windows. It was a very crazy and exciting night. Fun was definitely in the air. We didn't have to have drugs or alcohol to have fun tonight and that was all right.

It was getting late and Pat and Jennifer were "tired"—I've heard that before. They came up and said good night, "We'll see you two tomorrow." They left. The other three were gone already because they had better things to do. So Dick and I went back to the apartment. Mom and Dad where sitting on the couch watching TV. I didn't dare ask them what they did—it wasn't none of my business. I asked mom if it was alright for Dick to stay here. She said, "Yes I guess it's all right, but where is he sleeping? Your dad is sleeping on the couch." I said in my room on the floor. She just looked at me and said, "I've heard that one before." I said, "Mom I learned my lesson. Nothing is going to happen. I'm not ready for that yet." Dick said, "Sally, I'm too tired to do anything anyways—she really tired me out tonight." We had to leave the door open. Dick and I talked just about the whole night. Before mom went to bed she checked on us. She asked, "How can you guys still be up and talking at this time of night?" I said, "It's easy when you have something interesting to talk about and you're in love!" Five o'clock came before I knew it. We fell asleep holding each other. At 8 am, Shallon came in and just stood there staring at us. I can always sense someone in my room looking at me. I opened my eyes and I jumped. I said get out of here you little turd. She ran out. I guess she was having a hard time figuring out what to do, since my dad was on the couch snoring quite loudly. I got up went to the bathroom, went to her room and said, "You know you can still go watch TV. Just turn down the volume to low, so you won't wake my Dad." She did that and I went back to bed. Dick put his arm around me and just held me—it was the most beautiful feeling I had ever experienced. It felt like we were one or something. I loved it. I was able to sleep a couple more hours. Excitement woke me up. I got up went to see what Shallon was up too. She was sitting right in front of the TV like I told her too. Dad was sitting up on the couch. I said, "Dad, did she wake you up?" He said, "No, I wake up early no matter what time I go to sleep. Well it was only 10:30 in the morning so I wasn't worried too much." The phone rang, Shallon ran to the phone, but I got it first. It was Pat, who wanted to know what we were doing for breakfast. He suggested we all go to Alice's for breakfast about 11-11:30. I said hold on let me see if I can wake up Dick. I went to my room and gave him a gentle kiss on the cheek. He opened his eyes and looked at me. I said, "Pat wants to meet us at Alice's this morning." He got up—actually jumped up—and said, "Hell of a deal!" I went to the phone and told him what Dick said. Pat laughed and said that we'd see you soon. I asked Dad to go, but he was relaxing on the couch.

On the way to breakfast, Dick suggested pack up the truck today and begin moving. "I have to work Monday, he frowned, "I can't get out of it, since I took Thursday and Friday off for your big event." I said, "I know it's not that much, I promise. You saw all the boxes in my room, all we have to do is tear the bed apart. I'll see if I can get everyone to help pack the truck." We made it to Alice's and sat down. We had to take two booths, but we didn't mind because we were going to eat to our heart's content. We ordered a whole bunch of food—pancakes, home fries, eggs, French toast, and biscuits and gravy, my favorite thing on Alice's menu. It was the first to go. Dick asked if everyone would help us pack the truck, and, of course, Pat and Jennifer were in.

Everyone showed up on time to the apartment. Mom was in the kitchen cooking dinner. I've never seen her cook so much in a week. While, Dad was sitting on the couch, Pat brought some beer and wine coolers. Mom gave him some more money to go and get some more because there wasn't enough for everyone. We started packing my things in the truck. We tore the bed apart and put it in sideways so the other things would secure it. Pat finally came back and he helped finish loading the truck. Jennifer and I just watched to make sure the guys didn't break anything. The truck was packed in an hour and a half. I had to leave a few things, but mom said I could come back and get it. The guys covered my things, so the elements wouldn't ruin it.

We were drinking and having a great time at Mom's place. She made Goulash for dinner and everyone ate it, even Dad, who never liked Mom's cooking. He admitted she had become a much better cook in the years since their separation.

It was midnight and Pat said, "It's time for us to go." Mom asked if he was ok to drive and Pat winked and said, "I've driven in worse condition." Pat and Jennifer gave us a hug and I said, "Don't be strangers! We know where you live." Larry, Richard and Chris left too. I wanted to take Chris with me. There were things about him that I just adored—his personality, his perky smile, and crazy laugh. He lived life to the fullest. I would miss him with all my heart.

On the morning of June 8, 1987, two days after graduation, Dick and I said our goodbyes to my family. We were on our way to Phoenix to start our lives together. What an exciting adventure we were about to take together.......

I was just thinking that if I ended my book with "And we lived happily ever after together," I would destroy the concept of reality in my life. So, I will continue my story in another book.

Chris Burdon passed away May 12, 2008. He was unexpectedly and tragically taken away from us for reasons that could have been dealt with differently. I will always love and miss him dearly.

Everyone is affected by the reality we live in, like ripples in the water. Someone must have started the ripple somewhere and somehow. Everyone is affected in their own way. We are all connected in one way or another. It's your choice whether you believe it or not. To me I believe it.

-Conclusion-

I have to admit after all these years of being alive, I have no idea what to do. I struggle everyday trying to find the answers that have been bugging me.

Am I doing this right?

Why do I feel I have failed in this life?

Why do I have to see things differently than others?

Why do I feel alienated by others?

How come I always assume negativity in my life is normal?

These are agonizing questions I ask myself everyday. I reassure myself that one day everything will fall into place and I will figure it out and see things a lot clearer. I sought help in all angels, churches, new age, and spiritual awareness, through the studies I have done myself. I always end up in the same place where I started. Maybe because there isn't anyone out there with the knowledge that everyone is looking for. I hope that one day I will find what I'm looking for and live my life to the fullest.

Everyone has or will experience some sort of negativity in their life. It's how they perceive or cope with negativity and how they endure life is the important part. I hid from others most of my life, thinking everyone was the same. In fact, if you think about it, it's true. Everyone in one way or another is connected. Don't deny this to be true. In the subconscious, your mind knows it to be true. We are here to learn from our mistakes and then continue on with our lives no matter how hard it may seem. Eventually in time, it will become easier to deal with. By the time your old, you'll realize you wasted you whole life over something you could have complete control after all.

Like I say—things happen for a reason!!!

We are here to experience and to learn.

Who are we to judge one another? When, in fact, we are judging ourselves.

216